WHAT'S LEGIT?

WHAT'S LEGIT?

CRITIQUES OF LAW AND STRATEGIES OF RIGHTS

EDITED BY
LIZA MATTUTAT, ROBERTO NIGRO, NADINE SCHIEL,
HEIKO STUBENRAUCH

DIAPHANES

GEFÖRDERT DURCH DIE DEUTSCHE FORSCHUNGSGEMEINSCHAFT (DFG) – PROJEKTNUMMER 2114
FUNDED BY THE DEUTSCHE FORSCHUNGSGEMEINSCHAFT (DFG, GERMAN RESEARCH FOUNDATION) –
PROJECT NUMBER 2114

DFG Deutsche
Forschungsgemeinschaft

**KULTUREN
DER KRITIK**

K

⊛
LEUPHANA
UNIVERSITÄT LÜNEBURG

d **K**

ISBN 978-3-0358-0243-6

LAYOUT AND PREPRESS: 2EDIT, ZURICH
PRINTED IN GERMANY

WWW.DIAPHANES.COM

Contents

**Liza Mattutat, Roberto Nigro,
Nadine Schiel, Heiko Stubenrauch**

What's Legit?

Introduction

Once considered a stepchild of social theory, legal criticism has received a great deal of attention in recent years, perpetuating what has always been an ambivalent relationship. On the one hand, law is praised for being a cultural achievement, on the other, it is criticized for being an instrument of state oppression. While some theoreticians seek to transcend the institution of law altogether, others advocate a transformation of the form of law or try to employ counter-hegemonic strategies to change the content of law, deconstruct its basis or invent rights.

With regard to both their starting point and their theoretical background, all of these critical strategies differ greatly. When examining their starting points, one can observe that they either target the *content* or the present *form* of law and rights. In his contribution to this volume, Christoph Menke explains that this distinction is the distinction between *what* is presented and *how* it is presented.[1] While approaches advocating to fight for rights or to invent new rights seek to either change the definition or the scope of specific rights (i.e. their content), approaches aiming at overcoming, deconstructing or transforming law altogether focus on the way in which rights entitle and law functions (i.e. its form). Philosophically, legal criticism refers to a wide range of theoreticians reaching all the way from Marx to Derrida.

---

1   See p. 223 in the present volume.

It is not by accident that there has been a lot of dispute amongst positions of legal criticism, since at times their conceptions of law couldn't be more diverse. On the one hand, Marx, in a popular yet contested reading of his writings, considers legal criticism focusing on the content of rights to be utterly naïve. He argues that "legal relations arise from economic ones."[2] Therefore, a "[r]ight can never be higher than the economic structure of society and its cultural development which this determines."[3] Authors who, on the other hand, fight for specific rights accuse positions focusing on the form of law of being abstract. "It's jurisprudence, ultimately, that creates law," analyses Deleuze, "and we mustn't go on leaving this to judges."[4]

Since these discussions tend to be highly conflictual, different approaches to legal criticism are rarely published within one and the same volume. Yet it was exactly these conflicts we found to be highly interesting and productive when we were planning this volume. The question we asked ourselves and the contributing authors goes as follows: Which kind of critical practice and standpoint will emerge from which kind of theoretical model of law—and why? We received a variety of answers, spread out over the whole field of legal criticism. Some of the contributions were the subject of a controversial discussion amongst the publishers and between the publishers and the authors—they don't necessarily coincide with the publishers' opinion. On the following pages, we would like to sketch out five different concepts of law and rights, which are the foundation of different strategies of legal criticism: inventing rights, fighting for rights, overcoming law, deconstructing law and transforming law. These different strategies

2   Karl Marx and Friedrich Engels, *Collected Works, vol. 24: Marx and Engels 1874–1883* (London: Lawrence & Wishart, 2010), p. 84.
3   Ibid., p. 87.
4   Gilles Deleuze, *Negotiations, 1972–1990* (New York: Columbia University Press, 1995), p. 170.

also serve as titles of the five chapters within this volume, since the articles specify our sketches and elaborate on them in a number of ways. Some of them think about the relation of the concept and the critique of law, while others are exemplary of a certain style of critique.

1. Inventing Rights

Deleuze and Guattari's philosophy serves as one of the theoretical foundations of the strategy of inventing new rights. Responding to the question *What is Philosophy?*— the title of the last book they wrote collectively—they state: "philosophy is the art of forming, inventing, and fabricating concepts."[5] This claim is far-reaching—and in need of an explanation. For by inventing new concepts, philosophy not only poses new words, it also (and above all) poses new ways of experience and existence. Philosophy has the power of creating new forms of life. By establishing this idiosyncratic definition of philosophy (as a creative activity of generating new concepts and new ways of experience and existence), Deleuze and Guattari turn their backs on a multitude of common and influential conceptions of philosophy. For a different kind of function has repeatedly been ascribed to philosophy, namely that philosophy organizes our ways of experience and existence on the basis of existing concepts or that it uses these concepts in order to compare, hierarchize and hold on to given ways of experience and existence. Traditional forms of philosophy tend to regard a concept as an instrument for grasping that which is universal, permanent or even eternal within a changing world. With their creative interpretation of philosophical practice, Deleuze and Guattari

5   Gilles Deleuze and Félix Guattari, *What is Philosophy?* (New York: Columbia University Press, 2014), p. 2.

attack those notions of the concept that conceive the concept as an institution of order and control.

Authors interested in the invention of new rights oftentimes aspire to a similar change of perspective. According to them, Deleuze and Guattari's statements regarding the relation of concept and philosophy have to be applied to law and rights in a similar way. Instead of considering law to be an institution of organization, hierarchy and comparison, they argue that law can be approached creatively. Rather than characterizing law as a movement of subsumption, measuring individual phenomena against a background of general rights, they try to think of law as an instrument that can, by creating new rights, help to express new (not only human) forms of life and experience.

In his contribution "Against Law: The 1960s Anti-Juridical Moment in France," Laurent de Sutter specifies this creative way of dealing with law by examining French post-structural philosophy. Contrary to common belief—according to which this kind of philosophy was anti-juridical through and through—he paints the picture of a movement that saw its philosophical premises fulfilled in the practice of jurisprudence and the creation of new rights.

In "On Thinking and Feeling: The Law of Cultural Heritage," Susanne Krasmann poses the question of whether (and how) cultural objects can become legal subjects. She puts the creative capacities of law to a test by attempting to extend law beyond the realm of human actors, thus pursuing the call for a post-human law.

In his essay "Intensive Listening: Unfolding the Notion of Justice Through Reading the Work of Lawrence Abu Hamdan," Fares Chalabi suggests that a certain mode of listening might be the condition of dealing with law in a new and creative way. Whether a legal system silences those whom it excludes or endows them with rights, he argues, depends on whether it incorporates including or excluding practices of listening.

2. Fighting for Rights

Although they are related to the approach of inventing rights, approaches of fighting for rights are a distinct form of legal criticism. On the one hand, this approach involves the attempt to break through the crust of a mechanism of domination (and therefore deals with the question of how to overcome law altogether). On the other hand, it might involve the invention and creation of new rights. Paraphrasing an argument made by Jacques Rancière, fighting for rights can be understood as a political process, including a removal from the naturalness of a place.[6] Pursuing Rancière's train of thought even further, we might say that the approach of fighting for rights could be referred to as a form of political subjectivization that, at the same time, has the ability to produce polemical and paradoxical scenes that reveal a contradiction between two kinds of logic, by positing non-existing forms of existence. Political subjectivization redefines the frame of experience that gave rise to the identity of the political subject. It decomposes and recomposes the relationship between ways of doing, being and saying (something) that are constitutive of the perceptible organization of a community. As such, the political subject fighting for rights is not an entity "becoming aware of itself," finding its own voice or imposing its rights onto society. Rather, it is an operator connecting and disconnecting different areas, regions, identities, functions and capacities; all of which exist within the configuration of a given mode of experience. This approach thus renders it possible to think of the democratic multitude as something that is neither always already constituted as a community, nor a community in its becoming, a community that is going to be constituted in the future. Instead, the democratic mul-

---

6   Compare Jacques Rancière, *Disagreement. Politics and Philosophy* (Minneapolis: University of Minnesota Press, 1999).

titude can be thought of as being something that exists *outside*, regularly interfering with the temporary order of every constitution.

Yet this *outside* has to be determined more precisely. How can it be inscribed into the framework of new rights, if it is exterior to this exact framework? This question lies at the core of Carl Schmitt's political theology. Put in Schmittian terms, we have to ask how the state of exception can be articulated in a legal context. According to Schmitt, the exception is more interesting than the rule, since it is in the exception that the power of real life breaks through the crust of a mechanism that has become turbid due to repetition. In order to explain the way in which an exception can be integrated within the framework of a legal order, Schmitt establishes the distinction between constituent power and constituted power. The constituent power is not a pure or a simple kind of force. Instead, it is understood as a founding power. Put in different terms: it is the basis upon which the constituted power rests. Constituent power is the operator enabling the state of exception to be inscribed within the legal order. Schmitt therefore tries to think of this inscription by referring both to the distinction between constituent power and constituted power and to the distinction between regularity and decision.

Opposing Schmitt's concept of a decisionist sovereignty, Michel Foucault's concept of governmentality examines the governmentalization of the state. The crucial point of his analysis is that the state isn't a cold monster extending its tentacles over the entire civil society. Rather, it is a form of practice, a kind of governmentality, a general effect of governmental practices.

The importance of this approach lies in the fact that it puts an end to the confusion between law and sovereignty. We should thus separate state and law, since law does *not* emanate from the activity of a state. Instead, there is a constitutive place where rights form themselves. This place is not necessarily linked to an institution or to the sovereign form of an institution. Jurisprudence must not be confused with normativity. The interdependence of actions between subjects is characteristic of the legal sphere and foundational of the ensemble of social connections. This field of instituting practices is the point at which the formula "fighting for rights" assumes its true meaning.

In their respective contributions, Paolo Napoli and Alisa Del Re approach these questions. Napoli's essay aims at liberating the concept of institution from an invasive presence of the subject-person while trying to circumvent the incorporation of norms in the person-institution. With his materialist conception of law, Napoli tries to avoid understanding law as being an automatic reflection of society.

The problem of instituting practices lies at the core of Alisa Del Re's contribution, too. In her essay, the question of "fighting for rights" is examined by looking at the fight for European citizenship for women. Del Re argues that if, in Europe, citizenship is essentially based on the definition of the citizen as worker, the status of women's work has to be reconsidered. In her account, the reproductive work of women (still considered to be a "non-productive" activity by patriarchal society) can produce a polemical scene and serve as a starting point to extend the frontiers of European citizenship.

3. Overcoming Law

Whereas the first two strategies opt for a reformation of the legal realm, the strategy of overcoming law altogether tries to locate a normativity that lies underneath, besides or beyond law. Its question can be exemplified by the discussion of the state of exception. By commenting on Schmitt's account of the state of exception, Giorgio Agamben points out that it is an empty state of law, an ambiguous zone within which any legal determination is abandoned. The state of exception is neither a state of law, nor a state of nature. It is a space without any rights, a non-place, where the force of law is suspended. Yet that doesn't mean that law is absent. Rather, it is effective by being absent or by being suspended. It is the force of law that separates itself from law.

These considerations point towards another perspective of legal criticism that was sketched out by Walter Benjamin's *Critique of Violence*. Benjamin tries to elaborate on violence as something that lies outside or beyond the law. What does that mean? It means that he tries to break up the dialectics of a violence which establishes law and a violence which secures the functioning of the law. Law cannot tolerate the existence of violence outside its own sphere and thus perceives this violence—a violence that is immune to being absorbed by law—to be a threat that is impossible to overcome. A form of violence that is immune to an absorption by law is a form of violence that does not pose, but discharges law; it is a form of violence that neither preserves nor secures law, but dismisses it. If Schmitt tries to reincorporate violence in a legal context, Benjamin tries to think of violence in its purest form, beyond law. For Schmitt, a pure form of violence—a violence existing outside the law—is impossible. The state of exception is Schmitt's attempt at incorporating violence within law. Regarding the question of pure violence, Schmitt employs a concept of sovereignty that revolves around sovereign violence and poses sovereignty as a place of extreme decision and extreme violence. This form of sovereignty is located at the limits, it is a limit-concept [*Grenzbegriff*]. If, to Schmitt, the sovereign decides on the state of exception, Benjamin poses the question of sovereign indecision, of a sovereign being *unable* to decide (which is different from the fact that the sovereign is able to *not* decide). Benjamin poses a gap between power and the exercise of power, and this gap cannot be filled by any decision. It's not a *counter*point, nor is it a power that negates the sovereign as if power and the exercise of power were connected by a dialectical relationship. Instead, this gap is thought to be an act that pushes the sovereign to his limit, his *impotence*. As Agamben points out, we face catastrophe—instead of facing the miracle of a sovereign decision that resolves any given crisis and that will be part of a new legal order. Benjamin's insistence on the term pure violence—his term for any form of human action that neither poses nor restrains law, but dismisses it—is not an original figure of human action. It would be illusory to imagine a pure violence, a violence beyond and outside of law, that can be reintegrated by law. The pure violence Benjamin speaks of is no original state: it's what is at stake in the conflict revolving around the state of exception; it is that which is produced by the state of exception.

The problem of violence is at the center of Daniel Loick's paper "'...as if it were a thing': A Feminist Critique of Consent." He challenges the usefulness of a juridical notion of consent in descriptions of sexual violence and sexual assault. By referring to the international #MeToo campaign, he focuses on a paradigmatic case of what can be called juridicism, i.e. the problematic dominance of law within the ethical life of our society.

Franziska Dübgen discusses the question of violence in her contribution, "Rethinking the Law: Taking Clues from Ubuntu Philosophy," by looking at the idea of transformative justice employed by Ubuntu philosophy. She tries to rethink the legal system by finding new ways of solving interpersonal conflict. Rather than demanding a punishment that is inflicted upon the individual by the state, she asks how social deviance can be dealt with differently, thus overcoming the existing form of law. Dübgen provides an in-depth account of the way in which social activists increasingly refer to an idea of transformative justice while fighting for rights.

4. Deconstructing Law

In a similar way to approaches that aim at overcoming
law, deconstructive forms of legal criticism problematize
the foundations of law. According to Derrida's famous
formula, a successful deconstruction will show that the
condition of the possibility of an institution or a practice
is, at the same time, the condition of its impossibility.
This is Derrida's method in *Force of Law*, within which
he describes the relationship between law, justice and
violence. In his discussion of Benjamin, Derrida shows
that law distinguishes between "sanctioned and unsanctioned force."[7] The form of violence justified by established norms of law is "sanctioned" (e.g. a punishment
imposed by a court). Unsanctioned violent acts, on the
other hand, are acts which lack this authorization, e.g.
an illegal interference with the integrity of a person.

In this model, the generality of law is the condition of
the possibility of justice, since it is only through this generality that a complete justification of law can be conceived of. Verdicts that cause violent legal consequences
are justified by the rights they execute. These rights are
justified, because they were passed by the use of constitutional means. Constitutional laws are established, if
they have been implemented by constitutional amend-
ments. This is what the Viennese School of legal positivism calls the "hierarchical structure of the legal order,"[8]
to which it attributes the overcoming of arbitrariness
and violence. Derrida points out that this regress of justification cannot be continued indefinitely, but has to
come to an end at some point. An unjustified act has
to lie at the beginning of a chain of justifications—that
is, a violent act. At the same time, therefore, law is the

7 Walter Benjamin, *Selected Writings, Vol. 1: 1913–1926*, ed. Marcus
Bullock and Michael W. Jennings (Cambridge MA and London: The
Belknap Press of Harvard University Press, 1996), p. 237.

8 Hans Kelsen, *Pure Theory of Law* (Berkeley and Los Angeles: University of California Press, 1967), p. 221.

impossibility of justice, since the violence at its root constantly continues to have an effect. In the tradition of deconstruction, law is determined by an essential aporia, which has to be recognized rather than overcome.

In his contribution "Specters of Critique: Hauntology and the Ghosts of Law," Peter Goodrich examines the status and future of this deconstructive tradition and critique within legal theory. In order to stay up to date, it has to explore the potentials of present media conditions, which Goodrich understands to be determined by a new form of visuality. He suggests that previously invisible forms of critique could be made visible in phantasmagorical forms. According to Goodrich, starting points for critical inventions can be located in an affirmation of the radical situatedness and the sensual and bodily experiences of theoreticians working on the project of critique. "The radical project of critique continues, and survives, in potential at least in law, in the mode of counter-memory and its bodily materializations."[9]

Manuela Klaut demonstrates the deconstructive potential of the medium of film in her essay "On the Run from the Law: Alexander Kluge's *Yesterday Girl* as Cinematic Institution of Subsumption." According to Klaut, the depiction of the fate of Anita G., who tries to establish herself in West Germany after having fled from East Germany, explores the limits of legal representation. Klaut analyses the account of the trial within which Anita is sentenced to prison for having committed theft. By embedding the crime within the reality of Anita's life and setting it in contrast with the way it is presented within the trial, the untranslatability of an individual case into the language of law becomes evident. "The crucial thing about Kluge's cases is that they reach the limits of what can be assessed in legal terms and thus become legal impossibilities."[10]

---

9 See p. 195 in the present volume.
10 See p. 207 in the present volume.

5. Transforming Law

The aporias and ambivalences of law, which deconstructive forms of critique concentrate on, are also a motivation for transformative approaches. Theodor W. Adorno and Max Horkheimer's diagnosis in the *Dialectic of Enlightenment* can serve as a model for this attitude. In the preface, they summarize the ambivalent result they arrived at in their study: "We have no doubt [...] that freedom in society is inseparable from enlightenment thinking. We believe [...], however, that the very concept of that thinking, no less than the concrete historical forms, the institutions of society with which it is intertwined, already contains the germ of the regression which is taking place everywhere today."[11] The diagnosis of this ambivalence is immediately turned into an appeal: "If enlightenment does not assimilate reflection on this regressive moment, it seals its own fate."[12] Adorno and Horkheimer demand that enlightenment and its social institutions have to be reflective of their own shortcomings, since they produce repressive consequences. Enlightenment is in desperate need of enlightenment, if it is not to perish and drag away its unfulfilled promises. The approaches in this volume which pursue the goal of transforming the legal form adopt an attitude towards law that is similarly ambivalent. They cannot imagine any form of freedom in society without the institution of law. This is why they don't want to overcome law. Yet they are convinced that liberal theories have employed a fundamentally flawed concept of law. To them, it is thus not enough to demand new rights within the liberal legal system. Individual rights could not remedy the deficiency of the liberal legal system. Instead, they try to rethink the liberal concept of

11 Max Horkheimer and Theodor W. Adorno, *Dialectic of Enlightenment* (Stanford CA: Stanford University Press, 2002), p. xvi.
12 Ibid.

law and enlighten it, by confronting it with the repressive consequences law entails. They respond to the diagnoses of ambivalence not by overcoming law, nor by constructing, deconstructing or creating individual rights, but by transforming the liberal form of law.

In his contribution "Genealogy, Paradox, Transformation: Basic Elements of a Critique of Rights," Christoph Menke ascribes a depoliticizing effect to subjective rights, identifying this effect as the fundamental shortcoming of liberal law. That which subjective rights give entitlement to has to be presupposed by law. Liberal law thus naturalizes those areas it wants to protect and detracts them from political formability. Menke pursues the concept of a fundamental transformation of the liberal form of law by proposing the introduction of a second category of rights. He recommends the creation of counter-rights in order to counteract the naturalizing effects of subjective rights.

In his contribution "The Anarchy of Rights: On the Dialectic of Freedom and Authority," Benno Zabel questions the assumptions Menke presupposes in order to accuse the liberal form of law of this fundamental shortcoming and to render his proposal of counter-rights plausible. Is it the implicit idea of an aesthetic form of life that forms the background against which a transformation of the form of law can be demanded? And are the counter-rights the only plausible answer to the problem Menke suggests is the fundamental problem of liberal law?

Jonas Heller's approach also reacts to the shortcomings of the liberal understanding of law, yet in other conceptual terms. In his contribution "Deforming Rights: Arendt's Theory of a Claim to Law," he uses Hannah Arendt's concept of a right to have rights as an aid, in order to find a perspective from which these shortcomings can be defined more clearly. While liberal law interprets (human) rights as being the unconditional protection of every subject, the conceptual figure of a right to have rights clarifies that membership in a community must be understood as a condition of any right and that the liberal understanding of law has to become aware of these conditions in the course of its self-enlightenment.

By presenting a variety of heterogeneous approaches to legal criticism, this volume points out transitions and exhibits the irreconcilable differences of these approaches. Without denying the diversity of different forms of critique, they are put into relationship with each other with the aim of broadening the debates which all too often are conducted only within a singular theoretical current. In the end, therefore, there is not *one* answer to the question *What's Legit?*, but a multitude of answers not only questioning law, but also questioning each other.

What's Legit? Critiques of Law and Strategies of Rights began as part of the conference "Critical Stances", that was hosted by the DFG research training group "Cultures of Critique" at Leuphana University Lüneburg in July 2018. The book is part of the series "Critical Stances" and will be accompanied by two other books: "Critique: The Stakes of Form" and "Critique and the Digital." We thank all participants for their contributions and for the engaged discussions. Catharina Berents supported both the event and the publications with invaluable commitment. Mimmi Woisnitza kept the whole project from falling apart during the final steps. We wish to thank Stephanie Braune, Jasmin Camenzind, Jonas Ehret, Maximilian Gebhardt, David Mielecke, and Niklas Roth for manifold support. The translators, namely Alan Nixon, Aaron Shoichet and Aaron Zielinski worked patiently with both authors and editors on multiple revisions. Catherine Lupton copy-edited this volume with care and diligence. Our sincere gratitude goes to Michael Heitz from diaphanes for his confidence in the series and all his efforts to ensure its timely release. Finally, we also have to thank the German Research Foundation DFG for the generous funding that facilitated the entire venture.

Inventing Rights

Laurent de Sutter

Against Law

The 1960s Anti-Juridical Moment in France

§ 1
From Law to Justice

It was a complete misunderstanding. When Jacques
Derrida addressed the crowd gathered to hear him open
the conference organized at the Benjamin N. Cardozo
Law School, New York, by Drucilla Cornell and Michel
Rosenfeld, as a homage to his work, he was completely
out of tune. The conference, titled "Deconstruction and
the Possibility of Justice" indicated that there was a possible link between what he had developed since the end
of the 1960s, and what was the main business of Cardozo, namely law—and he somehow approved.[1] Yet
this approval, which was part of a more general move
of his, displacing the main locus of his work towards
a systematic questioning of the very nature of violence, democracy and politics, was based on a deliberate attempt at re-reading his own past. Despite Derrida's
repeated refusal to consider that his views had changed
over time, or that some topic had been left aside from
his previous works, the tone of his meditations was
changing—a change that would be epitomized by his

---

1 Drucilla Cornell, Michel Rosenfeld and David Gray Carlson, eds.,
Deconstruction and the Possibility of Justice (London: Routledge,
1992). For more information on the context of this conference, see
also Benoît Peeters, *Derrida* (Paris: Flammarion, 2010), p. 552 *sq.*

dialogue with Jürgen Habermas after September 11.[2] Yet
it was not changing fast enough to explain why, suddenly, a law faculty could decide to dedicate a conference to the "possibility of justice" that "deconstruction"
was exploring, displacing, creating, or simply rendering
thinkable. For someone who had been following Derrida's work since the publication of his first books on Hus-
serl, or the seminal volumes that were *De la grammatol-
ogie* or *L'écriture et la différence*, there must have been
something striking to witness which could appear as
contradictory. If one took for granted that the interrogation haunting any form of law was the one of guarantee,
then "deconstruction" could only seem anti-law —as it
was mainly a way to look at ideas through the lens of
the impossibility of any guarantee, or of any ground. Of
course, the title of the conference immediately implied
a distinction, which Derrida decided to adopt and elaborate: the possibility that was at stake with deconstruction was not so much the possibility of law as the possibility of justice—as if justice was something else than
law.[3] Derrida's opening address made it perfectly clear
from the outset: what the French philosopher was about
to discuss was the strange, but indispensable, move that
could lead from law to justice—or, to put it in the terms
of its original heading, "Du droit à la justice."[4] If law,
said Derrida, was what "deconstruction" was targeting,
there was something else that resisted any "deconstruction," and even was its motor—and this something else
was none other than justice itself.[5]

2   Giovanna Borradori, *Philosophy in a Time of Terror: Conversations
    with Jacques Derrida and Jürgen Habermas* (Chicago: University of
    Chicago Press, 2003).
3   Compare Jacques Derrida, *Force de loi: Le "Fondement mystique de
    l'autorité"* (Paris: Galilée, 1994), p. 18 *sq.*
4   Ibid., p. 11.
5   Ibid., p. 26 *sq.* On all this, see also Roberto Buonamano, "The Econ-
    omy of Violence: Derrida on Law and Justice," *Ratio Juris* 11:2 (1998):
    p. 168 *sq.*; John P. McCormick, "Derrida on Law; Or, Post-Structur-
    alism Gets Serious," *Political Theory* 29:3 (2001): p. 395 *sq.*; Florian
    Hoffmann, ed., "A Dedication to Jacques Derrida," *German Law Jour-*

§ 2
The Violence of Being

This distinction was not only a latecomer in Derrida's work; it was also the sign that something was evolving, and that the political radicalism of a certain moment of thought was slowly turning into a different affair, where ethics were taking the lead.[6] Of course, ethics had always been present: Derrida's first major article was his almost book-length study of the work of Emmanuel Lévinas on "Violence et métaphysique," published in 1964 in two issues of *Revue de métaphysique et de morale*.[7] Twenty-five years later, "Du droit à la justice" was still exploring some of the paths opened in this article, but the distinction between law and justice suddenly implied that a much greater attention had to be devoted to what may allow going past violence. The status of ethics in "Du droit à la justice" was indubitably obscure. To be honest, the word was barely mentioned; and Derrida would have immediately replied that the very word *justice* was already heading far beyond ethics, involving politics and law as well. Of course, this would have been true; yet there was something, in the attempt to look at justice as what cannot be deconstructed, that resembled a safeguard, an exit from a world where everything was always-already "deconstructing." The possibility of such

nal 6:1 (2005); Pierre-Yves Quiviger, "Derrida: de la philosophie au droit," *Cités* 30 (2007): p. 31 *sq.*; Peter Goodrich, Florian Hoffmann, Michel Rosenfeld and Cornelia Vismann, eds., *Derrida and Legal Philosophy* (London: Palgrave Macmillan, 2008); Pierre Legrand, ed., *Derrida and Law* (London: Routledge, 2009); Jacques de Ville, *Jacques Derrida: Law as Absolute Hospitality* (London: Routledge, 2012); Jérôme Lèbre, *Derrida: la justice sans condition* (Paris: Michalon, 2013); Simon Glendinning, "Derrida and the Philosophy of Law and Justice," *Law and Critique* 27:2 (2016): p. 187 *sq.*

6   Compare François Cusset, *French Theory: Foucault, Derrida, Deleuze & Cie et les mutations de la vie intellectuelle aux Etats-Unis* (Paris: La Découverte, 2003), p. 201 *sq.*

7   Jacques Derrida, "Violence et métaphysique: Essai sur la pensée d'Emmanuel Lévinas," *L'écriture et la différence* (Paris: Le Seuil, 1967), p. 117 *sq.* On this text, see, Peeters, *Derrida*, p. 173 *sq.*

a safeguard was precisely what "deconstruction," maybe misleadingly, had radically "deconstructed" in the eyes of the early readers of Derrida's work—helped, in truth, by several statements uttered by the man himself. For instance, the "deconstruction" of the American Declaration of Independence, offered during a conference held in Virginia for its bicentennial, and later published as *Otobiographies*, didn't mention any instance that could be excepted from its movement.[8] What Derrida suggested was that the dominant logic of the Declaration was, in fact, the logic of division—the fact that the Declaration, those who signed it, and the people at its core, were ceaselessly dividing themselves, so that they would never coincide with their own being.[9] What was to be understood was that being itself was the very name of division; there is no such thing as being, if one is to conceive it as something compact and stable, something capable of claiming an identity beyond its own permanent self-"deconstruction." To put it more properly: *there is nothing*—nothing can be considered as being, except if this being was the very movement of deconstruction of Being, the permanent self-differing of oneself towards oneself for which Derrida had coined his most famous neologism: "différance."[10]

§ 3
Against Human Rights

Derrida's attempt at indirectly saving something from its own "deconstruction" came as a surprise—but a

---

8   Jacques Derrida, *Otobiographies: L'enseignement de Nietzsche et la politique du nom propre* (Paris: Galilée, 1984).

9   Ibid., p. 23.

10   Jacques Derrida, "De la différance," *Marges – de la philosophie* (Paris: Minuit, 1972), p. 1 *sq*. The word appears for the first time in Derrida, "'Genèse et structure' et la phénoménologie," *L'écriture et la différence*, p. 239 (the article reproduced the text of a paper presented in Cerisy-la-Salle in 1959). Compare Benoît Peeters, *Derrida*, p. 134 *sq*.

surprise that was very soon accepted by his followers, who didn't seem to find bizarre his sudden surrender to human rights or parliamentary democracy. However, at the same moment, other figures of his generation adopted another path, and decided to show less appreciation for what was the then current state of political and juridical affairs, so remaining faithful to the tradition inaugurated several decades earlier.[11] Jean Baudrillard's ironic criticism of human rights in the second volume of *Cool Memories* in 1990, or Gilles Deleuze and Félix Guattari's variation on the same topic in *Qu'est-ce que la philosophie?* in 1991, were two examples of the survival of this tradition.[12] In both cases, the critique of human rights was part of a more general agenda whose main tenet was to consider law as a problem rather than a solution—and every attempt at solving this problem as the source of more problems, difficulties and aporias. For Baudrillard, human rights are nothing but a form of superstition blinding those who believe in them to the fact that there are things which escape our responsibilities—and that these things precisely are what we most long for for (while denying this fact).[13] The law in general, he added in a fragment of *Cool Memories III*, is the last fetish of those who have surrendered desire after having surrendered pleasure; to put it otherwise, law is nothing but the very result of the disappearance of life. When life vanishes, and with it the power of the instances that, through *jouissance*, could be counted among various forms of transgression, what we are confronted with is law, as the attempt to replace what was given by something resembling a guarantee. If life is the very name of what is without any guarantee, then one has to conclude that law is the antinomy of life, its

---

11 Compare François Cusset, *French Theory*, p. 279 *sq.*
12 Jean Baudrillard, *Cool Memories II: 1987–1990* (Paris: Galilée, 1990); Gilles Deleuze and Félix Guattari, *Qu'est-ce que la philosophie?* (Paris: Minuit, 1991).
13 Jean Baudrillard, *Cool Memories II*, p. 80.

definite loss under the *rule of law*, and the various apparatuses aimed at serving it—the first of them being the
modern nation state.[14] Despite the difference in terms
of vocabulary, Deleuze and Guattari somehow shared
Baudrillard's criticism; for them, too, human rights had
to be considered as one "axiom" of the market among
others—one more tool used by the "democratic State"
against its own subjects.[15] A true philosophy should look
at this axiom with contempt, and turn rather towards
the "possibilities of life," and the critique of the way
these possibilities are annihilated by the functioning of
the "democratic States," their police, their army, and
their self-satisfied capitalists.[16]

§ 4
Two Moments

With the fall of the Berlin Wall, something happened.
For some, it was the End of History, and the entry into a
new era of triumphant liberalism; for others, it was the
universalization of a certain type of political and juridical thinking, which was becoming more powerful than
ever. Despite his lengthy critical discussion of Francis
Fukuyama's best-seller dedicated to the defense of the
former, Derrida was the heir to a stream of thought necessarily leading to the latter; the fact that he eventually
took a path leading somewhere in between was the indication of a change.[17] After almost a decade of neoliberalism, during which critical thinking had been considered
with the bemused pity reserved for useless archaeological

---

14 Jean Baudrillard, *Fragments: Cool Memories III: 1991–1995* (Paris:
    Galilée, 1995), p. 118.
15 Deleuze and Guattari, *Qu'est-ce que la philosophie?*, p. 103.
16 Ibid., p. 104. On all this, see also Laurent de Sutter, *Deleuze: La pra-
    tique du droit* (Paris: Michalon, 2009), p. 67 *sq.*
17 Jacques Derrida, *Spectres de Marx: L'Etat de la dette, le travail du deuil
    et la nouvelle Internationale* (Paris: Galilée, 1993), p. 97 *sq.* See also,
    Peeters, *Derrida*, p. 568 *sq.*

artefacts, one had to make a choice: either continue the fight, or displace its cursor towards something more realistic. Derrida took one path; Deleuze and Guattari (and Baudrillard) took another; a few of their companions were still hesitating (Pierre Bourdieu, Jean-François Lyotard); while others were dead or almost (Louis Althusser, Michel Foucault, Roland Barthes, Jacques Lacan). However, together they constituted the incarnated map of the late moment of what should be called the *anti-juridical moment of the 1960s* in France—a moment which was strictly homogeneous with its *philosophical moment*, to use a concept of Frédéric Worms.[18] During the quarter century between the middle of the 1960s and 1989, a general operation of critique of law had been deployed by a whole generation of thinkers, as the necessary consequence of the revolution that they had brought to the realm of thought. At the moment when Derrida pronounced his Cardozo keynote address, the map showed many signs of dereliction; yet one could still decipher the main features of the moment that was about to end, if one wanted to—but apparently, there was nobody in the queue. The *anti-juridical moment* had passed unnoticed, even though its relationship with the philosophical revolution of the 1960s was crucial, not only for its own understanding, but also for the understanding of this revolution as such. Looking at it from a distance, one could even go as far as to state that the *philosophical moment* of the 1960s, in France, could be named as such only insofar as it was an *anti-juridical moment*, as if the latter was the very condition of the former. Without a revolution in the way law is conceived, it is impossible to talk of a philosophical revolution *tout court*, since philosophy has always relied upon its attempt at subjecting law to its power in order to constitute itself.

18 Compare Frédéric Worms, *La philosophie en France au XXe siècle. Moments* (Paris: Gallimard, 2009). For a more focused overview, see Patrice Maniglier, ed., *Le moment philosophique des années 1960 en France*, foreword by Frédéric Worms (Paris: PUF, 2011).

§ 5
Nomos versus Logos

Deleuze was maybe the most consistent in his attempt at bridging the philosophical conceptual creations for which he became famous with an in-depth dialogue with law—a dialogue that, nevertheless, never took the form of a proper book.[19] Still, from his very first researches on Locke up to his final collaboration with Guattari, *Qu'est-ce que la philosophie?*, Deleuze never ceased to dedicate efforts to the understanding of how law and philosophy were dancing a menacing dance. At first sight, Deleuze's main claim was as simple as one could get: law, he suggested, was the future of philosophy—if philosophy was to follow the path of transcendental empiricism, and forget about its past attempts at thinking grounding and guarantee.[20] Instead of considering law as the enemy of philosophy, Deleuze insisted on seeing it as an adjuvant in philosophy's own quest to escape transcendence, and reconcile with the casuistry of life—so postulating that law itself has nothing to do with transcendence altogether. To put it differently: Deleuze wanted to get rid of philosophy's desire for the transcendent Law of *logos*, and put as its keystone another kind of law, devoid of any reference to *logos*—another law for which he still decided to keep the name "Nomos."[21] Deleuze's intellectual move was a twisted one: on the one hand, he designated law as the new horizon of philosophy; on the other, he was reinstating philosophy as the discipline capable of making the difference between *nomos* and *logos*, between a "good" and a "bad" law.[22] The fact remains, though, that, in insisting on the inner divide of law, Deleuze was restaging, for the contemporary era,

19 Compare de Sutter, *Deleuze*, p. 11 *sq.*
20 Ibid., pp. 14–15.
21 Compare Gilles Deleuze and Félix Guattari, *Mille plateaux. Capitalisme et schizophrénie 2* (Paris: Minuit, 1980), p. 458.
22 de Sutter, *Deleuze*, p. 91 *sq.*

the millennia long discussion about its intellectual status, and also its practice: was law a principle of order, or was it a form of life? In the first case, best exemplified by the Greek concept of *logos*, law was only the name for a form of policing, that could be exercised in the realm of thought as well as in the realm of society—a form of policing based on generality, abstraction, and so on. However, in the second case, whose Roman concept of *ius* was the most famous expression, law had nothing to do with unity and principles, but rather with diversity and bricolage—that is, with a sense of construction of consequences rather than with the verification of fidelity to causes. Whereas Law (as *logos*) always implied contempt for its practice in the name of its ideal, law (as *nomos*) was entirely practical, entirely turned towards concrete experimentations and specific inventions—as, according to Deleuze, philosophy should be too.[23]

§ 6
Is Another Truth Possible?

Deleuze was not alone in his rejection of Law as *logos*; on the contrary, one could even say that this rejection constituted the fundamental trait uniting the conceptions of his French contemporaries, whatever their disciplinary origin or approach. What differentiated them, how-

---

23 Ibid., pp. 93–94. See also Nathan Moore, "Icons of Control: Deleuze, Signs, Law," *International Journal for the Semiotics of Law* 20:1 (2007): p. 33 *sq.*; Alexandre Lefebvre, *The Image of Law: Deleuze, Bergson, Spinoza* (Stanford CA: Stanford University Press, 2008); Rosi Braidotti, Claire Colebrook and Patrick Hanafin, eds., *Deleuze and Law: Forensic Futures* (London: Palgrave Macmillan, 2009); Edward Mussawir, *Jurisdiction in Deleuze: The Expression and Representation of Law* (Abingdon and New York: Routledge, 2011); Laurent de Sutter and Kyle McGee, eds., *Deleuze and Law* (Edinburgh: Edinburgh University Press, 2012); Jamie Murray, *Deleuze and Guattari: Emergent Law* (Abingdon: Routledge, 2013); Russel Ford, "Humor, Law, Jurisprudence: On Deleuze's Political Philosophy," *Angelaki* 21:3 (2016): p. 89 *sq.*

ever, was how they conceived *logos*—as an overarching order or a metaphysical concept, as a political system or a social logic of beliefs, as a symbolic instance or the materialization of the desire of its defenders. Althusser's critique of law, for instance, was foremost a critique of the way it serves as an "Ideological State Apparatus" aiming at enforcing a certain relationship of production upon the dominated class—a critique of *logos* as a policing device.[24] By contrast, Bourdieu's powerful analysis of the "force of law" (*droit*, in the French original, and not *loi*, as in Derrida) focused on the strategic dimensions at stake with an object whose definition was up for grabs—not a policing device, but a device to be policed.[25] The same goes for Foucault, whose deep historical insights aimed at showing, as Deleuze puts it, that the relationship of power towards law is not a relationship based on the enforcement of *the* legal, but of the definition of realms of legalities.[26] Yet all of these

24 Louis Althusser, *Sur la reproduction*, 2nd ed. (Paris: Puf, 2011), p. 197 *sq*. On this, see Laurent de Sutter, ed., *Althusser and Law* (London: Routledge, 2012). See also Francine Demichel, "Althusser et le Droit," *Politique et philosophie dans l'oeuvre de Louis Althusser*, ed. Sylvain Lazarus (Paris: Puf, 1993), p. 117 *sq*.; Nina Power, "Althusser: The Law, the Cop and the Subject," *Los Angeles Review of Books*, May 15, 2016, https://lareviewofbooks.org/article/althusser-law-cop-subject/ [consulted on the 13/03/20].

25 Pierre Bourdieu, "La force du droit: Eléments pour une sociologie du champ juridique," *Actes de la recherche en sciences sociales* 64:1 (1986): p. 3 *sq*. Compare Jacques Commaille, ed., "La place du droit dans l'oeuvre de Pierre Bourdieu," *Droit et société* 56–57 (2004): p. 11 *sq*.; Mikael Rask Madsen, ed., *Pierre Bourdieu: From Law to Legal Field*, *Retfaerd* 114 (2006); Lucille A. Jewel, "Bourdieu and American Legal Education: How Law Schools Reproduce Social Stratification and Class Hierarchy," *Buffalo Law Review* 56:4 (2008), p. 1155 sq.; Yves Dezalay and Mikael Rask Madsen, "The Force of Law and Lawyers: Pierre Bourdieu and the Reflexive Sociology of Law," *Annual Review of Law and Social Sciences* 8 (2012): p. 433 *sq*.; Jean-Jacques Sueur, "Pierre Bourdieu, le droit et les juristes: La méprise," *Droit et société* 85 (2013): p. 725 *sq*.; Bernard Voutat, "Penser le droit avec Pierre Bourdieu," *Swiss Political Science Review* 20:1(2014), p. 31 *sq*.

26 Compare Gilles Deleuze, *Foucault* (Paris: Minuit, 1986), pp. 37–38. See also Gerard Turkel, "Michel Foucault: Law, Power and Knowledge," *Law and Society* 17:2 (1990): p. 170 *sq*.; Alan Hunt and Gary Wickham, *Foucault and Law: Towards of Sociology of Law as Governance* (London: Pluto Press, 1994); Anthony Beck, "Foucault and

thinkers displayed a strong suspicion towards law as an instance deserving respect; whatever their differences, they all considered that the respect in question was undue, and that, contrary to social democrats like Raymond Aron, the least one could do was to question it. All too had instated this questioning as the defining feature of their enterprise of reformulation of either philosophy or sociology, psychoanalysis or history; as if a renewal of these disciplines was possible only on condition of a general attack on law. *The ruin of law is the condition of thought*—there can be thought only insofar as it is not made a norm: this was the common presupposition underlying the various intellectual endeavors of the *philosophical moment* of the 1960s in France. But the problem with law is that it tends to permeate every aspect of social, political, ethical, aesthetic, and even ontological life; law, under one form or another, incarnates the dimension of what we must get past if we want to formulate a novel truth about life. In the end, this was indeed the problem which the thinkers of this generation wanted to deal with: in the renewal of the concept of truth (even through its deconstruction), what was at stake was its possible separation from the idea of norm, of *logos*, of law.

Law: The Collapse of Law's Empire," *Oxford Journal of Legal Studies* 16:3 (1996): p. 489 *sq.*; Victor Tadros, "Between Governance and Discipline: The Law and Michel Foucault," *Oxford Journal of Legal Studies* 18:1 (1998): p. 75 *sq.*; Carole Smith, "The Sovereign State v. Foucault: Law and Disciplinary Power," *The Sociological Review* 48:2 (2000): p. 283 *sq.*; Peter Fitzpatrick and Ben Golder, *Foucault's Law* (London: Routledge, 2009); Bertrand Mazabraud, "Foucault, le droit et les dispositifs de pouvoir," *Cités* 42 (2010): p. 127 *sq.*; Ben Golder, *Foucault and the Law* (London: Routledge, 2010); Mario Alves de Fonseca, *Michel Foucault et le droit*, trans. Thierry Thomas (Paris: L'Harmattan, 2014); Ben Golder, ed., *Re-Reading Foucault: On Law, Power and Rights* (London: Routledge, 2014).

§ 7
On the Politics of Being

They were children of Karl Marx, Sigmund Freud, Friedrich Nietzsche (and Martin Heidegger), as revised by the great French tradition of rationalism incarnated by professors such as Georges Canguilhem or Jean Hippolyte, Jules Vuillemin or Léon Brunschvicg. From the latter two, they had learned the necessity of method, and the possibility of developing a path of thought different from the one set up by the Germans, especially the post-Kantians; from the former two, they understood the possibility of finishing with the old conception of truth.[27] This conception was the one grounded on Being—the fact that truth, whatever its features, always has something to do with Being, as the ultimate horizon that its unveiling should designate, or as the ecology without which it is unthinkable. Imagining another journey towards truth, and another version of what it could be, was what all the thinkers of the *philosophical moment* of the 1960s in France had in common, up to the point where the mere utterance of the word *truth* became unbearable. The law that they wanted to attack was then the law of Being itself; thinking truth without any connection to a norm implied destroying Being as the source of any norm, as the very place of Law itself; it required thinking the possibility of the absence of Being, or of its ruin. As a matter of fact, the affair looked tricky, since it was hardly obvious to determine whether Being was the source of Law, or Law the source of Being, or even that they were one and the same thing —but, to a certain extent, these questions were unimportant. What mattered was the shared certainty about the close relationship between Being and Law, and the intuition that succeeding in ruining the first would necessarily lead to ruining the other as well, so liberating philosophy from its two heaviest

---

27 On all this, see Frédéric Worms, *La philosophie en France.*

burdens. Furthermore, speaking of *liberation* was not a euphemism: what was at stake with the attempt at defining an ecology of thought devoid of any reference to Being or to Law was a struggle that was expected to have consequences well beyond the frontiers of metaphysics. For Deleuze, Derrida, Althusser, Foucault, et al., the fight was primarily conceived as a political one—not in terms of academic intrigues, or national revenges, but insofar as the imposition of Being as the key to truth was indeed the imposition of a certain type of politics. By putting Being (or Law, or the Good) on the top of the metaphysical edifice, the conditions for accessing the power to reign over this edifice were also defined—and, with them, the monopoly of the only class capable of satisfying them.

§ 8
Revolution at the Gate (of the Concept)

The politics of Being, for the French thinkers of the 1960s generation, translated into a series of effective short-circuits between thought and action; that is, between the realm of concepts, and that of the practice of intellectuals, militants and so on. The two most obvious forms of translation offered at the time were those of Althusser and Bourdieu, even though the vocabulary of the fight against the type of monopoly which benefitted the defenders of Being could be found everywhere. The famous definition of philosophy formulated by Althusser, stating that thinking was nothing but "class struggle in theory," transforming it into some sort of effective "practice" as such, indicated what the logic behind this short-circuit was.[28] Whereas the passage from theory to practice had

---

28 Louis Althusser, *Réponse à John Lewis* (Paris: Maspero, 1973), p. 41. For more detailed accounts on this claim, see Louis Althusser, *Sur la philosophie* (1984) (Paris: Gallimard, 1994), pp. 55–56; Louis Althusser, *Initiation à la philosophie pour les non-philosophes* (1975),

long been considered a complicated, or even impossible, task to pursue, Althusser considered that it had always-already been at work, especially when its mere possibility was altogether denied. Such a denial was nothing but an attempt at securing the monopoly that a close examination of the effectiveness of the short-circuit between theory and practice would immediately outline—denying its possibility was simply a way to hide it from the critical gaze in order to protect it. By contrast, emphasizing the dimension of "class struggle in theory" aimed at bringing it into the open, at making it appear in such a manner that the intellectual realm could be accepted for what it was: a dramatic battlefield between antagonistic forces. Of course, the context of Althusser's claim provided some reasons for such a clear-cut recognition of the short-circuit between theory and practice: in the 1960s, the French Communist Party (PCF) was still leading the fight for revolution—and for theory. Party Communism, at that time, provided an economy of thought not simply in terms of concepts, but also in terms of their immediate application within the political program of the party, which was, by all means, an ultimately theoretical program.[29] Bourdieu's understanding of "social fields" as a place for competition between different social classes looking for domination, or belonging to the dominant class, only expanded these ideas to the different political sub-worlds, outside the scope of the party.[30] What his sociology achieved was precisely to

ed. G. M. Goshgarian (Paris: Puf, 2014), p. 361 *sq.*; Louis Althusser, *Être marxiste en philosophie* (1976), ed. G. M. Goshgarian (Paris: Puf, 2015), p. 375 *sq.*

29 Compare Stéphane Courtois and Marc Lazar, *Histoire du Parti communiste français*, 2nd ed. (Paris: Puf, 2000). On the link between Althusser and the PCF, see Jacques Rancière, *La leçon d'Althusser*, 2nd ed. (Paris: La Fabrique, 2012). Some early biographical elements are presented in Yann Moulier Boutang, *Louis Althusser, une biographie: La formation du mythe: 1945–1956: Ruptures et plis* (Paris: Grasset, 1992), p. 198 *sq.*

30 The concept of "field" ("*champ*") was formulated by Bourdieu very early on. See for instance *Esquisse d'une théorie de la pratique* (1972),

show how the short-circuit between theory and practice was an everyday phenomenon; that one could observe, down to the most apparently insignificant detail, how it testified to the place occupied by a person in the social hierarchy.

§ 9
The Metaphysical Police

There is no innocence in the realm of concept. Truth always bears consequences; political choices shape its structure, object and capacity to grasp a certain state of things situated way beyond metaphysics—and the defence of Nomos is one of them. It was only natural, then, that Deleuze wanted to replace Being by becoming, inasmuch as he wanted to substitute *logos* with *nomos*, or law with casuistry; the general move of his whole generation was a move towards what had been left aside by the dominant philosophical tradition. Against the regulation of life, we have to focus on life as a means to ruin regulation, to show that regulation never succeeds in anything but securing the position of those advocating it—even though, in the end, the latter know that regulation is pointless. Being, to a certain extent, is not even a proper metaphysical category, if one is to consider metaphysics as a rigorous science consisting in extracting the exact consequences from its assumption; as Law itself, metaphysics never has been anything but tentative policing. Such policing is tentative because, in the end, never bypass its own failures, impossibilities or contradictions, so always-already showing how inconsistent it ultimately is, and how its only grounding is in its effective violence. Lacan might

2nd ed. (Paris: Le Seuil, 2000). For detailed discussions of this concept, see Bernard Lahire, ed., *Le travail sociologique de Pierre Bourdieu* (Paris: La Découverte, 2001), p. 23 *sq.*; Jean-Louis Fabiani, *Pierre Bourdieu: Un structuralisme héroïque* (Paris: Le Seuil, 2016).

very well have been the most explicit proponent of this claim: to him Law, despite its alleged symbolic majesty, was always based on a void or a crack—its power only relied upon the deliberate refusal of those who obeyed it to even consider that it was fundamentally null, that it didn't even exist at all.[31] Barthes, too, in the small theory of the contract that he offered in a passage of *Roland Barthes par Roland Barthes*, hinted at a similar conclusion, suggesting that the truth of any contract, of any legal mechanism of convention, was none other than prostitution.[32] Behind the social justification of the contract, as a device allowing for equilibrium of exchange, and rejecting any immoral use of its machinery, hides the fundamental expression of desire that the apparent neutrality of the contract tries to mask. In reality, no contract has ever served as a mere tool for balancing interests in an exchange society; rather, it has always served as a blueprint for the expression of the type of desire considered legitimate in a given society—namely, the bourgeois one. By foreclosing prostitution as illegitimate, although it was based on a financial negotiation leading to some sort of conventional agreement, bourgeois society was simply trying to dissimulate that every type of exchange belongs to the same logic.[33]

31 Compare Laurent de Sutter, "Reciprocal Portrait of Jacques Lacan as Gilles Deleuze," in Bostjan Nedoh and Andreja Zevnik, eds., *Lacan and Deleuze: A Disjunctive Synthesis* (Edinburgh: Edinburgh University Press, 2016), p. 32 *sq.*
32 Roland Barthes, *Roland Barthes par Roland Barthes*, in *Oeuvres complètes IV: 1972–1976*, ed. Eric Marty, 2nd ed. (Paris: Le Seuil, 2002), pp. 638–639.
33 Ibid., p. 629. See also Laurent de Sutter, "Prostituer la loi: La figure du contrat dans l'oeuvre de Roland Barthes," forthcoming.

§ 10
After Law

Yet appearances can be deceived. Behind the ruined landscape of law within which the thinkers of the French *philosophical moment* of the 1960s abandoned us, nothing had completely been destroyed; it was even the contrary. The case of Deleuze was paradigmatic: on the one hand, he wanted to get rid of Law, understood as a set of general and abstract principles affiliated to the Greek concept of *nomos*; on the other, he was a fierce proponent of law, as endless casuistry, on the model of the Roman *ius*. He was not the only one to think thus; if one was to read through Althusser's nostalgia for the trial that he was denied after he murdered his wife, Hélène Rytmann, there was also something to be saved of the world of law in his theory.[34] Althusser's case is trickier than Deleuze's since, on several occasions, Althusser expressly claimed that with the future advent of a Communist society, we would abandon law altogether, and turn towards other forms of managing coexistence.[35] As usual, he didn't mention which forms he had in mind—something typical of the Marxist tradition, whose embarrassment with law has always been slightly comical, as in the case of Marx himself, or of the official Marxist legal theorist Evgeny Pasukanis.[36] Belonging to a universe of sensibility whose standards had been devised by the Historical School of Jurisprudence, one could imagine that Marx and his followers would rely on the spontaneous organization of society

34 Compare Laurent de Sutter, "Louis Althusser et la scène du procès," *Décalages* 2:1, http://scholar.oxy.edu/decalages/vol2/iss1/24 [consulted on the 13/03/20].

35 See for instance Louis Althusser, "Eléments d'autocritique," (1972), in *Solitude de Machiavel, et autres textes*, ed. Yves Sintomer (Paris: Puf, 1998), p. 171, n. 22.

36 Compare Evgeny B. Pasukanis, *La théorie générale du droit et le marxisme*, trans. Jean-Marie Brohm (Paris: EDI, 1970). See also Michel Miaille, *Une introduction critique au droit* (Paris: Maspero, 1976).

to settle eventual conflicts.[37] One could even have gone as far as to state that, in a true Communist world, conflicts would become inexistent, which would immediately recall the very specific regime of "law" of China or Japan, based on a customary order of the world prohibiting conflict.[38] But Althusser was a rationalist, well aware of the fact that conflicts are a mechanical part of coexistence, and that some device would be needed in order to solve them—or, at least, to live with them in a way that wouldn't lead to the ruin of the whole Communist project. If modern law, as incarnated by the Civil Code and the judiciary system, was an intrinsically bourgeois device, based on a reactionary figure of the subject, it was supposedly possible to imagine, from another point of departure, another system of "law." Althusser hadn't any name for this system; the only thing he knew was that, instead of being based on the figure of the subject, it should be based on its very opposite; if there was to be a "law" for the Communist society, it had to be a law without the subject.[39]

§11
Structuralism's Last Stand

The idea of an impersonal law, without the subject and without normative power, was a structuralist's dream—

---

37 See Mikhaïl Xifaras, "Marx, justice et jurisprudence: Une lecture des 'vols de bois'," *Revue française d'histoire des idées politiques* 15 (2002), p. 63 *sq.* For the broader context, see Olivier Jouanjan, *Une histoire de la pensée juridique en Allemagne (1800–1918): Idéalisme et conceptualisme chez les juristes allemands du XIXe siècle* (Paris: Puf, 2005).

38 Compare Yosiyuki Noda, *Introduction to Japanese Law* (Tokyo: University of Tokyo Press, 1976); Jean-Hubert Moitry, *Le droit japonais* (Paris: Puf, 1988); Geoffrey MacCormack, *The Spirit of Traditional Chinese Law* (Athens GA: University of Georgia Press: 1996); John Owen Haley, *The Spirit of Japanese Law* (Athens GA: University of Georgia Press, 1998); Olivier Beydon, *Introduction à la pensée juridique chinoise* (Brussels: Larcier, 2015).

39 Laurent de Sutter, "Louis Althusser et la scène du procès."

and indeed, in Althusser's desire for a post-legal legal system, or Deleuze's eagerness to witness the triumph of a *nomos*-free *ius*, there was something structural at work. Of course, one had to understand structure in a non-coercive sense, as underlying the fabric of society, accompanying it without framing it; the structure at stake was mostly, as Foucault put it, a web of ever-changing relations rather than their fixed organization.[40] In his study of the functioning of the French Conseil d'Etat, *La fabrique du droit*, Bruno Latour has offered the perfect synthesis of what was in the making in the thought of Deleuze, Derrida, Foucault and the others, by calling law a web holding everything together without being anywhere—an impersonal constitution of relations.[41] The only specific feature of this web, according to Latour, is its robustness; that is, the fact that it gives to the relations that it establishes (or destroys, or reconfigures) a certain kind of solidity, born out of their inscription within the web itself. The structure of law is then not a given; it is an ever-moving landscape whose power only lies in its extension, in the fact that every new legal relation gives birth to other legal relations, retrospectively providing their strength to the previous ones.[42] In the vocabulary of Deleuze, law is nothing but a set of impersonal opera-

40 Compare Michel Foucault, "Le sujet et le pouvoir," (1982), *Dits et écrits, II: 1976–1988*, ed. Daniel Defert and François Ewald, 2nd ed. (Paris: Gallimard, 2001), pp. 1041–1062. For the place of this claim in the history of structuralism, see François Dosse, *Histoire du structuralisme, II: Le chant du cygne, 1967 à nos jours* (Paris: La Découverte, 1992).

41 Bruno Latour, *La fabrique du droit: Une ethnographie du Conseil d'Etat* (Paris: La Découverte, 2004), p. 283 *sq*. For a commentary, see Laurent de Sutter, "Plasma! Notes on Bruno Latour's Metaphysics of Law," in Kyle McGee, ed., *Latour and the Passage of Law* (Edinburgh: Edinburgh University Press, 2015), p. 197 *sq*. See also Kyle McGee, *Bruno Latour: The Normativity of Networks* (London: Routledge, 2014).

42 Bruno Latour, *La fabrique du droit*, pp. 294–295. This claim finds its source in Gabriel Tarde, *Les transformations du droit: Etude sociologique* (1893) (Paris: Berg, 1994), p. 76. See also, for a discussion, Laurent de Sutter, *Magic: Une métaphysique du lien* (Paris: Puf, 2015), p. 107 *sq*.

tions whose sole object is the rendering possible of other operations, constructing a potentially endless chain, ramifying through its development so as to encompass everything.[43] If there was a meaning to *ius*, it was this: behind *lex*, behind the tentative overarching of a general principle of order, something is always at work that may, or may not, allow this principle to become effective—something that is as weak as it gets. The weakness of law, compared to the bombastic majesty of Law, was what interested almost every thinker of the generation of Deleuze and Althusser—with the exception of those who, like Derrida, eventually found refuge in ethics. It was the key to their structuralism redux, and the point of departure for any endeavor in the world of law that would not take Law, *nomos*, rules, norms or legislation either for granted, or as even important, since its only objects were none of these, but instead mere operations. There is a Law that renders everything impossible; and then there is a law whose purpose is void, except that it opens up new possibilities, including the possibility of imagining a society without subjects—as well as its very opposite, if needed.

§ 12
In Praise of Practice

The long history of the conflicts between philosophy and law is best exemplified by Cicero's famous rant against lawyers—whom he wanted to replace with wise men defending the eternal principles of "natural law," so redeeming the flaws of practice.[44] Deleuze's move was

43 Compare Laurent de Sutter, *Après la loi*, forthcoming.
44 Compare Pierre Grimal, *Cicéron* (Paris: Fayard, 1986), p. 272 *sq.* See also Michèle Ducos, *Les Romains et la loi: Recherches sur les rapports de la philosophie grecque et de la tradition romaine à la fin de la République* (Paris: Les Belles Lettres, 1984); Marie Theres Fögen, *Histoires du droit romain: De l'origine et de l'évolution d'un système social*, trans. Denis Trierweiler (Paris: Editions de la Maison des sciences de

rather the opposite: it was an attempt at redeeming the flaws and dangers of trying to impose something like eternal principles of justice by a greater focus on the virtues of practice itself, as it is not concerned with such principles. Even though lawyers are part of the dominant classes of society, or are the defenders of a form of social reproduction aimed at repressing any possible change, there is still something in their practice that exceeds the boundaries of class or capital. This excess is law as such—that is, as a practice of imagination of new operations leading to the construction of new consequences beyond the actual chain of operations already in place— a practice of *technical*, rather than ethical or political, imagination. This is what explains why, despite their apparently devastating critique of law, all of the thinkers of the 1960s *philosophical moment* in France were not completely against law. If they were against something, it was the social order that used legal tools in order to enforce impossibilities. But law, understood as the modest practice of constructing more or less robust chains of consequences, had nothing to do with this order, and could very well be used, under certain conditions, for other purposes, including revolution. Instead of speaking of the *anti-juridism* of this generation of thinkers, as some have tried to do, it would be more suitable to speak of their *anti-legalism*, of their hatred of the position of domination given to a certain state of norms, weighing upon law as a deadly constraint.[45] This is why they could participate in struggles that seemed strangely

l'homme, 2007); Aldo Schiavone, *Ius: L'invention du droit en Occident*, trans. Geneviève and Jean Bouffartigues (Paris: Belin, 2008).

45 See for instance Hernando Vallencia-Villa, "Foucault and the Law: An Antijuridical Jurisprudence?," *Philippine Law Journal* 56:3 (1981): p. 355 *sq.*; Rares Piloiu, "Deleuze's Concept of Immanence as Anti-Juridical Utopia," *Soundings* 87:1–2 (2004): p. 201 *sq.*; Juliette Grange, "Statophobie, antijuridisme et critique du libéralisme dans les dernières oeuvres de Bourdieu et Foucault," *Cités* 51 (2012): p. 79 *sq.*; Julie Allard, "La philosophie, un anti-juridisme?," in Thomas Berns and Julie Allard, eds., *Pensées du droit, lois de la philosophie: Mélanges en l'honneur de Guy Haarscher* (Bruxelles: PUB, 2012), p. 39 *sq.*

democratic to the most radical revolutionary eyes, such as the experience of the *Groupe d'information sur les Prisons* which gathered many of them around Foucault, Pierre Vidal-Naquet and Jean-Marie Domenach.[46] What the *Groupe* wanted was not to abolish the penitentiary system as such, but only, if one looks closely, to augment its malfunctioning: by obtaining hidden information, and establishing new networks of solidarities between prisoners, lawyers, doctors, etc. There was nothing openly revolutionary in this, even though the circumstance that gave birth to the *Groupe* was the state censorship of the member of the Maoist group *Gauche Prolétarienne*, which was tempted by terrorism at some point in its history.

§ 13
Down the Family Tree

This was perhaps the most misunderstood point of the relationship between Derrida, Althusser, et al. and law: the fact that their anti-legalism was not intended to lead to some sort of generalized anti-juridism, but rather to a renewal of law per se. The embarrassment of the disciples (faithful or not) of the members of the group towards law most probably found its origin in their underestimation of the importance of this distinction—a distinction, indeed, that had never been made explicit. From Alain Badiou to Jacques Rancière, Slavoj Žižek to Jean-Luc Nancy, Antonio Negri to Fredric Jameson, Judith Butler to Ernesto Laclau, those who have been considered as the continuators of the work of the great French thinkers of the 1960s avoided the question of law. In *Multitude*, Negri, with Michael Hardt, dedicated a few pages

46 Compare Philippe Artières, Laurent Quéro and Michelle Zancarini-Fournel, *Le Groupe d'information sur les Prisons: Archives d'une lutte (1970–1972)* (Paris: IMEC, 2003).

to the necessity of elaborating a new legal pact, without really going into the details; Nancy, in *L'impératif catégorique*, offered some powerful pages on the act of judging, but never elaborated them further. That was basically it.[47] The most important exception, here, is Giorgio Agamben, whose masterwork *Homo Sacer* could be considered as a genuine theory of law, even though this theory would lead to some apocalyptical visions concerning the power attributed to law in the contemporary world.[48] To some extent, Agamben even radicalized the anti-legalism of his predecessors up to the point where there was nothing left for law, as a set of operations— as if law had been completely contaminated by Law, without any chance of return (yet Agamben still trusts law as a hermeneutical tool).[49] The same can be said of the bunch of law professors who found in the French thinkers of the 1960s *philosophical moment* resources to question their own practice, and ended up defining the ill-fated program of "Critical Legal Studies."[50] For what was Critical Legal Studies, if not an anti-legalism turned anti-juridism, as if it was impossible to make the distinction between the two—or, to put it differently: as if law was so alienated and alienating that there couldn't

---

47 Jean-Luc Nancy, "Lapsus Judicii," in *L'impératif catégorique* (Paris: Flammarion, 1983), p. 33 *sq.*; Michael Hardt and Antonio Negri, *Multitude: Guerre et démocratie à l'âge de l'Empire*, trans. Nicolas Guilhot (Paris: La Découverte, 2004), p. 341 *sq.* See also Laurent de Sutter, ed., *Žižek and Law* (London: Routledge, 2015).

48 Giorgio Agamben, *Homo Sacer: L'intégrale (1997–2015)* (Paris: Le Seuil, 2016).

49 On this point, see Laurent de Sutter, "Contra Iurem: Les deux ontologies de Giorgio Agamben," forthcoming. See also Catherine Mills, "Playing with Law: Agamben and Derrida on Postjuridical Justice," *South Atlantic Quarterly* 107:1 (2008): p. 15 *sq.*; Justin Clemens, Nicholas Heron and Alex Murray, eds., *The Work of Giorgio Agamben: Law, Literature, Life* (Edinburgh: Edinburgh University Press, 2011); Thanos Zartaloudis, ed., *Agamben and Law* (London: Routledge, 2015).

50 Compare Peter Goodrich, "Sleeping with the Enemy: On the Politics of Critical Legal Studies in America," in *Law in the Courts of Love: Literature and Other Minor Jurisprudences* (London: Routledge, 1996), p. 185 *sq.*

be any "good" lawyer who wouldn't base his or her practice on the very refusal of law. This might be why Derrida was cheered with such enthusiasm by the crowd gathered at the Benjamin N. Cardozo Law School when he pronounced his address on "Du droit à la justice": they recognized in his insistence on justice, and then on ethics, something they could rely upon. But, in doing so, they actually forgot to acknowledge the much more sophisticated lesson of Derrida's own thought, as an important member of a community who, in the end, hadn't lost all hope for law.

Susanne Krasmann

On Thinking and Feeling

The Law of Cultural Heritage

1.
Man's disappearance and the question
of the legal subject

In the *Order of Things* Michel Foucault famously fore-shadowed "man's" disappearance from history, "like a face drawn in sand at the edge of the sea."[1] As an epistemological figure, the human being, or humanity, is a rather recent invention. It was not until the end of the eighteenth century that the human sciences, claiming their position between fundamental science, or philosophy, and empirical sciences,[2] began to conceive of man as both the very subject of thought and an object of knowledge, as the human being that was able to speak, work, live their life and that would become the subject of interest of psychology, sociology and the study of literature and myth. Less than two centuries later, the truth of man began to crumble. In a further epistemological volte-face, the human being came to appear to be enmeshed in general structural conditions that far exceed individual existence: the subject of psychoanalysis sees itself inhabited by an unconscious that withdraws from autonomous self-mastery,[3] the subject of ethnology is placed in the historicity of societies

---

1 Michel Foucault, *The Order of Things. An archaeology of the human sciences* (London and New York: Routledge, 1989), p. 422.
2 Ibid., p. 377.
3 Ibid., p. 388.

thanks to the invariable logics of cultural formation,[4] and finally the subject of linguistics speaks only on account of the general laws of language. Yet these epistemologies, this is Foucault's point, are themselves thrown into history, and so is the human subject and its truth: it is conditioned by what can be said or thought at a certain moment in history.

Although humankind, as we all know, survived the twentieth century, today this species seems again to be "on the verge of its expiration date."[5] This time, it seems to be a question of physical extinction in view of global environmental degradation in the Anthropocene. As things stand, human beings are well on the way to destroying their own basis of existence, Earth, and now find themselves in the impossible situation of having to realize that the planet might survive independently of the human species.[6] If this crisis of humanity is considered an existential one, it also poses a question that is epistemological as well as ethical: how to conceive of a world that would exceed the destructive force and limitations of human politics?[7]

A new awareness relating to anthropocentrism has also emerged in an only seemingly disparate field: the debate on the value of cultural heritage for "humanity." It was an International Criminal Court's (ICC) decision that spurred this debate: the case of the Malian citizen Ahmad Al Faqi Al Mahdi, who on September 27, 2016 was found guilty of the war crime of intentionally attacking historic and religious buildings in Timbuktu

---

4   Ibid., p. 411.
5   "'Man' is a recent invention on the verge of its expiration date," *Heterodoxia: Heretical topics that challenges orthodox philosophy*, 18 September 2008, available at: http://www.hyperboreans.com/heterodoxia/ [consulted on the 09/02/20].
6   Kevin Grove and David Chandler, "Introduction: resilience and the Anthropocene: the stakes of 'renaturalising' politics," *Resilience* 5 (2017): pp. 79–91, 82.
7   Claire Colebrook, "A Globe of One's Own: In Praise of the Flat Earth," *SubStance* 41 (2012): pp. 30–39, 30.

and sentenced to nine years' imprisonment.[8] Following the orders of the Islamist group *Ansar Dine*, which had enforced sharia law in Mali, Al Mahdi executed the destruction of nine mosques and the Sidi Yahia Mosque door, all but one of them designated as World Heritage objects. The ICC judgement received considerable international attention and was widely perceived as a landmark decision, if not a precedent, as it was the first time a person had been brought to international justice on the grounds of destroying cultural heritage alone.

The verdict was not without controversy, however. The lively debate to which it gave rise can be said largely to be split between two poles. One side argued that "serious crimes" that had also been committed, such as murder, rape or torture of civilians, had received comparatively limited attention by that time.[9] Instead, the court had sought an "easy win" in view of existing video footage that provided compelling proof of al Mahdi's guilt.[10] For others the decision did not go far enough, given that the court had valued "the culture that binds a community together less than the toll on human lives."[11] The

---

8 *The Prosecutor v. Ahmad Al Faqi Al Mahdi*, Judgment and Sentence (Public), ICC-01/12–01/15, 27 September 2016, available at: https://www.icc-cpi.int/CourtRecords/cr2016_07244.pdf [consulted on the 09/02/20].

9 Compare, for example, Amnesty International, "Landmark ICC verdict against Al-Mahdi must be first step to broader justice in Mali conflict," September 27 (2016), available at: https://www.amnesty.org/en/latest/news/2016/09/landmark-icc-verdict-against-almahdi-must-be-first-step-to-broader-justice-in-mali-conflict/ [consulted on the 09/02/20]; International Federation for Human Rights, "ICC orders reparations for destruction of cultural heritage: a limited step in the prosecution of crimes committed in Timbuktu," August 17 (2018), available at: https://www.fidh.org/en/region/Africa/mali/icc-orders-reparations-for-destruction-of-cultural-heritage-a-limited [consulted on the 09/02/20].

10 Recent Cases, "Prosecutor v. Ahmad Al Faqi Al Mahdi. International Criminal Court Imposes First Sentence for War Crime of Attacking Cultural Heritage," *Harvard Law Review* 130 (2017): pp. 1978–1985, 1982.

11 Lucas Lixinski and Sarah Williams, "The ICC's Al-Mahdi ruling protects cultural heritage, but didn't go far enough," *The Conversation* 18 (2016), available at: https://theconversation.com/the-iccs-al-mahdi-ruling-protects-cultural-heritage-but-didnt-go-far-enough-67071 [consulted on the 09/02/20].

ICC Trial Chamber VIII had in fact stressed that "crimes against property are generally of lesser gravity than crimes against persons," but it had also recognized that the destruction of the World Heritage sites affected "the faithful and inhabitants of Timbuktu, but also people throughout Mali and the international community."[12]

Obviously, this debate set up a rivalry between the vulnerability of people, concerning their body or life, and the symbolic—or, to use the standard legal term, "intangible"—value cultural objects, in this case the religious buildings, have for a particular community, if not for humanity. Yet the matter is even more complex. At stake is not merely the juxtaposition between body and culture, human being and object, the value of human life and symbolic or emotional value, but the value of cultural objects as such. As Marina Lostal points out, the Office of the Prosecution in the Al Mahdi case espoused an "anthropocentric reading," bolstered by the increasing prevalence of human rights discourse in the last few decades, by positing human suffering as a requirement to assess and establish the gravity of the crime.[13] The decision would thus impede appreciating and protecting cultural heritage independently in future cases.

This idea of attributing to cultural heritage a value "per se"[14] is an intriguing figure of thought, as it seems to imply that cultural objects that have been created by human beings should henceforth maintain their existence independently of human ownership. Moreover, in a way it echoes the argument of the debate on the Anthropocene and thus shares the concern with revisiting humanity's self-positioning in the world. In both cases, human-

---

12 *Prosecutor v. Ahmad Al Faqi Al Mahdi*, Summary of the Judgment and Sentence, September 27 (2016), para 36, 39, available at: https://www.icc-cpi.int/itemsDocuments/160926Al-MahdiSummary.pdf [consulted on the 09/02/20].

13 Marina Lostal, "The Misplaced Emphasis on the Intangible Dimension of Cultural Heritage in the Al Mahdi Case at the ICC," *Inter Gentes* 1 (2017): pp. 45–58, 55.

14 Ibid., p. 45.

ity is portrayed as the responsible actor who has either destroyed or created something that is now to be recognized as an independent entity. Like Earth, cultural heritage should be appreciated as something that stands for itself, independent of the ownership of particular populations or human beings. And in both respects, humanity is needed to perform exactly this move: to recognize and at the same dissociate itself from its destructive or creative force. According to Claire Colebrook, what is required is not simply a withdrawal but a way of retaining our sense of thought. Thought here refers to humans' ability to anticipate their situation in such a way as to surpass it, as well as to text and theory that deploy their own anonymous force, not owned by anyone, of evoking as well as of dislocating meaning. They exceed human being as they are able to speak by themselves.[15]

Before taking a closer look at this conundrum of how to conceive of cultural objects as independent fellow entities that are nonetheless particularly valuable and meaningful for us, we need to briefly reconstruct the genealogy of the laws of cultural heritage to understand the singularity of the current situation, and with it the relevance of the case. As we will see, the problem is not that cultural objects were not already protected by the law. Rather, the notion of cultural heritage has come to be increasingly tied to a particular idea of ownership and representation of humanity that the ICC judgement allegedly reinforced, and that allowed for playing the vulnerability of human beings off against the value of cultural objects. The critique of this development coincides with a more general motif in legal theory that problematizes one of its key figures: the legal person or subject of law. While the modern version of this figure presupposes that men are, in principle, equal

---

15 Claire Colebrook, "Not Symbiosis, Not Now: Why Anthropogenic Change Is Not Really Human," *Oxford Literary Review* 23 (2012): pp. 185–209, 197.

subjects before the law, the legacy of political philosophy as well as of legal reasoning has endowed it with the
hierarchical division between human being and animal,
or non-human being, and human reason and body, or
biology.[16] Hence, a critique of law in the present context
approaches the classical question of who is entitled to
be "the subject of the rights of man"[17] by inquiring into
a "jurisprudence" that is concerned with humankind's
self-understanding.[18] To see how the law can be open
to revision, one needs to take into account the force
that brings it into action. Drawing on affect theory, we
might conclude that the same holds for cultural objects:
to the extent that they are considered valuable, they are
in need of recognition and advocacy; but like the law,
they are also able to speak for themselves.[19]

2.
The laws of cultural heritage

The prohibition of deliberately targeting or plundering
religious, historic, and cultural sites during war is a set-
tled principle in international law today, and in the history of the laws of war it appears as early as the eighteenth century. One of the constitutive regulations on the
way to the present situation was the Lieber Code, which
established a precedent at the height of the American

16 For the recent theoretical debate, see Roberto Esposito, "The *Disposi-
tif* of the Person," *Law, Culture and the Humanities* 8 (2012): pp. 17–
30; Ukri Soirila, "Persons and Things in International Law and 'Law
of Humanity'," *German Law Journal* 18 (2017): pp. 1163–1182.
17 Jacques Rancière, "Who Is the Subject of the Rights of Man?," *The
South Atlantic Quarterly* 103 (2004): pp. 297–310.
18 As Gilles Deleuze holds, jurisprudence that "deals with singularities" is what creates law, not codes and declarations. See *Negotiations, 1972–1990*, trans. Mark Lesser (New York: Columbia University
Press, 1995), p. 153.
19 While taking on a slightly different focus, the present article draws
on Susanne Krasmann, "Abandoning Humanity? On Cultural Heritage and the Subject of International Law," *Law, Culture and the Humanities* (2019).

Civil War in 1863 determining that monuments, places of worship and works of art be spared from destruction in times of war.[20] Proscriptions for the protection in the event of armed conflict of what today is known as cultural heritage appeared in, among other documents, the Hague Conventions of 1907 and 1954, which are considered further milestones. However, it was not until the rulings of the International Criminal Tribunal for the former Yugoslavia (ICTY), established in 1993, that responsibility for offences such as the destruction of cultural and religious objects was further defined and established. These rulings also contributed to shifting the focus away from state sovereignty toward the human being.[21] From the Rome Statute—which constituted the ICC and entered into force in July 2002—expressly recognizing the intentional destruction of cultural objects or sites as an act of war (pursuant to Article 8, 2),[22] more than a decade would elapse before the verdict on the Timbuktu case; prosecution of and conviction for the destruction of cultural heritage remains an exception today.

However, observers complained about the early focus of the court on the crime of destroying protected objects instead of primarily pursuing the harm directly done to people, in cases of mutilation, cruel treatment, or rape, which the prosecutor had taken into consideration when opening the investigation.[23] The prosecutor was thus criticized for being "overly focused on getting

20 Available at: https://uscbs.org/1863-lieber-code.html [consulted on the 09/02/20].
21 Compare Armin von Bogdandy and Ingo Venzke, *In Whose Name? A Public Law Theory of International Adjudication* (Oxford: Oxford University Press, 2014), p. 73.
22 Text of the Rome Statute circulated as document A/CONF.183/9 of July 17, 1998 and corrected by process-verbaux of November 10, 1998, July 12, 1999, November 30, 1999, May 8, 2000, January 17, 2001 and January 16, 2002, available at: https://www.icc-cpi.int/resourcelibrary/official-journal/rome-statute.aspx [consulted on the 09/02/20].
23 See ICC, Office of the Prosecutor, "Situation in Mali. Article 53(1) Report," January 16, 2013, para 133, available at: https://www.icc-cpi.int/itemsDocuments/SASMaliArticle53_1PublicReportENG16Jan2013.pdf [consulted on the 09/02/20].

a quick conviction" and seizing a political opportunity, at the cost of punishing "more heinous crimes,"[24] in particular sexual and gender-based crimes that Al Mahdi had allegedly also committed.[25] And indeed, when Chief Prosecutor Fatou Bensouda, immediately after Al Mahdi's transfer to The Hague, referred "to the attacks against the mausoleums as a 'callous assault on the dignity and identity of entire populations, their religious and historical roots'," she seemed to be all too "wary of the perception that crimes against property are too detached from human suffering," referring to the inhabitants of northern Mali in particular.[26] In the confirmation of charges hearing in 2016, the prosecution eventually maintained: "Let us be clear: What is at stake here is not just walls and stones. The destroyed mausoleums were important from a religious point of view, from an historical point of view and from an identity point of view."[27]

Over the second half of the twentieth century, a gradual move in legal discourse toward the subjective and "intangible" dimension of assessing and appreciating cultural objects can be observed.[28] The value of cul-

---

24 Marie Forestier, "ICC War Criminals: Destroying Shrines is Worse than Rape," *Foreign Policy*, August 22 (2016), available at: www.foreignpolicy.com [consulted on the 09/02/20].

25 Valérie V. Suhr, "The ICC's Al Mahdi verdict on the destruction of cultural heritage: two steps forward, one step back?," Voelkerrechtsblog, October 3 (2016), available at: https://voelkerrechtsblog.org/the-iccs-al-mahdi-verdict-on-the-destruction-of-cultural-heritage-two-steps-forward-one-step-back/ [consulted on the 09/02/20].

26 Lostal, "Misplaced Emphasis," p. 52.

27 ICC, "Statement of the Prosecutor of the International Criminal Court, Fatou Bensouda, at the opening of the confirmation of charges hearing in the case against Mr Ahmad Al-Faqi Al Mahdi," March 1, 2016, available at: https://www.icc-cpi.int/Pages/item.aspx?name=otp-stat-01–03–16 [consulted on the 09/02/20].

28 The UNESCO Convention of 2003 adopted this notion; in Art. 2 (1) it states: "The 'intangible cultural heritage' means the practices, representations, expressions, knowledge, skills – as well as the instruments, objects, artefacts and cultural spaces associated therewith – that communities, groups and, in some cases, individuals recognize as part of their cultural heritage." (UNESCO: Convention for the Safeguarding of the Intangible Cultural Heritage, Paris 17 October 2003, MISC/2003/CLT/CH/14.)

tural objects, it became more and more obvious, cannot be assessed by their "intrinsic quality" alone, but depends "on our ability to recognize their aesthetic, historic, scientific, social values."[29] This was also a shift in focus toward the immaterial or symbolic value cultural objects have for particular communities—though further specification of how to determine the vulnerability of the people affected is only beginning to take shape: how to estimate the material and the immaterial value of cultural objects; and in what sense is the destruction of cultural objects also to be assessed as material harm that affects the cultural life, the identity, the psyche or body of particular people? The Al Mahdi case, indeed, is instructive here. For example, in her briefing, the UN Special Rapporteur in the Field of Cultural Rights, Karima Bennoune, quotes a witness and person affected by the destruction of heritage in Timbuktu as follows: "Al Mahdi humiliated us, and made our humiliation known throughout the world […] It was a total humiliation". Subsequently she associates this experience with the Convention against Cruel, Inhuman or Degrading Treatment:

"Given the sometimes severe physical and mental suffering and humiliation occasioned, the destructions in this case of heritage so central to the enjoyment of human rights, could also be said for some victims to have risen to the level of cruel, inhuman or degrading treatment."[30]

Nonetheless, some critics pointed to "a missed opportunity," as the court had failed to further specify the legal

29 Marilena Vecco, "A definition of cultural heritage: From the tangible to the intangible," *Journal of Cultural Heritage* 11 (2010): pp. 321–324, 323.
30 Brief by Ms. Karima Bennoune, UN Special Rapporteur in the Field of Cultural Rights, *The Prosecutor v. Ahmad Al Faqi Al Mahdi*, ICC-01/12–01/15, Reparations Phase, 27 April 2017, p. 29–30; available at: https://www.icc-cpi.int/RelatedRecords/CR2017_05022.pdf [consulted on the 09/02/20].

regulations of the Rome Statute:[31] what exactly constitutes the cultural value of an object, even independent of its prior designation as a World Heritage site? Instead, as Lostal argues,[32] the court decision fell behind earlier legal provisions. The Hague Convention of 1954, for example, determines in Article 1 that "the term 'cultural property' shall cover, irrespective of origin or ownership." "Damage to cultural property, belonging to any people whatsoever, means damage to the cultural heritage of all mankind, since each people makes its contribution to the culture of the world."[33] Destruction of cultural property may be carried out without the intention of affecting a particular population or "the wish to re-write history:"[34] this indispensable element for the protection of cultural heritage is, according to the critics, what the judgement in the Al Mahdi case failed to regulate.

3.
The conundrum: Vulnerability and be-longing

What does it imply to demand that cultural heritage be acknowledged as a value in itself? Who acknowledges? And if it is human beings' signature that they "value

31 Recent Cases, "First Sentence for War Crime," pp. 1983–1984.
32 Lostal, "Misplaced Emphasis," p. 53.
33 See Article 1 and the preamble of the Convention for the Protection of Cultural Property in the Event of Armed Conflict with Regulations for the Execution of the Convention 1954, The Hague, 14 May 1954, available at: http://portal.unesco.org/en/ev.php-URL_ID=13637&URL_DO=DO_TOPIC&URL_SECTION=201.html [09.02.20]. See similarly the Convention concerning the Protection of the World Cultural and Natural Heritage, adopted by the General Conference of UNESCO at its 17th session, Paris, 16 November 1972, available at: http://whc.unesco.org/en/conventiontext/ [consulted on the 09/02/20].
34 Lostal, "Misplaced Emphasis," p. 58. On the different motives for attacking objects representing cultural heritage during armed conflict, see Johan Brosché, Mattias Legnér, Joakim Kreutz, and Akram Ijla, "Heritage under attack: motives for targeting cultural property during armed conflict," *International Journal of Heritage Studies* 23 (2017): pp. 248–260.

what values,"[35] how can value be thought of as being independent of the human eye? First of all, speaking of an independent value is not to deny the importance of cultural objects for local communities, their social life or religious practices, their identity and, not least, their "well-being."[36] Rather, it is to transcend the binary opposition of universalism versus particularism.[37] Furthermore, speaking of an independent value, obviously, precludes considering it an expression of "our" civilization.[38] Rather, we are urged to revisit the notion of "humanity as a whole" and to address the conundrum of cultural objects being produced by "us" but deserving appreciation and protection independent of any ownership.

Famously, we find in Kant, prior to any nationalist connotation of civilization, a relational conception of cosmopolitanism and humanity that could be useful for our purpose. For Kant it is culture, our ability to "cultivate our mental powers", that instills a "subjective sense" of solidarity, a "feeling of belonging to humanity." The fine arts and sciences carry the potential of a universally conveyable "pleasure."[39] It is the sensual experience, and the inspiration it unleashes, that invokes our sense of being in-common in the world—and that refers us back to ourselves as human beings: to

35 Claire Colebrook, *Death of the PostHuman* (Ann Arbor: Michigan Publishing, 2014), p. 203.
36 For the relevance of these criteria, see Derek Gillman, *The Idea of Cultural Heritage*, revised edition (Cambridge: Cambridge University Press, 2010), p. 21; Brosché et al., "Heritage under attack," p. 252.
37 See Francesco Franconi and Lucas Lixinski, "Opening the Toolbox of International Human Rights Law and the Safeguarding of Cultural Heritage," in Andrea Durbach and Lucas Lixinski, eds., *Heritage, Culture and Rights – Challenging Legal Discourses* (Oxford and Portland, OR: Hart, 2017), pp. 11–34.
38 Pheng Cheah, "Cosmopolitanism," *Theory, Culture & Society* 23 (2006): pp. 486–496.
39 Immanuel Kant, *Kritik der Urteilskraft*, ed. W. Weischedel, *Werkausgabe* X (Frankfurt/M., Suhrkamp, 1968, §83), quoted in Cheah, "Cosmopolitanism," p. 488. To be sure, Kant did not shy away from considering this ability as what distinguishes humanity from the limited capabilities of animals and constitutes human superiority.

our capacities to sense and to recognize that which transcends us as individual beings. What we are, or who we are, we might also learn from Kant, relies on our being interwoven with the environment. It is our *being with*.[40]

This perspective has further implications. Whether with regard to local communities or to the idea of humanity as a whole, it means that there is no self-evident nexus between cultural objects, origin and ownership. It is nothing simply given or natural, but has to be established. As Ryan Trimm contends, "Our legacies only become ours when we lay claim to them"—which empirically as well as theoretically involves the question of who the presupposed "we" of "our legacies" is and who is authorized to lay claim to that.[41] To appreciate the value of cultural heritage in its uniqueness, and even as an expression of human craftsmanship,[42] then, is to step back from the idea of cultural property being something that we possess or that represents us. To embrace the notion of a "feeling of be-longing" instead introduces a more dynamic and relational understanding of cultural value being something that has to be performed or processed, literally brought in to being: it is to relate and to connect to these objects, to reach out and feel attached, to long for and imagine, and, ultimately, to create narratives and meaning.

Note that the German notion of *Denkmal*, monument, entails the term "thinking," and thus the activity of engagement, of familiarizing oneself and becoming affected so as to understand the significance of cultural

40 Jean-Luc Nancy, *Being Singular Plural* (Stanford CA: Stanford University Press, 2000).
41 Ryan Trimm, "Heritage as trope: conceptual etymologies and alternative trajectories," *International Journal of Heritage Studies* 24 (2017): pp. 1–12, 10.
42 To be sure, to the extent that this appreciation draws on an "aesthetic value," it hinges on human evaluation and perhaps also cultural biases. See Alice Palmer, "Legal Dimensions to Valuing Aesthetics in World Heritage Decisions," *Social & Legal Studies* 26 (2017): pp. 581–605.

objects.[43] There is no given value of cultural objects, and not even a given object. Evaluation may presuppose values, but at the same time values emerge out of such "'perspectives of appraisal'". Evaluation and appreciation, which bring values into being, therefore always involve a moment of "creation." [44] Speaking in terms of affect theory allows us to capture these dynamic processes of cultural objects unfolding "into worlds"[45] and becoming what they are to us in a multilayered course: of affecting where "we" are affected by those objects (they involve us), we appreciate them (our appreciation addresses them), and we judge or evaluate them (our feeling about them makes them "good"). Affect thereby alludes not merely to the moment of bodies affecting and being affected but, particularly important in this context, is also what ensures continuation. It is, according to Sara Ahmed, "what sticks, or what sustains or preserves the connection between ideas, values and objects."[46] Affect, that is to say, is also cultural and "textual". Moreover, if value is the effect of recognition, this means that "humanity", as a reflection of these activities, is something instable. It is not something we can sit back and rest on, but must time and again in such activities be imbued with life. How, then, does the law step in?

43 Lyndel V. Prott and, Patrick J. O'Keefe, "'Cultural Heritage' or 'Cultural Property'?," *International Journal of Cultural Property* 1 (1992): pp. 307–320, 311.

44 Gilles Deleuze, *Nietzsche and Philosophy*, trans. Hugh Tomlinson (London, New York: Continuum, 1986), p. 1.

45 Sara Ahmed, "Happy Object," in Melissa Gregg and Gregory J. Seigworth, eds., *The Affect Theory Reader* (Durham NC and London: Duke University Press, 2010), pp. 29–51, 30.

46 Sara Ahmed approaches the question of valuable objects in terms of "happiness as a happening," (ibid., p. 29) meaning that it involves contingency or unpredictability: the "hap" of happiness and "a happening," (ibid., p. 36).

4.
Advocacy through thinking and feeling

The law, or "juridical involvement", is said to typically enter the scene in a reactive mode, that is, when prevention of "imminent loss" and preservation for the future are indicated.[47] Similarly, we might concede that concern for cultural heritage increases in times of crisis: societies, as it were, cling to what they have and what represents the best side of humanity, their ability to imagine and create, and that which promises to outlive generations. Criminal trials, and in particular outstanding international judgments concerned with such matters, thus do not merely communicate legal norms and determine the limits of what is permitted. Especially when sparking broader public debates, they may be read as also reflecting social and political concerns of their time and, along with this, the self-understanding of certain communities. Take, for example, the briefing of the UN Special Rapporteur in the Field of Cultural Rights in the ICC case. Her reference to the Hague Convention for the Protection of Cultural Property of 1954 may not merely be read as an actualization of its legal determinations and emphasis of its relevance but also as a form of enactment: it envisions humanity—"all mankind"—as relying on cultural heritage and as cultural subjects to be:

"While specific aspects of heritage may have particular resonance for and connections to particular human groups, damage to any cultural property damages the cultural heritage of all mankind, since each people makes its contribution to the culture of the world".[48]

A law that is able to renew itself appeals to a hope: it promises that there is progress. It may take up prior

---

47 Cornelia Vissmann, "Cultural Techniques and Sovereignty," *Theory, Culture & Society* 3 (2013): pp. 83–93, 89.

48 Brief by UN Special Rapporteur in the Field of Cultural Rights, p. 6.

motives of self-description and displace or reinvent them, but may also discover new territories or entities. The law is not blind to its own limitations. As Christoph Menke, drawing on systems theory, expounds: "By knowing itself, the law knows of non-law [...] it knows [...] that there is something that eludes its distinguishing."[49] Following Menke, we may designate "matter" as the yet "unmarked or formless" of the law as form.[50] It is exterior to the law but at the same time constitutes "the materialism of law":[51] it is potentially part of and being inscribed into the law. This is how the law materializes. Being in a position to reflect upon itself and proceed with the differentiation between law and non-law, the law is able to "processualize" matter into form. Matter here is not to be confused with object or the material. It is "rather impulse: that which is effective in the form-process, that which drives it."[52] The law, and we may also read this in affect-theoretical terms, needs to be motivated, literally *enforced*.

Nonetheless, cultural objects cannot by themselves claim the rights that they do not have in order to constitute themselves as legal subjects, as Jacques Rancière would put it.[53] And unlike us, human beings, the law might not by itself feel attracted, or affected, by the beauty of cultural objects. As it does not act without "impulse," cultural objects are in need of recognition, of appreciation and advocacy for the law to be motivated to speak in their name. It is through legal reasoning or other forms of care that they may eventually be counted in as equal (legal) subjects.

---

49 Christoph Menke, "Materialism of Form: On the Self-Reflection of Law," trans. Javier Burdman, in Kerstin Blome, Andreas Fischer-Lescano, Hannah Franzki, Nora Markard and Stefan Oeter, eds., *Contested Regime Collisions. Norm Fragmentation in World Society* (Cambridge: Cambridge University Press, 2016), pp. 281–297, 284.
50 Ibid., p. 286.
51 Ibid., p. 281.
52 Ibid., p. 289.
53 Rancière, "Subject," p. 305.

The debate surrounding the ICC decision articulated itself under the "improbable conditions"[54] of coinciding with the crisis of the Anthropocene, when humanity has again and urgently become aware of its own entanglement in the world. If cultural objects under these conditions seem to be particularly worth saving, they may not merely remind us of our ability to create something, and to think and be affected; but also bring us to realize that cultural objects develop their own force: as matter they are "textual", readable. They affect us, and as texts they speak by and for themselves.[55]

If the law, in this instance, also raises its voice, it may remind us of previous forms of recognition. When the eighteenth-century Swiss jurist Emer de Vattel codified the laws of war, determining that edifices "such as temples, tombs, public buildings, and all works of remarkable beauty" be spared from destruction, he realized that they "do honour to human society."[56] In retrospect, we might appreciate this formulation saying that cultural objects indeed have been created by human beings, but then deploy their own force. They consider themselves not too good to "honor" their creators and fellow (human) beings.

54 Michel Foucault, *Subjectivity and Truth: Lectures at the College de France 1980–1981* (Basingstoke: Palgrave Macmillan, 2017), p. 222.
55 Colebrook, 'Not Symbiosis', p. 196–7.
56 Emer de Vattel, *The Law of Nations, or Principles of the Law of Nature, Applied to the Conduct and Affairs of Nations and Sovereigns* (Indianapolis: Liberty Fund, 2008 [1758]), para 168, quoted in Lostal, "Misplaced Emphasis," p. 53.

Fares Chalabi

Intensive Listening

Unfolding the Notion of Justice Through Reading the Work of Lawrence Abu Hamdan

The first aim of this essay is to present the theoretical work of Lawrence Abu Hamdan[1] as an entry point to his artistic work. As the focus of this essay is the theoretical work as such, the description of the artistic works will be relegated to footnotes. The second aim of this essay is to expose the arguments and analysis of Abu Hamdan for their own relevance to the conception of justice. The third aim is to formalize the work of Abu Hamdan in order to reveal the different layers that are operating in

1   "Lawrence Abu Hamdan reincarnated in Amman in 1985 and is currently living in Beirut. He is a 'Private Ear.' His interest with sound and its intersection with politics originate [sic] from his background as a touring musician and facilitator of DIY music. The artists [sic] audio investigations has [sic] been used as evidence at the UK Asylum and Immigration Tribunal and as advocacy for organizations such as Amnesty International and Defense for Children International together with fellow researchers from Forensic Architecture. Abu Hamdan received his PhD in 2017 from Goldsmiths College London.In 2019 Abu Hamdan was nominated for the Turner Prize for his exhibition *Earwitness Theatre* and his performance *After Sfx*. In 2017 his film *Rubber Coated Steel* won the Tiger short film award at the Rotterdam International Film festival, The audience award at 25 FPS Festival in Zagreb, and the Dialog Award at European Media Art festival in Osnabruk. In 2016 he won the Nam June Paik Award for new media. Abu Hamdan is a fellow at the University of Chicago, was 2017/2018 guest of the DAAD Kunstler Program in Berlin and the 2015–17 fellow at the Vera List Centre [sic] for Art and Politics at the New School in New York. His solo presentations have taken place at Witte De With, Rotterdam (2019), Tate Modern Tanks & Chisenhale Gallery, London, Hammer Museum L.A (2018), Portikus Frankfurt (2016), Kunsthalle St Gallen (2015), Beirut in Cairo (2013), The Showroom, London (2012), Casco, Utrecht (2012). His works are part of collections at MoMA, Guggenheim, Van AbbeMuseum, Centre Pompidou and Tate Modern." http://lawrenceabuhamdan.com/info [consulted on the 07/03/20].

his analysis of juridical situations. I will use a Deleuzian conceptual grid in order to undertake such formalization, by showing that Abu Hamdan unfolds[2] the juridical situations into an extensive, intensive and problematic dimension. It remains that the aim of this formalization is not to expose Deleuze's conception of justice, but to use Deleuze's ontological dimensions with a view to highlighting the implicit structure of Abu Hamdan's argument. By revealing this structure, I will show how in each juridical situation we can frame what it means to be just or unjust. This essay will explore three juridical situations: civil rights, political rights and natural rights.

I. Civil Rights: From Hearings to Electronic Ears

By *civil rights*[3] I understand a well-defined juridical situation, i.e. a situation where the law and juridical practices are instituted and accepted by the subjects governed by these laws. By *subject*[4] I understand an individual that accepts to be part of some institution, and by *subject of the law* an individual accepting the juridical institution as whole. In this section I will expose the analysis of Abu Hamdan that shows how the practice and conception of justice evolve in relation to the listening techniques that are used to record and analyze the testimonies of the juridical subjects.

---

2   The basic three concepts of the problematic, the intensive and the extensive are exposed in *Difference and Repetition*. Deleuze shows how the problematic is progressively specified and actualized by passing through an intensive dimension before ending up in an extensive organization. For more details, see Gilles Deleuze, *Difference and Repetition*, trans. Paul Paton (New York: Columbia University Press, 1994), pp. 277–281.

3   On the different definitions and distinctions related to rights, I refer to Robert Audi, ed., *The Cambridge Dictionary of Philosophy* (Cambridge and New York: Cambridge University Press, 1999), entry "right."

4   On the distinction between individual and subject I refer to Louis Althusser, *On the Reproduction of Capitalism*, trans. G.M. Goshgarian (London: Verso Books, 2014).

64

The Semantic Intensity: Hearings and Liable Speech

"Oyez ! Oyez ! Oyez!"—"to hear, to hear to hear,"[5] is the ritualistic utterance that traditionally opens the juridical space for hearing testimonies. In this space, speech is transformed, by the ritual of oath[6], from its everyday ordinary use into its extraordinary use as testimony, i.e. into a speech that now has juridical weight. It is for this reason that the defendant must carefully craft his or her speech, because anything that he or she says could backfire on him or her. In this regard the Miranda Warning[7] brings to the awareness of the suspect that his or her speech has now crossed the legal threshold and will be scrutinized by legal listening. The Miranda Warning is then able to momentarily and locally institute a mobile space for juridical hearing outside the courts of justice. The "right to remain silent" is then a protective measure aiming at sheltering the suspect from the treachery of his or her own speech. The juridical subjects are hence liable for *what they say*, the content of their speech. A *fair hearing* then is a hearing where one is aware that he or she is being legally heard, be it because he or she was warned or because he or she is under oath.

The legal writ *habeas corpus*—"may you have a body"—requires that the accused is physically brought before the judge, in order for the judge to evaluate the materiality of his or her presence by looking for bodily

---

5   "Oyer, Oyez: The former derives from the n use of AF oyer (as in legal oyer and terminer): OF oïr (F ouïr), to hear: L audi re: f.a.e., AUDIBLE. AF oyer has imperative oyez, hear ye." Eric Partridge, *Origins, a Short Etymological Dictionary of Modern English* (London: Routledge, 1966), p. 2244.

6   On the performative use of language, see J. L Austin, *How to Do Things with Words* (Oxford: Oxford University Press, 1962).

7   "You have the right to remain silent. Anything you say can be used against you in court. You have the right to talk to a lawyer for advice before we ask you any questions. You have the right to have a lawyer with you during questioning. If you cannot afford a lawyer, one will be appointed for you before any questioning if you wish. If you decide to answer questions now without a lawyer present, you have the right to stop answering at any time." https://en.wikipedia.org/wiki/Miranda_warning#cite_note-3 [consulted on the 07/03/20].

signs and gestures. It remains that these material signs only reinforce, or trouble, the clarity of what is being said and can't stand on their own as valid testimonies. Juridical hearings rely first then on the semantic function of speech, what Abu Hamdan refers to as *logos*, while the non-verbal effects, or *phone*[8]—such as pitch, accent, glottal stops, intonations, but also other bodily signs such as blushing, sweating etc.—play a secondary role in relation to the semantic function. In liable speech, then, *logos* dominates *phone* and truth is established on the ground of an investigation that will secure the relation between the content of speech and the referent of speech. In this configuration of speech, truth is fact while evidence is what sustains and grounds these facts. A witness will be the one that brings about evidence by speaking the truth. A *fair speech* is a truthful speech, i.e. a speech that is adequate to the speech referent and doesn't distort the facts.

It remains that the space of juridical hearing and liable speech opens up a problematic dimension that requires a higher form of listening and a higher form of speaking. In fact, some sentences uttered in the juridical space might have a double meaning, playing on the dichotomy between the conversational use of speech and its liable juridical use. The prosecution or defense might ask the defendant, suspect, witness or expert a question that will reveal their political, emotional, or other personal biases in relation to the case and by that nullify their testimony: one can be baited by well-crafted questions.

---

8   For the distinction of *phone* and *logos*, Abu Hamdan refers to Aristotle: "And whereas mere voice [phone] is but an indication of pleasure and pain and is therefore found in other animals […] the power of speech is intended to set forth the expedient and inexpedient, and therefore likewise the just and the unjust. And it is a characteristic of man that he alone has any sense of good and evil." Aristotle, *The Basic Writings of Aristotle* (New York: Modern Library, 2001), 1253a, pp. 7–18. Quoted from Lawrence Abu Hamdan, "Aural Contract, Investigation at the Threshold of Audibility." (Ph.D. diss., Goldsmith's College, University of London, 2017), p. 51.

Liable speech and juridical hearings can then be used to exclude those who are unaware of the technicalities of the juridical maneuvers. The exclusion relies on invisible and problematic thresholds, on this thin line where words can reverse their meaning from an everyday fluent use into a hardened juridical acceptation. This blurriness between everyday speech and liable speech opens the possibility for baiting and trickery, and hence it is on this thin blurry line that one must decide for or against justice. This decision is itself the correlate of the indetermination inherent to speech in the juridical space. Fairness will consist in an inclusive use of these thresholds, while unfairness will use these thresholds and ambiguities to exclude. An *inclusive* use of the inaudible thresholds will aim at avoiding trickery, while an *exclusive* use of these inaudible thresholds will aim at baiting the defendant against his or her own will. Many movies made that game of trickery visible, in the interjection "objection your honor," where an attentive lawyer, harkening to these imperceptible reversals of words, tries in extremis to save his client from being baited.[9]

A critique of liable speech will reveal the existence of this problematic dimension, will uncover the invisible lines of demarcation before they close on the defendant. To be able to hear implicit trickery requires experience and an alert ear, but also points to a *higher form of listening*, a form that doesn't stop at the immediate meaning of the uttered words but is able to harken at their inaudible counterpart. In the same movement, this higher form of listening calls for a *higher form of speech*, a speech that objects, prevents, and cuts the invisible web that is being woven in the shadows, or a speech that speaks in full awareness of these thresholds, placing them at a distance when questioning. Without the

9   In *Mr. Deeds Goes to Town* there is a mock trial scene where the prosecution reverses any everyday behavior of Mr. Deeds into a proof of his mental instability. *Mr. Deeds Goes to Town*, directed by Frank Capra (Columbia Pictures, 1935).

higher exercise of the faculties[10] many will be silenced by their own speech, opening up a *higher form of silencing*, which is the highest form of injustice. Injustice, at this problematic level, will consist then in nullifying the speech of a juridical subject and excluding him or her because of the technicalities of the juridical procedures. Silencing is a higher form of silence because it requires one to speak and be heard in order to become juridically inaudible, and such silencing can only be heard in the interstices of the audible words.

The Analogical Intensity:
Audio Analysis and Speech Sampling[11]

This juridical configuration will be shattered by the introduction of analogical recording technics in the vicinities of the juridical sphere. In 1984, the UK Police and Crimi-

---

10 I will use the Deleuzian notion of a higher exercise of the faculties to show that injustice as silencing produces a silence that bypasses the empirical use of our senses. To bypass such empirical use, one needs to disorganize the normal organization of the faculties, in this case by coupling conceptual analysis with the capacity to hear. As Deleuze puts it: "In whichever tone, its primary characteristic is that it can only be sensed. In this sense it is opposed to recognition. In recognition, the sensible is not at all that which can only be sensed, but that which bears directly upon the senses in an object which can be recalled, imagined or conceived…It is not the given but that by which the given is given. It is therefore in a certain sense the imperceptible [insensible]. It is imperceptible precisely from the point of view of recognition—in other words, from the point of view of an empirical exercise of the senses in which sensibility grasps only that which also could be grasped by other faculties." Deleuze, *Difference*, p. 139.

11 The art work corresponding to this section is *The Freedom of Speech Itself*, an audio piece of 35 minutes. Abu Hamdan describes this work as follows: "*The Freedom of Speech Itself* is a [sic] audio documentary which examines the contemporary application of forensic speech analysis and voice-prints, focusing on the UK's controversial use of voice analysis to determine the origins and authenticity of asylum seekers' accents. Here, Testimonies [sic] from lawyers, phonetic experts, asylum seekers and Home Office officials reveal the geo-politics of accents and the practice of listening that led to shocking stories of wrongful deportations. When combined with the experimental audio composition and appropriated radiophonic techniques these interviews are designed to question the legal status of vowels and consonants." This work can be consulted by following this link: https://labuhamdanphdpracticeportfolio.squarespace.com/chapter-1/ [consulted on the 07/03/20].

nal Evidence Act, PACE[12], made it mandatory to audio record all police interviews. These techniques signal a new intensity in listening where it becomes possible to amplify voices, accelerate and decelerate the speed of utterance, decompose a word into its syllables, etc. This new intensity of listening then allows diving into the molecular dimension of speech and listening at a subhuman or superhuman auditory level. This intensive mutation has, as its counterpart, an extensive mutation of the juridical space. In fact, the audio-recording techniques allow the juridical space to open, from the confinement of the interrogation rooms and courts of justice to the extent of the telecommunication lines.[13] Last, as we will see, the intensive mutation modifies the relation between *logos* and *phone*, between the semantic and material dimensions of speech, and by that modifies the notions of juridical truth, witnessing and what it means to be just.

The LADO test, i.e. Language Analysis for the Determination of Origin[14], exemplifies such mutation. In the port of Dover[15], the immigration authorities screen migrants by making them undergo an interview in their

---

12 See Code E full legislation: https://www.gov.uk/government/uploads/system/uploads/attachment_data/file/495716/52344_00_Pace_Code_E_Accessible_v0.3.pdf [consulted on the 07/03/20].

13 "Moreover, prior to PACE, if it was suspected that someone's voice was on an incriminating recording—for example a wire-tapped telephone conversation in which there was discussion of an illicit act, or a CCTV surveillance tape of a masked bank robber shouting "Hand over the money!"—that person was asked to come to the police station and give a voluntary voice sample. After PACE, doing so was no longer voluntary: the police simply had to hold an interview with the suspect to access their voice." Abu Hamdan, "Aural Contract," p. 45.

14 "This is LADO. Governments, or the agencies or experts they employ, record and analyze claimants' speech in order to ascertain whether someone really speaks the language of a group they say they belong to, at the level that should be expected (based on their story), as part of testing their claim to come from a certain nation, region or clan." Peter L. Patrick, "Language Analysis for the Determination of Origin (LADO): An Introduction," in *Language Analysis for the Determination of Origin, Current Perspectives and New Directions,* ed. Peter L. Patrick, Monika S. Schmid, Karin Zwaan (Basel: Springer International Publishing, 2019), p. 1.

15 Dover is the closest port to France and is used as an entry point to England.

own native language. The interview is recorded and then analyzed with a view to determining the origin of the asylum seeker. The analysis bears mainly on the dialectological features of speech—such as accent, grammar, vocabulary, etc.—marginalizing the proper semantic content of the speech—such as stories, content, explanations, etc. The supporters of the LADO procedure claim that the focus on the material basis of speech, the *phone*, allows the authorities to bypass their emotional involvement in the stories of the asylum seekers and by that arrive at a purely objective and rational judgement. Truth can now be established on the ground of the material dimension of speech, rather than on the ground of a factual investigation proving the validity of what is being said. For example, the immigration authorities rejected the asylum request of Mohamad Barakat[16], grounding their judgement on his pronunciation of the word "tomato." Barakat was seeking asylum as a Palestinian from Jenin, but he pronounced the word "banad*ou*ra" instead of "band*o*ra," betraying by that a Lebanese-Syrian accent. The immigration authorities were quick to conclude that his real origin is Lebanese or Syrian, and not Palestinian, and hence ended up rejecting his request.

The new intensity of listening then allows a syllable to be isolated and compared with another, but also for the audio recorded material to be presented as evidence in a court of justice. The LADO analysts seem then to have tapped into a source of objective evidence extracted from the material dimension of speech, similar to the extraction of DNA traces from crime scenes. It remains that the LADO procedure is highly flawed and relies on heavy presuppositions. A direct flaw in this procedure is that many asylum seekers are used to code-switching and adapt their accents to interviewers in order to make themselves understood, thus modifying their accents during interviews and so disturbing the

---

16 Compare Abu Hamdan, "Aural Contract," pp. 63–64.

purity of extracted samples.[17] To answer these critiques the forensic linguistic lab Verified[18] opted for a monologue version of the LADO test, where the applicant had to speak for fifteen minutes without interruption, thus bypassing the influence of the interviewer on the interviewed. It remains that, be it in its dialogical or monological form, the LADO test relies on two heavy presuppositions. The first is that the dialectological features overlap in a strict manner with the national borders, while many linguists argue that it is rather the community and the family that determine these features, overriding the national partitioning.[19] The second presupposition is that the biographical data doesn't affect the phonetic dimension of language, while in fact pronunciation adapts to the different places of residence of the speaker. It follows that the pretense to reach objectivity by separating the phonetic dimension of speech from its biographical content, is a maneuver that allows the reduction of the asylum seeker to a number of material phonetic traits as standing for his or her truth, and that can justify dismissive and exclusive maneuvers.

The analogical recording technologies and the corresponding intensity of listening not only expand the juridical space and reverse the hierarchy between *phone* and *logos*, they also break the Miranda right, given that the juridical subject is deemed to provide a recorded speech sample that can become material evidence testifying against him or her in a court of justice. With *speech samples* the notion of *fair speech* is damaged because now we disregard the content of speech and hence the possibility of honesty and truthful saying. In a similar

17 "The participants in the interaction, other than the asylum seeker, represent another dimension of variation." Tim McNamara, Carolien Van Den Hazelkamp, Maaike Verrips, "LADO as a Language Test: Issues of Validity," *Applied Linguistics* 37:2 (April 2016): pp. 262–283.
18 Compare Abu Hamdan, "Aural Contract," p. 68.
19 Diana Eades et al., "Guidelines for the use of language analysis in relation to questions of national origin in refugee cases," *International Journal of Speech, Language and the Law* 11:2 (2004): pp. 179–199.

fashion the notion of a *fair hearing* is damaged because now one is being judged on a number of speech elements that escape one's conscious control, while a fair hearing requires that one is heard and judged in full awareness of the liability of one's speech, and on the ground of what is consciously being said. One's unconscious pronunciation can now stand as a witness against one's conscious speech, and by that the principle *tetis unis, tetis nullus*—"one witness is not a witness"—is challenged.[20] In addition, truth now results from a simple correlation between a material trace and a pre-assigned meaning, thus dismissing the need for investigation and facts. Last, the nature of the juridical subject, as a subject characterized by truthful saying, also gets damaged, given that the reduction of *logos* to *phone* leads to the reduction of the subjects to the materiality of their voices. All these modifications open the gates for biased judgements, disguised as material evidence, which justify all kinds of exclusions and discriminations.

It is in this sense that a *critique of the technologies of legal listening* must reveal the problematic nature of these material traces. As we have seen, Abu Hamdan shows that the modification of the pronunciation of some words could point towards another place of origin, or towards the migration of the subject due to the violent situation in his or her place of origin. By carrying a double determination these traces become problematic. Hence any hasty decision for any particular side of the alternative will betray a political will for exclusion that grounds itself on a simplistic reductionist view and a facsimile of truth. To this form of reductionism Abu Hamdan proposes the conflation of *phone* and *logos*, arguing that "the instability of an accent, its borrowed and hybridized phonetic forms, is testament not to someone's origins but to an

---

20 "The voice is made to become a second source of testimony, in addition to the words it speaks, another witness or evidence to the event." Abu Hamdan, "Aural Contract," pp. 49–50.

unstable and migratory lifestyle."[21] By that, truth is no longer determined on the grounds of a simple correlation but becomes the horizon that needs to be attained by the complex and double implication relating *phone* and *logos*. With the analogical technologies the critique needs then to first build the space of the problematic, by revealing the biases of all forms of reductionisms. Second, and from that problematic stance, it needs to develop a *higher form of listening* and a *higher form of speech*. Abu Hamdan, by problematizing these technologies, allows us to hear how they silence the migrants. The amplification of voices, the increased intensification in the listening technologies are producing a deafening silence correlated to a profound injustice. The higher form of listening will consist then in hearing the silence induced by these technologies: a migrant is silenced and excluded by a syllable that he or she pronounces. In the same movement, a higher form of speech will consist in speaking against these maneuvers of silencing that aim at excluding in the most expeditious way those whom we don't have time to listen to.

Electronic Intensity:
Electronic Ears and Material Speech[22]

The LVA, the Layered Voice Analysis[23], is a further intensification of legal listening. With the LVA and similar

---

21   Ibid., p. 65.
22   The artistic work by Abu Hamdan related to the LVA technologies is the audio piece *The Whole Truth* (2012), and can be found under the following link: https://labuhamdanphdpracticeportfolio.square-space.com/chapter-2/ [consulted on the 07/03/20] Abu Hamdan describes this work as follows: "The trigger for the audio documentary The Whole Truth is the current application of voice analysis as a lie detection method recently piloted by European, Russian and Israeli governments as well as being employed in border agencies and insurance companies all over the world. This technology uses the voice as a kind of stethoscope, an instrument to measure internal bodily responses to stress and tension; a material channel that allows the law's listening to bypass speech and delve deeper into the body of its subjects."
23   "It is well known that human oral communication contains features, which can be used to provide useful information about a speaker

electronic technologies we reach the atomic layers of speech, its micro-vibrations and micro-silences. The amplification and decomposition of these micro-vibrations allow the detection of points of tension and hesitation due to the glottal contractions of the speaker. Relying on algorithms that match the voice's vibrations with a database of pre-recorded samples of embarrassed, hesitant, tense, etc. voices, the machine is able to emit its verdict regardless of the content of the speech, or even of its material traits. With this electronic advance the investigator doesn't even need to listen anymore, to slow down, accelerate and detect imperceptible syllables, given that the machine does the work on its own. With the LVA legal listening crosses a new threshold by injecting an electronic ear at the level of the materiality of the voice itself, an ear that can listen at the vibratory level. This new intensity gives a new extension for the juridical space, providing it with a grip over all spoken and written words. With text and voice recognition tools and search engines, a number of keywords— such as suicide, bomb, terrorist—automatically trigger recording machines and can lead to legal interrogation and police interventions, backed up by electronic analysis.[24]

If the Miranda Warning was the preamble for a fair hearing, and if the analogical technologies crossed through the limits of such fair hearing by forcing the interviewee to provide speech samples, with the electronic technologies we move even deeper in speech extraction. The sampling of speech now occurs in the open without any specificity of time or place: any con-

apart from the linguistic content, or meaning, of what was said, and that this indexical information can prove exceedingly helpful in forensic work. That is, indexical information includes all aspects of the speech signal in addition to the meaning of the utterance itself." James D. Harnsberger, Harry Hollien, Camilo A. Martin and Kevin A. Hollien, "Stress and Deception in Speech: Evaluating Layered Voice Analysis," *Journal of Forensic Sciences* 54:3 (May 2009): pp. 642–650.
24 Compare Abu Hamdan, "Aural Contract," p. 93.

versation using an electronic device can be sampled and analyzed if it is deemed suspect by the algorithm. The electronic intensity allows then an overlap between everyday speech and liable speech, destroying by that the grounds of a *fair hearing* and a *fair speech*, and practically turning juridical and police investigation into the equivalent of secret intelligence procedures.[25] This modifies the function of witnessing, where now the electronic detection and recording plays the role of a universal and omnipresent witness that can provide evidence from the electronic traces. With *phone* turning into a pure vibration that carries as such its semantic determinations, truth can now be detected in the physical constitution of the voice: the vibratory voice structure of a sexual offender, potential criminal or terrorist. From the reductionism of the analogical techniques we move towards a *correlationism* of data as the ground of truth. The correlation of a number of key words, visited internet sites, voice vibrations, etc. will screen out potential criminals and the like.[26] The LVA technology claims objectivity by constructing truth on the ground of quasi physical traces and by correlating these traces to databases. Yet these technologies are biased and the target of many criticisms. One of the first problems in this technology concerns the subjective sampling of the voices constituting the database as such.[27] Another flaw of the LVA is that

---

[25] On the extent of electronic surveillance, we can consult Glen Greenwald, *No Place to Hide: Edward Snowden, the NSA and the Surveillance State* (London: Picador, 2015).

[26] On the critique of correlationism as characterizing the electronic age we can consult Eric Sadin, *La vie Algorithmique, critique de la raison numérique* (Paris, Editions de l'échappée, 2015).

[27] "To produce a verdict, the algorithm needs to learn the logics of those verdicts— for example, in order for it to profile the voice of a sex offender it first needs someone to teach it the vocal attributes of a sex offender. Someone has to tell this machine in the first place what an embarrassed voice sounds like [...] These highly subjective inaugural judgments, then programmed into the system, are inaccessible to any of its subsequent users." Abu Hamdan, "Aural Contract," p. 100.

this technology often zooms down to the digital silences, rendering its verdicts completely biased.[28]

In the face of the electronic technologies the experts and critics must then build anew the place of the problematic, by using their technical expertise and knowledge to show that the direct correlation between *phone* and *logos* is not possible. The work of Abu Hamdan goes in this direction by showing that techniques similar to LVA are at best problematic, and hence any verdict decided on the ground of these algorithmic analyses simply expresses a biased will to exclude a number of subjects from a fair hearing. The revelation of this problematic dimension calls for *higher forms of listening and speaking*, requiring technical expertise to stand with justice rather than using such expertise to exclude and silence a number of juridical subjects.

II. Political Rights:
Silence Between Justice and Injustice

By *field of individuation* I understand the source, authority, principle, etc. that gives a human being his or her individuality, i.e. his or her political, historical, cultural, linguistic, religious etc. identity.[29] By *international politi-*

---

28 In other terms the LVA program sometimes detects voice variations that are the result of the recording of the voice on the electronic support and don't even pertain to the voice as such, disqualifying by that the credibility of this technique. Compare Anders Eriksson and Francisco Lacerda, "Charlatanry in Forensic Speech Science," *International Journal of Speech, Language and the Law* 14: 2 (2007): pp. 169–193.

29 The *field of individuation* is a Deleuzian notion that is characterized by intensities and pre-individual features from which the individual is actualized by a process of differentiation. I am using this notion to show that the Palestinian political stance is such a field of individuation from which Palestinians extract their individuality. "This difference in kind remains unintelligible so long as we do not accept the necessary consequence: that individuation precedes differenciation in principle, that every differenciation presupposes a prior intense field of individuation. It is because of the action of the field of individuation that such and such differential relations and such

cal rights I understand a juridical situation where we have a conflict between two fields of individuation leading to the rejection of the juridical institutions or juridical claims pertaining to these respective fields. By *national political rights* I understand a juridical situation where a group of individuals share the same field of individuation as the others but reject the subjectivation of some of the established institutions, while remaining part of the overall individuating field. Abu Hamdan exposes two cases that correspond to these two situations: the ghettoes of the black communities in the USA rejecting the authority of the police, as expressing the violence of that institution against their communities and thus refusing to be the subjects of that institution, and the Palestinians in the occupied territories rejecting the authority of the Israeli state, as a violence made by another state against their people, and thus refusing to be individuated by the Israeli state. We will see that in these situations the extension of justice, the technologies of listening and the problematization of justice will take a new turn.

Silencing the Ghettoes[30]

ShotSpotter[31] is a technology that relies on echo triangulation measurements to automatically localize gunshots. Using that technology, the police are able to detect and localize gunshots without the need to rely on the willingness of local communities to report these gunshots.

---

and such distinctive points (pre-individual fields) are actualized." Deleuze, *Difference*, p. 247.

30 The art work corresponding to this section is *H[gun shot]ow c[gun shot]an I f[gun shot]orget?*, mostly mentioned in artist talks where Abu Hamdan analyses the audio recording of the murder of Michael Brown. In this piece Abu Hamdan brings our attention to the indifference of the man hearing the gunshots while sending a private message. By that Abu Hamdan highlights the silence of the black community and makes it heard, not only focusing on the gunshots but also and mainly on why the man remains undisturbed. For more details about this piece, see http://lawrenceabuhamdan.com/blog/2016/3/7/hgun-shotow-cgun-shotan-i-fgun-shotorget [consulted on the 07/03/20].

31 For more details on ShotSpotter we can refer to their site: https://www.shotspotter.com [consulted on the 07/03/20].

ShotSpotter claims that its microphones are much more accurate in detecting gunshots than the human ear and this technological superiority allows them to report what humans do not usually report because of their incapacity to distinguish gun shots from other loud sounds.[32] In fact, as Abu Hamdan replies, there is nothing wrong with the human hearing capacity, especially when compared to the microphones used by ShotSpotter, and their rhetoric only aims at overshadowing the unwillingness of some communities to report police gunshots in order to avoid more police violence. Hence what ShotSpotter silences is the resounding silence of these communities and its heavy implications as to their feelings towards the police. Abu Hamdan invites us to listen to that silence as a meaningful silence, and by that he problematizes the unreported gunshots and the official interpretation of these silent communities. Silence is then a bifurcating problematic point: it could be the result of some negligence, or the willful expression of a feeling of distrust in the authorities. To determine univocally this problematic point the authorities have to rely on a biased technological rhetoric. Instead of *including* that silence and raising the question about why some communities do not report crime, the authorities *exclude* that dimension by relying on automated systems of listening and reporting, and thus double the exclusion patterns in which these communities are trapped. It follows that a simulacrum of a law-abiding community is set in place.[33] In this case we can see that

---

32 Compare Abu Hamdan, "Aural Contract," p. 115.
33 "Though calibrated by police gunfire, ShotSpotter is deaf to violence the police themselves bring to these communities, and ignores that the 80 percent of unreported incidents is a silence that is, at least in part, the result of police violence. In replacing the 80 percent of previously unreported incidents of gunfire, ShotSpotter algorithmically automates a law-abiding community. Rather than seeking to sensitively restore a communication breakdown, it digitally simulates a channel of communication between the community and the police." Ibid., p. 116.

ShotSpotter as an intensive form of listening is itself a consequence of a politics of exclusion in regard to some communities, and that the authorities could have reached or developed other forms of listening, if they had first listened inclusively to the silence of these communities. Some principles of justice can be valid—such as "law-abiding communities must report crime"—and yet they can be used as such to pervert justice. If the LADO and LVA techniques broke through the Miranda right by forcing the interviewees to speak and by turning everyday speech into liable speech, ShotSpotter perverts the witnessing function even further by producing ghostly ears, ears without subjects that hear and speak in place of the excluded communities, and thus turn their silence, refusal, and opposition into a facsimile of participation. The *higher form of political injustice* consists then in such a facsimile of a law-abiding community, where reporting crime doesn't express anymore a common will and reveal a trustworthy relation between the government and the governed, but rather reinforces sociopolitical divisions. It is by disregarding the refusal of these communities that the government exacerbates a situation of political injustice and exclusion.

To include these communities, one needs to hear their silence as a meaningful expression of refusal and suffering. It remains that this form of hearing is only possible when informed by historical and political analysis, i.e. a *higher form of listening*. When one problematizes silence, one is also able to hear how the authorities silence these communities by covering up their silence with a technological rhetoric and automated reporting systems. A *higher form of speech* will consist here in speaking with the excluded and standing with them in the face of oppression, by revealing the true nature of these reporting technologies as a will for silencing. Abu Hamdan shows how the mapping of the gunshots by ShotSpotter betrays its true intentions by showing how police gunshots are massively concentrated in some neighborhoods and not others. In this reversed engineering approach Abu Hamdan subverts this technology by turning it as a finger of accusation against the authorities.[34]

Silencing the Occupied Territories[35]

It is in this line that we need to hear the silence of the Palestinians as an expression of protest against the silencing imposed on them by the Israeli state. I will argue that the Israeli state uses the juridical form of subjectivation to shatter the source of individuation of the Palestinians. I will try to show, by relying on Abu Hamdan's analysis, how the trials of the Israeli military courts[36] operating in the occupied territories must

34 "The 'blue wall of silence,' an unofficial code amongst police officers to not testify against each other to what they have witnessed [...] The gunshots included here also include all of the police gunfire, and so unintentionally, the city of Minneapolis is building an archive that could help civil rights groups to gather data on when and where police gunshots are fired—data that was previously occluded by "the blue wall of silence." Ibid., p. 120.

35 The artwork corresponding to this section is the video *Rubber Coated Steel*. In this 21 minute video Abu Hamdan synthetizes in a fictional trial his criticism of the Israeli juridical proceedings in the cases of Abu Daher and Abu Nawara. The description of the piece is as follows: "A detailed acoustic analysis, for which Abu Hamdan used special techniques designed to visualize the sound frequencies, established that the Israeli border guard Ben Deri had fired live rounds, and moreover had tried to disguise these fatal shots to make them sound as if they were rubber bullets. These visualizations later became the crucial piece of evidence that was picked up by the news channel CNN and other international news agencies, contributing to the Israeli state renouncing its original denial of the crime. The investigation was also presented before the U. S. Congress as an example of Israel's contravention of the American-Israeli arms agreement. A little over a year after Abu Hamdan completed his work on the Forensic Architecture report, he returns to the case of Abu Daher and Nawara. The video, *Rubber Coated Steel*, acts as a tribunal for these serial killing sounds. This video tribunal does not only preside over the voices of the victims but also seeks to amplify silence, and suppression itself." For more details, we can consult: https://labuhamdanphdpracticeportfolio. squarespace.com/introduction/ [consulted on the 07/03/20].

36 Since the 1967 Israeli occupation of the Palestinian territories, Palestinians are under the rule of the Israeli Military Law and the local laws that were in place prior to the occupation. For crimes that don't involve the occupier the local law must be applied, or else the military one. If the Palestinians refuse the verdict of the military courts they can appeal to the Israeli Supreme Court of Justice. For more de-

be read as strategies of counter-individuation aiming at destroying the political identity of the Palestinians and hence their political claims.

A Palestinian teenager, Mohammad Abu Daher, was shot by an Israeli soldier during a protest. Earlier that day Nedeem Nawara was shot in the same location.[37] The family of Mohammad Abu Daher withdrew his body from the hands of the Israeli military authorities in order not to turn his dead body into the stage upon which the Israeli authorities play their auto-critique as a democratic civilizing state[38]. By that, "they place their son's body in a metaphorical mass grave of colonial violence. Mohammad Abu Daher does not become a victim but another martyred body in a collective struggle for liberation."[39] The refusal to participate in the juridical democratic masquerade, the refusal to be represented in an Israeli military court, the refusal to give one's dead to the cynical perpetrators of colonial[40] violence, are

tails, see Sharon Weill, "The judicial arm of the occupation: the Israeli military courts in the occupied territories," *International Review of the Red Cross* 89:866 (June 2007): pp. 395–419.

37 "On May 15, 2014, two Palestinian children were shot and killed by Israeli forces in the town of Beitunia. Nadeem Nawara, 17, and Mohammad Mahmoud Odeh Abu Daher, 16, were participating in protests to mark Nakba Day. Nawara was shot in the chest, while Abu Daher was shot in the back. Both were killed by live fire. Both deaths were captured on security cameras installed on a nearby shop. These videos show the teenagers to be distant from the Israeli forces and posed [sic] no immediate threat to them." https://labuhamdanphdpracticeportfolio.squarespace.com/introduction/ [consulted on the 07/03/20].

38 A possible reading of the Israeli juridical maneuvers to which I adhere is expressed among other points of view by David Kretzmer: "From a radically different perspective, it may be argued that the main function of the Court has been to legitimize government actions in the Territories. By clothing acts of military authorities in a cloak of legality, the Court justifies and rationalizes these acts. Even if this has not produced legitimization in the eyes of residents of the Occupied Territories themselves, it has done so both for the Israeli public, in whose name the military authorities are acting, and for foreign observers sympathetic to Israel's basic position." David Kretzmer, *The Occupation of Justice: The Supreme Court of Israel and the Occupied Territories* (Albany NY: The State University of New York Press, 2002), p. 2.

39 Abu Hamdan, "Aural Contract," p. 31.

40 Since I had a disagreement on the status of Israel as a colonial state with some of the editors, which remains unresolved, I'd like to give all acts of silent protest revealing how Palestinians are silenced when invited to speak. The legal instrument here is used to cover up political violence and collective resistance. It is used to turn the collective insurrection of the Palestinians into scattered individual actions leading to scattered personalized victims.[41] The legal discourse here functions as an instrument to silence political speech by giving voice to the individuals, and hence it is a vector of individualization that aims at covering up by these individuating procedures its political func-

some arguments that support my position on this topic. Henry Laurens provides a number of proofs showing that the Israeli state is colonial, given that it could have only constituted itself by the exclusion of the Palestinians from their lands as illustrated in his concept of "zero gain game." One of these proofs is the project of transfer of the Palestinians that was negotiated in the 1930s by Zionist representatives. As Laurens puts it: "Colonization is in the very dynamics of the original irredentism, hence the incompleteness of the normalization of the Jewish people and the paradoxical regression to a state of fear that Zionism wanted to make disappear." (My translation). See Henry Laurens, "Palestine, 1948. Les limites de l'interprétation historique," *Esprit* 266/267: 8/9 (2000): pp. 119–46. Other intellectuals share these views, such as Alain Badiou: "It is even less rational to pretend to find in the Nazi gas chambers what can confer to the colonial Israeli State, installed in the Middle-East (and not in Bavaria...), a derogatory status to the one we impart since decades to all colonial States, and where one must simply enunciate that they represent a form that is particularly detestable and highly obsolete of the oppression of the dispossessed people." (My translation). See Alain Badiou, *Circonstances 3, Portées du mot juif* (Paris: Editions Lignes et Manifestes, 2005), p. 5. Gilles Deleuze shares similar positions as shown in his article, which was omitted in the Semiotext(e) translation, "Greatness of Yasser Arafat": "Israel has never hidden its goal, from the beginning: to empty the Palestinian territory. And much better, pretending that the Palestinian territory was empty, forever destined for the Zionists. It was colonization, but not in the European sense of the nineteenth century: it would not exploit the inhabitants of the country, they would leave." (My translation). Gilles Deleuze and David Lapoujade, *Deux régimes de fous textes et entretiens, 1975–1995* (Paris: Éditions de Minuit, 2003), p. 222.

41 As Abu Hamdan underlines, the Israeli military courts separated the two cases of Abu Daher and Nawara, treating them as accidental casualties rather than part of the same criminal act aimed at taming all forms of political upheaval. The Israeli soldier, Ben Deri, was only sentenced for the murder of Nawara, and on account of "negligence." Abu Hamdan, "Aural Contract," pp. 16–17. For more details, see: https://forensic-architecture.org/investigation/the-killing-of-nadeem-nawara-and-mohammed-abu-daher [consulted on the 07/03/20].

tion. The Israeli state aims at individuating the Palestinians by turning them into defined voices and bodies, actual individuals with proper names, personal voices and individual wounds. Against this, the Palestinians bring these bodies back to the realm of the undefined: collective graves where names don't relate any more to individual bodies, and where speech resounds as one collective silence. By building this collective nameless body, the Palestinians are able to generate an impersonal individuation, a field of individuation without specific individuals, a field where proper names stand for events scarring a collective unified body: the thousand names of martyrdom, the thousand names of insurrection, the unified suffering of the Palestinian people. This field of individuation is the field from which each Palestinian becomes individualized and acquires his or her individuality as a Palestinian.

The maneuver of the Israeli state consists in silencing this collective individuality by offering the Palestinians a legal subjectivity, a personal body, a proper voice and name. In his art work *Rubber Coated Steel*, Abu Hamdan creates a fictional trial where he merges the trials of Nadeem Nawara and that of Mohammad Abu Daher, to show the collective and political nature of these crimes, while in fact the Israeli military court separated these two crimes and thus individuated their victims. Abu Hamdan then included his forensic analysis of the crimes showing how the two boys were shot in the same place by a gun bearing the same sonic signature, while in fact this material was not accepted in the official trial.[42] Last, towards the end of the video, he stages a moment where the prosecution, insistently inviting a number of witnesses to speak, is answered by a collective silence. In

---

42 Despite the evidence provided by Abu Hamdan to the campaign *No More Forgotten Lives* undertaken by Defense for Children International, and supporting the case of Abu Daher, the Israeli military court never tried any soldiers for this crime. Abu Hamdan, "Aural Contract," pp. 16–18.

this fictionalized trial, Abu Hamdan gives body to the silence of the young Palestinians as expressing an act of refusal of such personal individuality, and an act affirming their collective political individuality.[43]

If, however, the parents of Nadeem Nawara opted to give the body of their son to the Israeli authorities, in order to make his body speak, and further accepted to participate in the juridical trials, it remains that, as Abu Hamdan puts it, such strategies are risky and humiliating.[44]

It is then only if we place ourselves at the political level, by revealing how the Israeli military trials are strategies to break the collective individuality of the Palestinians, that we can dismiss the alternative between fair or unfair Israeli trials.[45] In that regard I think the theoretical and artistic work of Abu Hamdan is clear: the refusal of the Israeli trials even if they are fair is not a juridical question but a political one, and it is in this refusal of Israeli justice that Palestinians can build a collective individuality incarnated in one body and a thousand names as the expression of a whole people fighting oppression.

---

43 "It is intended that the reader of my transcript feels this injustice each time the protestors' voices are struck from the record, and yet the crescendo of tension does not come at the moment these voices are finally heard, but rather when they are implored to speak by the prosecution, their champion, when they choose rather to perform their own inaudibility to the court." Ibid., p. 23.

44 "It is clear that the hearing received is humiliatingly unjust in its verdicts and politically compromising, set within the parameters of the colonial state. Further, he risks being stigmatized by fellow Palestinians as collaborating with the occupiers, and risk his sons [sic] body being abducted by the Israeli state as a punitive measure against him and his family." Ibid., p. 34. On the Israeli abducting of the bodies of the Palestinians we can consult Zena al-Tahhan, "Why does Israel keep the bodies of Palestinians?," *Al Jazeera* (August 10, 2017): http:// www.aljazeera.com/indepth/features/2017/08/israel-bodies-palestinians-170810075805418.html [consulted on the 07/03/20].

45 "This is not how justice is done," said Nadeem's father, Siam Nawara, after the sentencing. "I never expected the Israeli court to do justice for my martyred son, but I had to do all I can to present a solid case and to expose the Israeli judicial system before the world and I did." https://www.theguardian.com/world/2018/apr/25/israeli-policeman-jailed-fatal-shooting-palestinian-teenager-nadeem-nawara-border-ben-deri [consulted on the 07/03/20].

The simulacrum of justice in this case consists in considering that individuality is a factual given by dissociating it from the political field of individuation. This cynical form of justice pretends that individuals can be neutrally judged without regard to their political individuation. Courts of justice operate among individuals that share the same source of individuation, and by sharing this common source of individuation they become the subjects of a common state, and the subjects of its laws and regulations. But when this common source is lacking, and even contended, we can't treat individuals as being already the subjects of the law, even a military law, without doing violence to the political individuality of these individuals. Violence reaches here a new level, it is not the intra-legal violence against citizen or future citizen anymore, but a violence that attains the core and the foundation of legality itself, as its condition of possibility. The Israeli legal institution and its hearing technics is used to silence another field of political individualization, and hence to silence a potential state and nation, and a potential alternative legal system. By offering the Palestinians a personal individuality to endorse, and by offering that in the name of justice and in the name of their victims, the Israeli legal institution is luring them into abandoning their political struggle and their political individuality. It is in this regard that the silence of the Palestinians and the withdrawal of their dead are the actualization of another field of individuation and of another political individuality, which the Israeli state is trying to render absurd and inexistent by opening the space of legal testimony. It is in this sense that this form of silencing is even deeper than the previous ones and different in its nature because it corrodes the core of the existence of those who are being silenced and not only their just claims under a common law. The Israeli state's inclusion of the Palestinian in its juridical space is then in fact an exclusion from their political field of individuation, and in this regard the juridical tools are turned into political instruments, legal justice a disguise for political injustice, inclusion a disguise for exclusion, justice a deeper form of injustice.

The withdrawal of the bodies and the silence of the witnesses have then a political weight and "post-mortem forensic examination cannot escape the politics of this situation and must proceed in a manner that exceeds the neutrality of science."[46] In order then to respect the political acts of protest while at the same time wanting to prove that the Israeli soldier did indeed shoot Mohammad Abu Daher with live ammunition, Abu Hamdan turns his analysis towards the footage of the event. By analyzing the audio traces of the gunshots, "the focus of the investigation is on the perpetrator, rather than seeking to speak for, or stand for, the victim."[47] While the Israeli state tries to annihilate the political stance of the Palestinians by offering them a place in the Israeli juridical space, Abu Hamdan uses the forensic techniques to reinforce the political protest of the Palestinians, by making the material traces of the event speak against the testimony of the Israeli soldier.[48] By making matter speak, by making colors and movements speak, it is the world, addressing an international audience[49], that testifies against the cynical claims of innocence of the Israeli soldier. We reach by that another layer of justice, a layer beyond the personal realm, a layer where justice is at play between fields of individuation and where the witness, arbitrator, and battleground of this

46 Abu Hamdan, "Aural Contract," p. 32.
47 Ibid. p. 33.
48 "Rather than submit them to police investigators, DCI intended to publicly release our findings in response to developments of the media narrative, intervening in the investigative process from the outside." https://forensic-architecture.org/investigation/the-killing-of-nadeem-nawara-and-mohammed-abu-daher [consulted on the 07/03/20].
49 We can refer to the first CNN report in relation to the Nawara case: https://www.youtube.com/watch?v=3ayr99E3AmU [consulted on the 07/03/20].

confrontation is the world itself. This means that even if the Israeli courts reject such forensic analysis, it remains that such analysis reveals evidence against and outside of these particular jurisdictions for the whole world to see. The work of art becomes the vehicle that makes visible these extra-juridical proofs, making the material world testify in a *higher form of speech* and making the political silence of the Palestinians heard in a *higher form of listening*.

III. Natural Rights: Silent Screams[50]

By *natural rights* I understand the basic rights of the living human being. In this juridical situation we are outside of all instituted laws, where the relation of domination becomes purely physical and aims at annihilating the psychic and organic life of the individuals. Terror will aim at debilitating the living dimension of the

---

50 The artwork corresponding to this section is *Saydnaya: Inside a Syrian Torture Prison*. The description of this work is as follows: "In 2016 Lawrence Abu Hamdan worked with Amnesty International and Forensic Architecture to produce an acoustic investigation into the Syrian regime prison of Saydnaya 25km North [sic] of Damascus, where over 13,000 people have been executed since the protests in 2011 began. The prison is inaccessible to independent observers and monitors. The memory of those few who were released is the only resource available from which to learn of and document the violations taking place there. However, the capacity of detainees to see anything in Saydnaya was highly restricted as mostly they were kept in darkness, blindfolded or made to cover their eyes. As a result, the prisoners developed an acute sensitivity to sound. Abu Hamdan worked with survivors' earwitness testimony to help reconstruct the prison's architecture and gain insight as to what is happening inside. The website linked above is an online platform that hosts the totality of this report, which includes not only acoustic but 3D architectural modelling and animation produced by Forensic Architecture. On this website, you will see videos documenting the interview process Abu Hamdan contributed to as well as all the sounds you hear were produced by Abu Hamdan based on the instructions he was given by the ear witnesses to Saydnaya." For more information and the consultation of the work: https://labuhamdanphdpracticeportfolio.squarespace.com/chapter-3/ [consulted on the 07/03/20].

individual in order to eradicate his or her individuation and any possible subjectivation.

In the Saydnaya Prison, the terrorist Assad regime uses silence as a control and torturing device. Prisoners are not allowed to make any noises, so can barely breath or move, in order to avoid being beaten, or even killed.[51] Thus the prisoners are subjected to a permanent stress condition of having to withhold any movements, speech or screams. The prisoners' permissible sound emissions shouldn't exceed 26 cm, which intensifies the confinement space.[52] By comparing the testimonies of two former detainees, one who was held in Saydnaya before the Syrian revolts and another after the Syrian revolts, Abu Hamdan was able to detect a drop of 19db in the sound tolerance at Saydnaya, a drop that expresses the transformation of the prison into a death camp.[53] Furthermore, by relying on the auditory memories of the detainees Abu Hamdan was able to reconstruct the space of the prison, using echo profiling technics and echolocation in order to translate the memory of sound into architectural components.[54] In fact, the imposition of

---

51 Compare Abu Hamdan, "Aural Contract," p. 146.
52 Abu Hamdan was able to retrieve this kind of information by interviewing the detainees and by asking them how loud they could speak. He recorded their whispers and made his calculations to determine how far their voices were allowed to reach: "So where the physical capacity of our voices to reach outside our bodies is 180 meters, the absolute limit in Saydnaya is just 26 cm. This demonstrates the range of audibility the detainees of Saydnaya inhabit, a 26 cm radius that confines the space in which they can be audible and creates an alternative image of the architecture of their incarceration." Ibid., p. 150.
53 "This 19db drop in whispers allows us to give a scale to what Diab describes as 'the levels of torture' being 'even worse.'" Ibid., p. 151. We can also consult Abu Hamdan's audio piece, *Saydnaya (missing 19db)*, by following this link: https://labuhamdanphdpracticeportfolio.squarespace.com/chapter-3/ [consulted on the 07/03/20].
54 "This meant studying the vibrations the survivors experienced through the walls and floors into their eardrums as a mediated event, through which the building was transmitted. The physics of sound propagation became one of the means by which we could build an argument for the inseparability of the violence perpetrated and the building in which it was contained." Abu Hamdan, "Aural Contract," p. 136.

a drastic silence in Saydnaya heightened the auditory capacities of the detainees and enhanced their auditory memory, allowing them to recall the names of those who were called for execution, to detect the sounds of torture, the times at which the truck used to leave loaded with dead bodies, etc.[55] If in these extreme conditions sound became the medium to apprehend space, by contrast spoken language itself passed through lip reading and the visual medium.[56] If death camps aim at an absolute silencing, a silencing in death and in the after death, the conditions in these prisons make possible an exacerbated form of life that discovers new capacities to hear, speak and sense in the bleeding of one sensorial field into the other, and in the disorganization of the normal use of the senses.[57] Walls start to speak through their vibrations, each type of vibration expressing a torture technique, each vibration expressing a type of scream, or of body impacts: "'breaking down a wall', 'tearing up a wall', and 'the worst one, which shook the walls'." Hunger amplifies sounds[58] and this amplification beyond measure and other psychological sensorial

---

55 "Despite constant exposure to the sounds of torture and extreme violence, their hearing was so accentuated in the silent conditions that they could accurately evaluate that the most destructive of all of the sounds they were exposed to in the prison, as it signified that mass executions were taking place, was this fifteen minutes of silence between the truck leaving and coming back." Ibid., p. 155.

56 "Entire images and scenes of the prison were built from the perceived sounds and audible events happening in its corridors, stairwells, and adjacent cells. Yet at the same time, as audible speech was forbidden, communication between the inmates, despite the darkness, became a visual experience, as they relied on silent and visually legible aspects of speech such as lip reading and hand gestures. Sound became sight and sight became sound." Ibid., p. 158.

57 "However, the position of the table in the main atrium, the size of the stairwell and number of stairs, and the colour of the outside wall were details that had been perceived across and between the senses, and the product of the sensory deprivation itself." Ibid., p. 159.

58 "This was the sound of a threshold at the threshold of the medium of sound itself, both the sound of hunger and hunger's effects on auditory perception, to the extent that the state of hunger made a box of food landing on the ground sound equivalent to the amplitude of a reverberant metallic impact resonating through a space equivalent to the Notre-Dame." Abu Hamdan, "Aural Contract," p. 164.

distortions become the faithful witness of the state of deprivation, fear, and violence in Saydnaya.

It follows that "these memories, which are in excess of the acoustic realities of the prison, can be understood to speak more comprehensively about the violence endured at Saydnaya than the impression that would emerge from a precise acoustic reconstruction of the prison's sounds."[59] A fair hearing will have then to listen across the senses, and the forensic techniques must be sensitive to the distortion and bleeding of the senses, use sound archives to establish a non-verbal language with the ex-detainees[60], but also express sounds with images in view of accuracy[61], or measure death and violence in decibel. In the face of absolute injustice, the silencing by death, intensive listening must retrieve traces that were meant to be erased, retrieve and reveal a form of life that can still speak at the borders of death. At that level hearing injustice is one that can hear life in the disorganization of life. We have to be able to hear the inaccurate depictions of the ex-detainees as accurate expressions of violence, but also to hear the bleeding of sound into images and images into sounds as faithful expressions of the state of fear and violence. At that level of violence all our faculties reach a point of discord, violence is transmitted from one faculty to the other, making us see with our ears and hear with our eyes. Our faculties and senses are subjected to a forced movement carrying them beyond their normal use and opening them at a higher power.[62] In such proximity to death and extreme

---

59 Abu Hamdan, "Aural Contract," p. 166. We can also consult the art work, *Saydnaya (ray traces)* on https://labuhamdanphdpracticeport-folio.squarespace.com/chapter-3/ [consulted on the 07/03/20].

60 Compare Abu Hamdan, "Aural Contract," p. 144.

61 "The cross-sensory ways in which the ex-detainees' memories were encoded meant that in order to access them, we also had to work across the senses; discussing details that they heard by using images rather than sounds could be, counter-intuitively, more effective." Abu Hamdan, "Aural Contract," p. 159.

62 I am using here the Deleuzian notion of a higher exercise of the faculties when subjected to violence. Applying Deleuze's analysis of the

violence life reaches a new form, it dissolves its human form and is able now to blend with walls, turn architectonic elements into new sensory organs, can see in darkness and hear silence. It is this new form of life that we need to be able to listen to. To reduce the testimonies to bare expressions of trauma that can't yield any evidence, to reduce them to pure psychological phantasmagorias, to reduce their verbal depiction to metaphors, would be to exclude this form of life from the realm of justice and by that commit an act of deep injustice.

The distortions of the senses, the inability to speak, the amplifications of memory, the construction of a new body, etc. are all evidence of a life facing death. To make justice for these lives one needs to have different ears and eyes to be able to listen, one needs to build new faculties by using archives, things, images, simulation technics, etc. in order to dive into the imperceptible. These constructed faculties will allow us to speak and hear that other form of life. Abu Hamdan's work consisted in creating such sensory organs that can hear beyond the normal sensorial fields in order to include the testimony of these lives as evidence, so opposing the death machine that wanted to eradicate their voices and reduce their testimonies to mere babble. A just hearing as a *higher form of listening* at that level consists then in building the capacity to sense, a capacity that itself reflects the disorganization of the senses and

sublime and the properly aesthetical experience, I consider that the detainees did reach this higher form and that the work of Abu Hamdan consists in building the tools and organs capable of collecting and recording this limit experience. "Discord of the faculties, chain of force and fuse along which each confronts its limit, receiving from (or communicating to) the other only a violence which brings it face to face with its own element, as though with its disappearance or its perfection." Deleuze, *Difference and Repetition*, p. 141. We can also consult Deleuze's analysis of the Kantian sublime: "The faculties confront one another, each stretched to its own limit, and find their accord in a fundamental discord: a discordant accord is the great discovery of the *Critique of Judgement*, the final Kantian reversal." Gilles Deleuze, *Kant's Critical Philosophy*, trans. Hugh Tomlinson and Barbara Habberjam (London: The Athlone Press, 1984), p. xii.

makes sensible in this disorganization that which can only be sensed, i.e. the absolute silencing of life. The Will-for-Life opposes the Will-for-Death, an opposition that reorganizes the senses, calls for new creative capacities and another conception of justice: justice as a will to include, hear, and understand another form of life that develops under extreme conditions. The *higher form of speech* in this case consists in speaking the language of this other living form, and building and creating the organs to do this. In his video *Saydnaya: Inside a Syrian Prison,* we can see this tremendous creative work undertaken by Abu Hamdan to be able to speak and listen to the ex-detainees of Saydnaya.

IV. Conclusion: The Idea of Justice

We can interpret the platonic motto *"Justice is Just"*[63] as stating the Idea of Justice, or that we can only be just if we reach the Idea of Justice. Abu Hamdan's work shows that justice is at play at the level of the Idea, meaning at the level of these problematic points that first need to be revealed and that are then the place of the decision for justice or injustice.[64] We have seen that this decision bears on inclusion or exclusion as two fundamental attitudes characterizing the just as opposed to the unjust. In its most general form the Idea of Justice has then inclusion and exclusion as two basic relations between abstract differential elements. The Idea of Justice is later specified when we determine the abstract

---

63 "Then justice is the sort of thing that is just. That's how I would reply to the questioner. Would you also?" Plato, *Plato*, 763 Protagoras, 330-C4–8.

64 Deleuze conceives the Idea as the expression of a problem that relates a number of abstract singularities and that gets actualized by a process of differenciation, first in the intensive realm and second in the extensive realm, as this article has tried to show. "Problematic Ideas are not simple essences, but multiplicities or complexes of relations and corresponding singularities." Deleuze, *Difference*, p. 163.

elements and the exact form of inclusion and exclusion between these elements. We have seen that phonetic traits, the silence of some communities or populations or the accounts of death camp survivors are problematic points. The relation of inclusion and exclusion will bear on the abstract elements characterizing these problematic points: to include / exclude the biographical in the phonetical, to include / exclude the political in the technical, to include / exclude the absurd in the reasonable.

The ascending path towards justice consists in showing that there is a problematic stance beyond the obvious, that beyond the obvious correlation of accent and origin the mispronunciation could itself express migration, that beyond the obvious refusal of justice the Palestinians are asking for another form of justice, that beyond the obvious negligence the black communities are actively refusing a form of violence, that beyond the obvious incoherence of the testimonies of those who experienced life at the border of death there might be a higher form of coherence. The ascending path of justice consists then in revealing these problematic points, and by that it reveals that injustice lies essentially in a decision for exclusion and a disregard for the Idea of Justice.

The inclusion of the Idea of Justice, of the problematic itself, is then justice itself, and it is from that fundamental attitude than we need to determine the intensities of listening, the qualities of juridical speech and the extensities of the juridical space, which constitute the descending unfolding of justice. The decision to exclude implements new intensities of listening in order to expand the space of exclusion. Yet it is only the inclusion of the Idea of Justice that will allow us to hear the silencing of the excluded, the colonized, and the tortured, a silencing that can only be heard and requires another form of listening, a listening from the stance of the Idea. *"Only Justice is Just"* would mean that we can only hear justly if we stand there, if we stand in the realm of the Idea, because it is only from that stance that

93

we will be able to hear silencing and speak against it in a higher exercise of our faculties to hear and speak: injustice being what can only be heard and spoken against.

	Idea—Problematic	Intensive	Extensive	
Civil Right Opposition between right and wrong	Problematic relation between phone and logos	Semantic	Verbal testimony	Performative Space
		Analogical	Reductionist Phonetics	Telecom Space
		Electronic	Correlationist Data	Open Electronic Space
Political Right Opposition between political fields	Problematic silence of the excluded communities	Technological reporting	Automated testimony	Surveillance Space
	Problematic silence of an oppressed people	Media Coverage	World and Media testimony	International Space
Natural Right Opposition between life and death	Problematic forms of life	Kinesthesia and creation of sensory organs	New living forms as testimony	Space of the Living

Fighting for Rights

Alisa Del Re

Women in Europe

A Variable Geometry Citizenship[1]

> *Before the law all citizens were equal,*
> *but not all, naturally, were citizens*
> Robert Musil[2]

1.
Preliminary remarks on European citizenship for women

While it is already complex enough to attempt to imagine European citizenship for both genders, given the disparity between men and women in European countries in terms of the enjoyment of rights, it is even more difficult to hypothesize its attainment by women, given the disparity between the female citizens of one country and another.[3] Moreover, other forms of inequality are now being added to this structure, such as the inequality between migrants and natives and the racialization of society. Analyzing Europe as a cultural construct in progress—even if it is in crisis or precisely because it is—allows us to observe and interpret the discursive

---

1   Alisa Del Re, *Una cittadinanza a geometria variabile* in Alisa Del Re, Cristina Morini, Bruna Mura and Lorenza Perini, eds., *Lo sciopero delle donne* (Rome: Manifestolibri, 2019), pp. 63–74.
2   Robert Musil, *The Man Without Qualities* (London: Pan Macmillan UK, 2017).
3   See also Alisa Del Re, "Per una cittadinanza europea delle donne," in Dino Costantini, Fabio Perocco and Lauso Zagato, eds., *Trasformazioni e crisi della cittadinanza sociale* (Venice: Ca' Foscari, 2014), pp. 151–166.

dynamic of the globalization of social space. Through it, citizenship emerges as a "field" of conflict, in which rights defined at supranational, national and local levels are interwoven, and in which forms of power, authority and rights, both centralized and dispersed, engage.[4]

2.
How is European citizenship made up today?

European citizenship is made up of two fundamental components: national citizenship and the status of wage-earner.

It should first be pointed out that since 1789 the concept of citizenship as a container for citizens' rights has been superimposed on that of nationality. There is a mix of citizenship, as a legal institution, and nationality, as a socio-cultural notion: both concepts are used as synonyms until we activate the predominance of citizenship, understood as belonging, against citizenship understood as a container of rights. A gender reading captures a strange aporia: the recognized members of a nation have not been citizens with all rights for long. Women and men were considered equal as national citizens, but different as holders of rights. What impedes women's freedom and citizenship is not an archaic legacy of the past, a series of obstacles and delays to be removed, but lies precisely in the founding act of modernity: the social pact arising out of the French Revolution.

Modernity bases the figure of individual and citizen on the male gender, extending it to encompass the very notion of humanity on which it claims to base the universalism of political forms. For example, women have long been excluded from politics not so much for their condition as for their essence, for what they are: the

---

4   See also Saskia Sassen, *A Sociology of Globalization*, (New York: Norton and Company, 2007).

other and the elsewhere of man[5], and the possibility of interpreting equality and citizenship, without inclusion/exclusion, within the differences, is thus invalidated.

The idea that an individual is entitled to rights of citizenship in Europe even in the place where he or she resides is an argument born *in* and *as a result of* the world of work, which claims worker status to be a condition for legitimizing rights of citizenship.

However, in the European Union, to enjoy social and labor rights in the country you reside in it is not enough to be resident and to pay taxes and welfare contributions—requirements generally necessary at national level—you also need to be a citizen of a Member State.[6] The criterion of residence is therefore still largely subordinate to the criterion of nationality; in fact, non-EU migrant workers residing in EU territory are not granted the same freedom of movement and access to the welfare state as internal migrants.[7]

The problems inherent in the union of citizenship and migration appear inseparably linked, like citizenship and gender, so much so that it is not possible to speak sensibly of any of the classical dimensions of citizenship

---

5   See also Maria Luisa Boccia, *La differenza politica* (Milan: Il Saggiatore, 2002).

6   European citizenship was established in 1992 by the Treaty of Maastricht, which established that "everyone who holds the nationality of a Member State shall be a citizen of the Union" (Art. 8). In 1997, the Treaty of Amsterdam (which came into force in 1999) integrated the previous Article 8 into Article 17, clarifying the relationship between European and national citizenship, with the addition of the paragraph: "Citizenship of the Union shall complement and not replace national citizenship." The Lisbon Treaty (2009) further revised the European citizenship statute: compared to the previous version, the formula "citizenship of the Union shall complement national citizenship" is replaced by the expression "shall be added to national citizenship."

7   See Andrew Geddes, *Immigration and European Integration: Beyond Fortress Europe?* (Manchester: Manchester University Press, 2008); Costanza Margiotta and Olivier Vonk, *Nationality Law and European Citizenship: The Role of Dual Nationality*, EUI Working Papers, RSCAS 66, Robert Schuman Centre For Advanced Studies EUDO Citizenship Observatory, 2010.

(political, civil, social or fourth generation rights) without taking into account their interlocking with the dynamics of migration and gender. This approach uses Thomas H. Marshall's concept of citizenship as a frame and a more or less integrated "package" of legal titles, access titles (requirements), as well as a way and means of enjoying rights.[8] This frame can be thought of both objectively, as a "constitution" of the European citizen, and subjectively, as variable and stratified conditions of possible recognition for acting in the public sphere. But it is also how that short circuit between European and national citizenship, which gives rise to an extreme differentiation of situations in the territory of the Union, comes about. If, in fact, the European institutions are not able to interfere in the way in which national citizenship is acquired, Member States are free to modify the laws on citizenship according to political convenience, which in their turn have an effect on European citizenship.[9]

Moreover, European citizenship is not only linked by birth and constitution to the universalist imperatives of equality proclaimed by the French Revolution, nor it is linked to its universalist ideals. The European Citizenship is linked to the possibilities, the quality and the definition of labor. In Marx's conception too, man is what his labor allows him to be. Marxist feminist scholars have noted a series of contradictions in the definition of women's labor in a society where labor builds identity and contributes to substantiate citizenship, and this

---

8   See Thomas H. Marshall, *Citizenship and Social Class* (Cambridge: Cambridge University Press, 1950).

9   For example, the recognition of dual citizenship for the descendants of second, third and fourth generation emigrants by a number of European states, as well as by the former colonial powers vis-à-vis the citizens of the former colonies, means that millions of citizens permanently residing outside the territory of the Union benefit from the rights guaranteed by European citizenship. The freedom that states enjoy to establish autonomously the criteria for the acquisition of citizenship currently translates into a confrontation between *non-resident citizens* and *resident non-citizens*.

has allowed a new vision and perspective of citizenship itself. Separated from labor, the issue of female citizenship is still almost an oxymoron, because women do not yet seem to be fully-fledged political subjects, not even in the most recent times when they have seen their citizenship formally recognized, but not fully expressed.[10]

Today, the citizenship of rights in Europe, in particular as regards social rights, is essentially based on the definition of the citizen as a worker, which is in conflict not only with citizens who are victims of crisis, the unemployed, precarious or undeclared workers, but also, and again, with the gender dimension of the definition of citizen, since women are statistically the "citizens" least defined as "workers." From the Treaties of Rome to the Treaty of Nice—now subsumed into the Treaty of Lisbon—it is only the citizen with a job—in most cases a male citizen—who can move around Europe claiming rights in every state he cares to reside in, and enjoing the rights that derive from this status.

About ten years ago, a group of French women jurists, lawyers, trade unionists and journalists made a proposal concerning the citizenship rights of women in Europe. In association with the organization "Choisir la cause des femmes" ("Choose the Cause of Women"), they developed and published the project *La Clause de l'Européenne la plus favorisée (The Most Favored European Women's Clause)*, which tried to establish a legislative package made up of the best laws in the Union concerning the rights of women, to be applied to all European female citizens.[11]

Is it possible today to contemplate implementing this project? Can we consider the project sound? It is a project that starts from laws that already exist (and from the fact of excluding *a priori* those women who

---

10 Marisa Forcina, "Donne: lavoro e cittadinanza," *Critica marxista* 6 (1 December 2006): pp. 37–43.
11 See Gisèle Halimi, ed., *La clause de l'Européenne la plus favorisée* (Paris : Des femmes–Antoinette Fouque, 2008).

are not (yet) citizens, i.e. migrants), so it starts from the sovereign powers of individual states to establish the laws that govern the lives of male and female citizens and those who are not citizens but who reside in different states. The expected change is not radical, it only represents the best today's national democracy has to offer; it will make no decisive change in the condition of women who are still, depending on which state they live in, second class citizens compared to their male counterparts. I believe, however, that we should start with the subjective conditions of women in Europe, whatever their legal status, by analyzing one of the component elements of European citizenship: work, and looking at women's work.

3.
How can citizenship be broken down from a gender point of view?

Given the premise that worker status is the basis for European citizenship, the first question to ask is what is and how do we define the work of women?

a) First, according to the traditional definitions of work, i.e. paid work, it is a question of seeing how much, how and where women work.[12] The latest report by the European Trade Union Institute (ETUI)[13] points out that among the countries of the European Union, Italy, with a gender employment gap of 18%, is currently second only to Malta (24.5%) followed immediately by Greece (17.7%). The countries where the gender gap is closest to zero are Lithuania, Sweden, Latvia and Finland. The report also recalls that those with the widest gender gap

12 I will discuss this topic starting from Italian analyses, which can in general be extended to the rest of Europe.
13 ETUI, *Benchmarking Working Europe 2018*, https://www.etui.org/ Publications2/Books/Benchmarking-Working-Europe-2018 [consulted on the 09/09/19].

also have the lowest employment rates for women. But when it comes to wage labor, it is not only a question of defining how many women work, but also of analyzing the quality of labor, which is an analytical dimension that cuts across and complements the market profile. Exploring gender differences in terms of equal opportunities for men and women to do a good job shows that women present more signs of disadvantage than men.[14]

Some empirical evidence from studies developed in Italy by the National Institute for Policy Analysis (INAPP)[15] reveals the existence of different profiles between men and women, with reference to the areas that define quality work. Working women are penalized by comparison with men in terms of autonomy (less ability to determine the intensity, the modalities and the conditions of their work), economically (reduced wages, less economic stability, greater job insecurity), job complexity (fewer chances to participate in on-the-job and career training activities, greater inconsistency between the training process and the work position held), and as regards the control of their work (less possibility to participate in decision-making processes and to lay down guidelines to improve work organization or work processes).

It would seem that the problems of reconciling professional and private life are an exclusively female prerogative; women frequently give up challenging working careers that require significant investment in terms of time and responsibility. A clear symptom of this mechanism is that when work involves women, a high propor-

---

14 See Valentina Gualtieri, "Quale lavoro," Ingenere, 23rd March 2018, http://www.ingenere.it/articoli/quale-lavoro [consulted on the 09/09/19].

15 See also Irene Brunetti and Valeria Cirillo, "Donne e mercato del lavoro in tempo di crisi, tra discriminazioni multiple e intersezionalità," Annual congress of the National Conference of University Equality Bodies, 2018, in https://oa.inapp.org; see also Valentina Guarnieri, "Lavoro dignitoso, equità e inclusione" (Padova: University of Padua, 2017).

tion of it is part time, and often voluntary. There has to be something aside or upstream of women's paid work that holds back a more active participation in terms of career.

b) So let's face the unspoken, or, if you want, the implicit: it's not easy to talk about work in relation to the citizenship of women if we cannot also consider as work the reproduction of individuals, work traditionally given a female gender.

The radical materialist feminists of the 1970s defined "work" as that free activity of reproduction of individuals and of the species historically attributed to women (to "female" roles).[16]

This reflection from the last century has continued to our own day, even within the Not-One-Less strikes that lumped together both productive and reproductive work. Especially decisive was the feminist analysis of the nature of "domestic work," the de-identification that was made of its being a "natural" function, according to the vulgate of ancient and modern patriarchies, and its recognition as a patriarchal performative social construction.[17]

By presenting the family as a hidden component of the economy—as the primary place of reproductive work necessary for productive work and as a mechanism whereby wages are distributed to persons that are marginal or cut off from the labor market—feminist theorists have shown that the spheres of work and the family,

16 A whole strand of Italian Marxist feminism (I am thinking of Mariarosa Dalla Costa, Antonella Picchio, myself and others) had already defined reproduction as work in the 1970s. At the beginning of 2012, a decision of the Venice labor judge, Margherita Bortolaso (not by chance a woman) defined a housewife as a "non-employee worker," granting her husband parental leave for childcare because "both spouses work." The husband, a policeman, was denied this permission by his employer, the Ministry of the Interior, hence the employment dispute. Thus, the definition of domestic work as work, and of the housewife as a worker, today also has legal sanction. The idea has come a long way.
17 See Silvia Federici, *Caliban and the Witch* (New York: Autonomedia, 2004).

instead of being independent of each other, are in fact a continuum.[18] The work of carers seems to be a separate matter, foreign to the world of production; but, particularly nowadays, when capitalist production has invaded our lives, and hence the reproduction process too, transferring its characteristics into the new "forms" of work, it is not possible to define a clear boundary between the two sectors. They are connected, even if historically differentiated, and in them capital prioritizes and organizes human activities for the purpose of its own reproduction. The bond develops in two directions: the first, more clear-cut, is that already described as the direct production of value, the second is that in which the qualities of care work as producer of value form part of wage labor and the production of goods. As for the social identity of the caregiver: "The caregiver is usually defined with reference to the role: family (e.g. wife, mother, daughter) or professional (e.g. maid, nurse) or specific (e.g. volunteer). The evocation is generically and usually feminine, so much so that it can be said that gender is a component part of the social identity of the caregiver."[19]

In neo-liberalism, women's care work has been identified with multi-tasking, which skill today dominates the supply chains of new techno-informatics markets and transcontinental financialization services. This is the famous *W factor*, which used to fill the financial pages of some great Italian newspapers, or was part of *womenomics* analysis.[20] In this case, one of the strengths of the neo-liberal economy was concealed behind the upheaval and capitalist refunctionalization of women's care work, in all the affective and sentimental dimen-

18 See Lucia Chisté, Alisa Del Re, Edvige Forti, *Oltre il lavoro domestico* (Milan: Feltrinelli,1979).

19 Grazia Colombo, Per una definizione del lavoro di cura, Accaparlante, 1st January 2000 http://web.accaparlante.it/?q=articolo/una-definizione-del-lavoro-di-cura [consulted on the 09/09/19].

20 Women's Forum Global Meeting of the Women's Forum for the Economy & Society (Paris, November 2018).

sion of "everything for the other" that women have been forced to deploy over the centuries.

So it is not enough to say that care work is part of the history of women, unless we want to reduce it to an aptitude for "complex" service available to anyone who wants to acquire it. From this point of view, the Argentine *Niunamenos* has forced us to face a new experience: we are all workers (*trabajadoras somos todas*). This creates common ground and breaks down the historical division between reproductive work and the work of production of goods and services. It disobeys the systematic subordination of women's work, whether unpaid work or wage labor, which is always paid less than men's work and is always less satisfying. The violence of capital requires that the work of reproduction remain invisible.[21] But when the needs of offspring (the reproduction of people has unavoidable rigidities) demand a choice between wage labor and the unpaid work of reproduction, the conditions of neo-liberalism today are unlikely to send women home: rather, the entry of many women into the labor market corresponds to an entry into the private sector of other female workers (often migrants) to perform reproductive work, so creating gender hierarchies and harshly cut wages.[22]

---

21 See Veronica Gago, "This world is already another," *Pagina* 12, 26 October 2018, https://www.pagina12.com.ar/151011-este-mundo-ya-es-otro [consulted on the 09/09/19]: "They call it love, but what it really is, is unpaid work. #TrabajadorasSomosTodas brings this unpaid but obligatory work into the open, recognises us all as producers of value and at the same time allows us to denounce the hierarchy imposed by systematically ignoring it. We need union organisations that take charge of the reproduction of life in general."

22 See Gennaro Avallone, *Sfruttamento e resistenze* (Verona: Ombre Corte, 2017), particularly on the exploitation of the migrant labor force and the often very harsh working conditions of foreign "carers," who are in charge of very sensitive and increasingly key sectors such as care for the elderly and domestic care. Kostadinka Kuneva and Tania González Peñas have proposed to the European Parliament a resolution on the rights of workers in the domestic and care sectors, approved on 28 April 2016. This step meant for the first time a formal recognition at European level of the importance of this work and of the protection of the people who do it, often women

This, then, is the work of women, which is fundamental to their European citizenship: largely unsatisfactory market work, and invisible reproductive work, which added together often lead to a halving in wages which are already below the market average.

4.
Reproductive work as the basis for a new definition of European citizenship

So, to define the European citizenship of women, why do we not start from what unites them all, native and migrant, national and resident in different countries, namely reproductive work? This is unquestionably complex, often ambiguous ground, which might suggest the "naturalization" of domestic work. But the fact is that failing to address it means, in the first place, being blind to a matter of fact regarding the material condition of women. Second, it means not taking into account the transformations of "doing work" that involve acquiring for all types of work the unpaid, exploitative qualities of reproductive work—qualities such as total availability of time and attention, love for the work object, empathy and relational aptitudes, and loneliness deriving from the individualization of work and from individual contracting in the work itself, with qualities that can hardly be contractually agreed. Furthermore, taking into consideration reproduction as work will have consequences for the whole population, both reproducers and offspring, that is, each of us for our rigid and ineliminable needs.

If we want democracy to take on concrete, non-formal connotations, if we want the representation of women

and migrants. Currently, in most EU countries, domestic work, especially when carried out by migrants, does not enjoy the rights recognised in other areas of work. It should be noted that the resolution is a "weak," non-coercive instrument in the EU.

not to be linked to their belonging to the family nucleus, if we think that the body of a citizen is not undifferentiated and at the same time independent of any reproductive relationship (as in Hobbes' *De cive*),[23] if we consider female citizenship to be asymmetrical and incomplete, in the presence of heteronomy, namely laws thought up by others, we must begin to take into consideration the reality of each of our daily lives. The European citizenship of women must reflect the concrete nature of the lives of the women themselves who live in these territories. In fact, as Rita Segato[24] suggests, the female way of doing politics is a pragmatic, practical way that has to do with the ability to improvise in order to be able to defend life. It is something topical, not utopian.

Utopia does not allow us to think about the present, and it is in daily life that we are able to find the sense of that domestic politicity that has forced us to forget. Abstract citizenship, without gendered bodies, without the needs of dependent individuals, can only build hierarchies of power and violence.

If there is any common ground linking all women, native or migrant, living in Europe, it is their reproductive work. In the last century, through the romantic image of heterosexual marriage, such work identified female citizens living in the nation states as second-class citizens because they were considered to be perpetually dependent. The massive, albeit unequal, entry of European women into the labor market, a poorer and in many cases a "service" market, was guaranteed by lower-cost workers whose status was more precarious, for the most part immigrants, who entered households to

---

23 Thomas Hobbes, in his work *De cive* (On the Citizen), 1642, describes the state of nature as formed by men (men, not women), ahistorically considered to have sprung from the earth like mushrooms and having reached full maturity with no relation to one another.

24 Paola Rudan, "Ragazze ribelli che non si adeguano. Un'intervista a Rita Segato," *Il Manifesto*, 5 July 2018, https://www.connessioniprecarie.org/2018/07/05/ragazze-ribelli-che-non-si-adeguano-unintervista-a-rita-segato/ [consulted on the 01/06/20].

replace European women in reproductive work. Natives and immigrants thus experience a radically differentiated access to citizenship and a partial and conditional recognition of their social and reproductive rights. The possibility of whether or not to outsource reproductive and care work, a possibility linked to greater or lesser financial resources, is becoming an increasingly decisive element in the real enjoyment of freedom, such as that of bringing a child into the world or of succeeding in reconciling work and family. The expansion of a low-income labor market, which rotates around the world of personal services and the mercantilization of care work, has favored the process of stratification of female citizenship on both a local and global scale. The Spanish collective "Precarias a la deriva" ("Casual workers adrift") has coined a neologism *cuidadanìa*, derived from the words *cuidado* (care) and *ciudadanía* (citizenship). It specifies that:

We define *citizenship* as the right to care and to be cared for without care implying that women, or any other caregiver/care receiver will be put in a position of subordination. If citizenship relies on the sexual contract as a heteronormative device, *citizenship* subverts this device through the proliferation of bodies, practices, and desires for the production of other forms of life.[25]

25 "Definimos la *cuidadanía* come derecho a cuidar y ser cuidado sin que el cuidado signifique subordinación para la mujeres, ni tampoco para ninguna otra posición de sujeto cuidadora/cuidada. Si la ciudadanía está sostenida en el contrato sexual como dispotivo heteronormativo, la *cuida-danía* subvierte este último mediante la proliferación de cuerpos, prácticas y deseos para la ducción de otras formas de vida" (Precarias a la deriva, "Precarización de la existencia y huelga de cuidados," in M. Jesús Vara, ed., *Estudios sobre género y economía* (Tres Cantos: Akal, 2006), p. 126.) See also Precarias a la deriva, *Precarious Lexicon. Provisional European lexicon for free copy, modification, and distribution by the jugglers of life by some precarias a la deriva*, trans. F. Ingrassia and N. Holdren, Caring Labor: An Archive, 14 December 2010, https://caringlabor.wordpress.com/2010/12/14/precarias-a-la-deriva-precarious-lexicon/ [consulted on the 01/06/20].

It seems to me that in this way we can bridge the gap that exists between natives and immigrants, between women citizens of one European state and another by eliminating radically differentiated access to citizenship and giving a partial, conditional recognition to social and reproductive rights. But placing reproductive work and the rights that derive from it at the center of the citizenship debate means redesigning the European welfare system, because care and reproduction require public services and institutions that work to create the conditions for the enjoyment of a good quality of life for all, changing the idea of the autonomous and unconnected citizen.

For some years now, NUDM (Non Una di Meno) demands have been formulated in this sense: the material content of citizenship—a European minimum wage, the recognition of reproductive work, an unconditional basic income for all men and women, a welfare system that guarantees living needs—has to be built up against the violence of living conditions. These reflections tend towards the elaboration of an alternative way of thinking about politics starting from needs, from corporeality, from the relationship of dependence on the natural and social environment, from the material conditions that make social reproduction possible.

Considering that social reproduction refers to the reproduction of the species, to the continuous reproduction of the labor force and to the environmental conditions of creation and maintenance of individual and collective life, of neighborhoods, communities and states, it becomes fundamental to rewrite the "gender contract" that revisits the sexual division of reproductive labor on a global scale and the citizenship of women, which is still highly stratified at national and European level.

Paolo Napoli

Instituting Revisited

For a Materialistic Conception of the Institution

Common sense, even before a serious intellectual examination, tells us that the concept of institution seems to
blur the borders between disciplines on purpose and,
consequently, not even the law would be able to exercise a technical hegemony as it does with many other
semantic constructs. In this essay, however, I would
like to put forward a reading of institutions that in no
way makes a secret of its debt towards a materialistic
approach in describing social phenomena if the latter,
in particular, impact the law and, more generally, that
region with much more fluid borders that are the forms
of normativity. In this attempt I would like to start from
two cornerstones of Marxian thought that dictate the
meaning and set the theoretical scene for the considerations proposed here.

As is well known, the first thesis on Feuerbach conceives practice as rational objectivity and not as an
enforceable reflection of an idea. If we want to fill this
principle with content, the concept of institution also
deserves to be revisited, shifting attention from the subject-person to which objective practice is traditionally
associated. The use of the gerund "instituting" instead
of the noun "institution" asserts itself in all its dynamic
plasticity because it is the result of the very objectivity of human action. This objectivity, however, cannot be reduced to pure sensuous data, but is reflected
in an artefact that is both material and ideal. Instituting means, first of all, assigning a name to things, qual-
ifying them as entities destined for a purpose, which

cannot be separated from an action that gives them a precise social status. In this sense, attributing a name is a profoundly materialistic gesture because it simultaneously denatures—in the sense of removing allnatural evidence—the reality and delineates the sensuous coordinates in which the actors are oriented. If the object is neither a stumbling block of nature nor a projection of the idea, but a sensuous human activity—that is, a practice—the artefacts produced by this practice tend to disengage from the domain of their maker and acquire an autonomous historical functioning, both as current events and as latent presences that are inscribed in an arrhythmic and long-lasting chronology. Hence the sense of the prologue of the *Eighteenth Brumaire*, the second cornerstone of Marxian thought examined here, on men making their own history:

> Men make their own history, but they do not make it as they please; they do not make it under self-selected circumstances, but under circumstances existing already, given and transmitted from the past. The tradition of all dead generations weighs like a nightmare on the brains of the living. And just as they seem to be occupied with revolutionizing themselves and things, creating something that did not exist before, precisely in such epochs of revolutionary crisis they anxiously conjure up the spirits of the past to their service, borrowing from them names, battle slogans, and costumes in order to present this new scene in world history in time-honoured disguise and borrowed language.[1]

In short, thinking about the institution from a materialist perspective means recognizing that the people, things and actions of the world are not the result of destiny but of a destination. In conceiving the destination and

---

1 Karl Marx, *The Eighteenth Brumaire of Louis Bonaparte* (1852) (Createspace Independent Publishing, 2015), p. 1.

bearing it in mind—that is, in instituting the world—
human labor finds in law a rather well-equipped ally.

Beyond the person

Once the issue is situated in this framework of intelligibility, the first step to be taken is to move away from the
more general concept of institution regarding the fig-
ure-person, the subject that, like a Moloch, is emblem-
atically represented by the Weberian concept of *Anstalt*:
a social group whose commands have been set relatively
successfully, within a given field of action, to each
action with certain characteristics. Here the institution
stands as a coercive apparatus devoted to establishing
order in a social environment, according to what is a
shared vision both in the analysis of Erving Goffman
and in that of Michel Foucault: the state, the church,
schools, charity organizations for the poor, barracks,
hospitals, asylums, prisons, but also corporations and
colleges form the variegated constellation of an organi-
zational model with precise structural and operational
qualities. An anthropomorphic creator of a well-regu-
lated life in all spheres, an institution with such characteristics proves to be an easy target for analyses that
pay more attention to historical situations and dynamics and are less seduced by ideal-typical models that are
inclined to drift towards reification. It is nevertheless
necessary to take these reactions, which find their field
of incubation in micro-history, with a pinch of salt. It
may not be true that the criticism of the great contriv-
ances of domination by the generalized normative force
must, on the contrary, come to an institution conceived
as the creation of actors from below; a position that
has the naive mistake of not recognizing the tendential
autonomy of the legal devices that live due to their own
potential and versatility, but also of imagining a local
dimension that is self-sufficient in expressing the criteria

of its comprehension.[2] According to this perspective the relations between actors and political-judicial-administrative apparatuses on the strictly environmental level should be favored, as institutions are meant as "the outcome of specific local behaviors, of localized actions."[3] Hence the centrality of the concept of action, based on the conviction that "the activity of institutions is realized in giving a political meaning to the relationship between the actions and the space in which they occur, with the aim of creating a field of competence."[4] In other words, social actions would be inputs that allow institutions to subsequently carry out actions that have a meaning that is institutional but, at the same time, is spatially defined; an institutional sense that would nonetheless be triggered by the solicitations of what systems theory defines as the "environment." In this way, according to Tigrino and Giana, the editors of the dossier:

> We intend to propose a model of alternative analysis both with respect to the one on which the proposal of microhistory was structured (in which the actions – practices – were interpreted mainly starting from social systems of localized relations, without, however, placing institutions at the center in their capacity as autonomous historical subjects), and with respect to the responses derived from neo-institutionalism, which has investigated the ability institutions have to determine and produce shared social behaviors through a process of standardization of relations between individuals (determining stable social economic relations).[5]

This second approach to the issue of institutions proves to be at the very antipodes of the first. By aiming to valorize the role of specific practices in the interaction

---

2   Vittorio Tigrino and Luca Giana, eds., "Istituzioni," *Quaderni storici* 139 (2012), compare the introduction, p. 3–11
3   Ibid., p. 5.
4   Ibid.
5   Ibid., p. 6. (Translation of the author)

between actors and established powers and to bring out the figure of the institution ex-post, as a consequence of this process primarily managed by the inventive force of men and women, such an approach risks becoming dangerously deficient in terms of critical evaluation, should it be discovered that the institution is already there—which is highly likely, since it is often ahead of human moves, as the Marxian prologue of *The Eighteenth Brumaire* warned. But despite this specious removal the other problem would still be unsolved; that of the Weberian model and its derivatives, namely the idea that the institution is a subject, natural or artificial, and as such personifies a position of power. And here lies the crux of the matter.

If the materialistic premises from which we started are valid, it is more difficult to adhere to a reading that apodictically represents the institution as a person. It should not be forgotten that the latter is a technical construction, and not a natural data or a social fact governed by the principle of causality. As a legal artifice, the person is a sterilized notion of natural and historical contingencies and functions as an empty center of imputation of rights and obligations, thus rendering a capital service to the thought and practice of law, but more generally to the organization of associated life. Imagining a concrete human being, the notion of a person was constituted in the tradition of Roman law as an expedient to compensate for a relational deficit that the flesh-and-blood subjects are not able to fill. The person is a mechanism that abstracts a general sense scheme that is reducible to the dimension of pure juridical relations from the particular determinations of each individual. The great intuition in Roman thought was that of having imagined a decorporealized prosthesis, which introduces the appropriate mediations where individual human beings are not able to set up immediate relations between themselves or where, more simply, these relations are not enough to guarantee the functioning of society. As Yan Thomas showed, the genuine sense of the person consists in offering an anchorage point for one's will, decisions and actions that duplicate the substantial identity of the subject, but, at the same time, increase the operational potential of a society's public and private relations. Being one's self and being a creditor, debtor, son, heir, etc. meant recognizing that that precise individual as well as his status, his authentic self and the typical role of the functional class to which he belongs found equal acceptance under the unique name of person. Only in the Middle Ages did the sense of the concept become the capacity to act within justice, a prerogative that indicates a proprietary relationship. Having a legitimate person or role (*personam legitimam habere*) meant being the permanent owner of a capacity to protect one's rights before a judge.[6] For example, whenever a number of entities (human beings and things) have had to be treated as a unit, the person has been invoked to socially construct a collective whole that is irreducible to the sum of its parts. The classic example is that of the legal person, a fiction that the canonist Sinibaldo dei Fieschi (later Pope Innocent IV) elaborated and classified in the thirteenth century, distinguishing the *collegia* amongst other ways in *realia* (cities, hamlets, churches) and *personalia* (professional, religious and student guilds or corporations).

Sociology also noticed the advantages that such a process entails, whose late attrition came from the very proponents of the individualist approach—the holists, it goes without saying, have less resistance to justifying the social relevance of collective identities. It is enough to think of a work such as *Foundations of Social Theory* (1990) by the American James Coleman, to which one of the most attentive Italian sociologists, Gian Primo

6   Yan Thomas, "Le sujet concret et sa personne. Essai d'histoire juridique rétrospective," in Olivier Cayla and Yan Thomas, eds., *Du droit de ne pas naître. A propos de l'affaire Perruche* (Paris: Gallimard, 2002), pp. 124–126.

Cella,[7] recently returned to valorize the contribution of law in defining collective agents; a notion that social analysis usually fails to grasp beyond the empirical data of individual behavior.

And yet, amongst the more socially perceptive jurists such as Gunther Teubner, there is now a critique of the inadequacy of the paradigm of the legal person, mainly perceived as a "curious fiction of jurists."[8] From the point of view of the theory of systems that Teubner borrows from Luhmann, the concept of a person as a center of imputation of law dissolves in the "the socially binding self-description of an organized action system as a cyclical linkage of identity and action."[9] In the 1920s, Kelsen himself had advised being wary of alleged substances that disguise the reality of functional operations. What was under attack was the systematic dualism where, according to the model of theology, behind the function the substance should always be sought, the person behind the institution, God behind the State.[10] It is not by chance that the concept of person, under the influence of medieval theology, has gradually lost its original quality of normative construction, and has ended up being hypostatized into a metaphysics of singular and authentic subjectivity. Catholic "personalism" after the Second World War gave a philosophical voice to this transformation of technique into essence. Moreover, in the legal field, German professors of public law of the late nineteenth century had found nothing better than the coining of the formula "State-person" with which to seal the anthropomorphic analogy, and therefore closer

7   Gian Primo Cella, *Persone finte. Paradossi dell'individualismo e soggetti collettivi* (Bologna: Il Mulino, 2014).

8   Gunther Teubner, *Ibridi e attanti. Attori collettivi e enti non umani nella società e nel diritto* (Milan: Mimesis, 2015), p. 38.

9   Ibid., p. 39.

10 Hans Kelsen, "Der Begriff des Staates und die Sozialpsychologie. Mit besonderer Berücksichtigung von Freuds Theorie der Masse," *Imago* 8: 2 (1922): pp. 97–141. Both Freud and Kelsen reject Gustave Le Bon's hypothesis, outlined in his 1895 book *La psychologie des foules*.

correspondence to the real world, of a purely nominal notion like that of State. A "person" with such unequivocal subjective traits, able to associate the bodily element to the spiritual one so as to define more or less extended groups of individuals—just think of a metaphor as a collective soul which the socio-psychology of the masses of the late nineteenth century used widely—decisively conditions the very notion of the institution. By wrapping the latter in its shell, the "person" as isomorphic subjectivity of the human individual casts shadows over all the work of normative developments, that is, of institutional practice, of which the institution is the result. Similarly, we tend to forget that the "person" is originally a practical artefact, and only due to extra-juridical contamination does it come to coincide with the specific and concrete individual. This, in turn, uniting with other individualities, generates the composite figure of the political and social body. A renewed materialistic look at the institution, capable of projecting it into spaces in which the law cannot appear as solitarily hegemonic, thus supposes the refounding gesture of playing instituting against the form-person.

Beyond the institution-Katechon

If the model of "person" shields the fact that instituting precedes the institution and, in this way, compromises the correct comprehension of social dynamics, another problem arises from the hasty way of conceiving the institution as a constraint; that is, as an antagonistic presence to the free movement of human praxis. Interpreted as a hierarchical filter of the most widespread applications for recognition, the institution is but an eminent negative place. It is a model that, in modern times, dates back to Hobbes, whose institution par excellence, the State, is considered to be the dam against wanton individual appetites and, therefore, a deterrent to violence. To tell the truth, the idea that the institution works with this katechontic spirit—or, at least, as a filter that reins in the forces, thoughts, feelings and desires of flesh-and-blood subjects—historically and conceptually goes back to the theological opposition between *charisma* and *officium*, between pneumatic anarchism on the one hand and ordered and prescriptive structure on the other. On this opposition between freedom and obedience, the Protestant debate arose about the authentic nature of Christianity, a debate developed in the favorable climate of the Bismarckian *Kulturkampf*. In the most radically Lutheran declinations of the polemics such as those of Rudolph Sohm, the institution is perceived as a political, juridical and social construction that essentially produces its effects in terms of command and subjugation, where the freedom of Christians and the communities formed by them is a direct result of the ungovernability of the grace that comes from the Holy Spirit. Expecting to marshal the free voice of divine grace in the sacraments, Catholic thought would initiate that progressive process of juridification of the Christian phenomenon culminating in the Gregorian reform in the eleventh century. Colonized by the law and its engineering of government, the Church would have definitively lost its authentic meaning of a horizontal, equal and ahierarchic community.[11]

The Protestant vision of the ecclesial institution coercing the freedom of the faithful acts as a critical model that is broad enough to be used in other contexts too. After all, an approach that relegates the institution to the narrow and sinister light of power and asymmetry is analogous to that which was used to justify the French sociological critique of the 1960s and 1970s (Bourdieu), which also became less extreme in its one-dimensional reading of the institutional phenomena. It is a perspective

---

11 Rudoph Sohm, *Kirchenrecht*, I: *Die geschichtlichen Grundlagen* (1892) (Leipzig and Munich: Duncker & Humblot, 1970).

that finds as much comfort in the rigid and totalizing patterns of structuralism as it does in the armor of the law that, as we know, at least in its formalist, structured and structuring declensions, is already so. In addition, as Luc Boltanski clearly showed in *De la critique*,[12] pragmatism has sought to devalue the very autonomy of the institution and the stable and independent nature of the semantic tools it uses (such as judicial norms) to show the situated character in each enunciation, the importance of the contextual component thanks to the inventive capacity of the actors who are always autonomously able to live together, independently or in spite of the constraints imposed by the institutions. The problem, as Boltanski rightly points out, is that pragmatism ends up hypostatizing an implicit agreement in society, which reabsorbs the uncertainty that characterizes men and women's being in the world, where the fundamental reason of social life and therefore the condition to elaborate the critical form is instead conflict, disagreement. Hence a reconsideration of the role of the institution that Boltanski paints on a procedural background no longer obsessed with the negative taboo: "An institution is a bodiless being to which is delegated the task of stating the whatness of what is [ce qu'il en est de ce qui est]. To institutions fall the task of saying and confirming what matters [...] In particular, institutions must sort out what is to be *respected* from what cannot be."[13]

Boltanski has certainly made a remarkable step forward in regard to measuring the role of the institution more on the issues and challenges (*enjeux*) than on the status of the collective subject and a priori holder of a position of power. Attention thus falls on the ways of institutionalization rather than on a hypothetical institutional identity. From time to time, those relatively well-organized presences that fulfil the function of say-

12 Luc Boltanski, *De la critique* (Paris: Gallimard, 2009).
13 Ibid., p. 117.

120

ing and confirming the agenda of a society in a given historical period are institutionalized. Every entity structured in continuity that is called upon to exercise this task boasts an "institutional" purpose. Hence the not insignificant consequence that is primarily valorized by the element of historical contingency from which the institution takes shape, which also makes it possible to no longer focus on the classic places of the *Anstalt*, but to equip oneself with critical tools when identifying what emerging realities are elected to be institutionalized from time to time and become stabilized in a relative duration.

This opens the gap to observe the work of the institution in its power to indicate and validate the presence of exemplary political, social, juridical turning points, but also the existential *lato sensu*, which are part of the scene in which the subject enters into relations with others, as well as with him or herself.

The thing-institution

Although possessing far more fluid properties and not being as shielded in a preconceived domain, Boltanski's institution still acts as a filter between an inside and an outside, between the admissible on the one hand and the negligible if not even eliminable on the other. This divergence recalls that gap between telling the truth and being truthful that in his *The Order of Discourse* Foucault took up from Canguilhem to describe the regime of circulation of the enunciations in modern societies. In particular, the transition from the moment in which the truth is affirmed but not yet admitted into official scientific discourse, because it does not correspond to the rational codes that regulate and validate the judgments, to that in which the enunciations are legitimized at the scientific level and acquire the character of accuracy. The institution would be placed in this second space, that of a procedural regularity in which the orthodoxy of the enunciations is based on their "orthology," that is, the respect for the rules of enunciation and the sequence of different cognitive and practical acts that allow the truth of being to be officially supported.

In order to take a further step and free the institution from the invasive presence of the subject-person, or rather the abstract personification of a publicly recognizable figure that rises above the private actors, we could paradoxically avail ourselves of the ideas offered by one of the founding fathers of institutionalism, namely Maurice Hauriou.

I say paradoxically, because when we consider a reference text such as *Théorie de l'institution et de la fondation* (1925), we find the most convinced appreciation for the person-institutions and a substantial underestimation of what Hauriou defines as the thing-institutions. Regardless of a distinction that retraces the juridical topic of "persons and things," it is interesting to note that in trying to catalyze our focus on the former, Hauriou allows us, in spite of himself, to question the consequences of a combination between the concept of institution and the world of things. In a nutshell, the problem he poses is the following.

After having challenged the limits of the subjectivist theory centered on the will of the State personality at the origin of the law (Gerber, Laband and, above all, Jellinek), and the objectivist theory of Duguit, according to which the law lies entirely in the objectivity of the legal norm in harmony with the Durkheimian supremacy of the *social milieu* on individual consciences, Hauriou intended to circumscribe the role of the legal norms. If these represent an element of continuity and duration for institutions, we cannot therefore say that they are the founding moment. While the objectivistic approach leads to attributing the *social milieu* with the ability to create the legal norms from which institutions arise, according to Hauriou this force is nowhere to be found in the *social milieu*. The *social milieu* will at most be able to confirm or inhibit individual initiatives, but not to generate a rule that creates institutions.

In order to elude these two models, Hauriou then proposes the famous definition of institution as an "idea of work or enterprise that is historically incarnated in a power that is organized in a social group that lives in communion with it."[14] It is clear, however, that with such characteristics Hauriou's institution can only identify with the personal or corporative form; the only one to be endowed with that vital force that would be lacking in thing-institutions like legal norms. However, and here is the best part, in clarifying the meaning of the thing-institutions, the French jurist gives arguments that can be used in their favor rather than to discredit them, as he actually wished to do. In fact, thing-institutions as legal norms work in social immanence, that is, do not inhere to a precise idea of the work internalized in this or that public or private person. Not representing the privilege of any constituted power, thing-institutions are nomadic agents that are virtually able to lend their "service" to any corporate subject, the State in the first place: "As an idea," says Hauriou "the legal norm [i.e. the thing-institution] spreads and lives in the social environment, but does not entirely generate a corporation that belongs to it; it lives in the social body, for example in the State, lending it its power of sanction and taking advantage of the manifestations of communion that take place there. It is not able to generate a corporation because it is not a principle of action or of an enterprise, but, on the contrary, a principle of limitation."[15]

In Hauriou's proposal it is possible to defend the idea that the legal norm adheres to social relations and not

14 Maurice Hauriou, "Théorie de l'institution et de la fondation. Essai de vitalisme social," in Maurice Hauriou, ed., *Aux sources du droit. Le pouvoir, l'ordre, la liberté* (Paris: Bloud & Gai, 1933), p. 96.
15 Ibid., p. 97.

to a self-referential elsewhere. Or rather, it should be said that this norm is inscribed in the immanence of history, to avoid fueling the age-old misunderstanding of a law —the thing-institution—conceived as an automatic reflection of society. These deterministic residues, which sometimes reappear between the lines of a social history albeit driven by the best intentions, ignore the very specific chronology of legal norms, which are current but also latent in the long term and, as such, call into question any hasty representation in terms of social reflection. At the same time, however, the idea that the legal norm is a source of limitation must be rejected from Hauriou's vision, because it is evidently the fruit of a reduction, typical of public law expert, of the concept of law to the expression of a sovereign will. A position of this kind loses the authentic origin of law that rests on the activity of private subjects, for whom legal norm is not a principle that simply prohibits and sanctions, but an opportunity to create and innovate material and symbolic relations.

The problem of a materialistic vision applied to the law and, in particular, to the issue of institutions, therefore consists in the efforts to avoid the incorporation of norms in the person-institution, by permanently calling into question this movement of subsumption—not by capital, but by the person—of the very immanence of those thing-institutions that are the legal norms. In this regard, perhaps the best example is the well-known evolution by the most pervasive institution of our age: the market. In the states of the Ancien Régime, the market would identify a precise portion of the urban territory. As Fernand Braudel said, "le marché, c'est faire surface."[16] For a long time the market was just a material sign of the city life that was essential to the subsistence

16 Fernand Braudel, *Civilisation matérielle, économie et capitalisme, XVᵉ-XVIIIᵉ siècles, vol. II: Les jeux de l'échange* (Paris: A. Colin, 1979), p. 12.

of the community. A space in which the needs of individuals were concentrated and for this reason worthy
of attention from political authorities, the market, in
its original form, was above all the empirical perime-
ter in which a combination between subjects and goods
was located. Material visibility is the condition that
exhausts the market's political-economic status since it
is a portion of territory in which there should be a guarantee that exchanges be carried out correctly. The market still works as a thing-institution, which implies a
series of divisions: of the urban territory, of the day, of
the actions, of the goods and of the money. By locating
and subdividing, the market ends up creating an environment. The original status of the market in modern
times began showing its inadequacy from the second
half of the eighteenth century, when the spatial dimension was no longer able to complete its significance.
The birth of political economy introduced an ontological shift: the market was no longer a mere portion of
urban territory, but also a criterion of intelligibility of
social interdependence represented by the supply and
demand for goods. In this sense, *market place* and *market principle* have been used to indicate the emergence
of the abstract meaning of the term alongside that of the
traditional one.[17] In this second stage, which evidently
does not cancel out the previous one but increases its
semantic dimension following precise social, economic
and demographic processes, the market fully asserts
itself as an institution of "veridiction," as Michel Foucault would say.[18] It may seem that this abstract dimension of the object overwhelmingly characterizes every
sector of the material and cultural life of the present,
given that the market acts as the ultimate thermometer

17 Steven L. Kaplan, *Les ventres de Paris* (Paris: Fayard, 1988), pp. 16–18.
18 See the courses delivered at the Collège de France in 1978 and 1979:
Michel Foucault, *Security, Territory, Population* (New York: St Martin's Press, 2009) and Michel Foucault, *The Birth of Biopolitics* (New
York: St. Martin's Press, 2010).

in evaluating the proper functioning of the other institutions. However, this role as a real institution of institutions, which might seem to place the market as a sovereign rank of *superiorem non recognoscens*, has for several years now been accompanied by a metamorphosis, essentially realized in the sphere of communications, which represents the market not only as a spatial object and as a principle of all-round social intelligibility, but as a real person, with its own emotional and cognitive sphere (market indices). We are constantly exposed to a relentless comparison with what the market thinks and expresses as if it were a ubiquitous subject that judges, condemns and absolves. This anthropomorphic dimension assumed by the market—whose causes should be investigated well beyond the sphere of the media that is too easily elevated to the convenient abode of being, that is, to a new ontology—appears all the more interesting and disturbing because its way of expressing itself is extensively drawn from the emotional register. One need only think about how many times a day one reads and hears how "nervous," "euphoric," "skeptical," "uncertain," "jumpy" etc. the markets are; all qualities we struggle to recognize in an abstract entity and which instead, precisely for this reason, succeed in making us accustomed to institutions by disguising the directive result in the form of a voluble and nameless human being. The anthropomorphized market reactivates and overpowers the classic status of the institution and gives us, in a more anonymous and decentralized way than in the past, the most obsessive paradigm of power: the person. In the face of this process concerning the ways of representing social constructions, ways that very often end up being reified into real substances, the usefulness can be seen of the torsion of method introduced by Foucault, who always preferred anonymous dispositives— that is, the naked mechanisms of exercising power. In this respect the Foucaultian discovery of that heteroclite field of normativities is very fruitful, as these are endowed with a relative autonomy with respect to empirical contexts, and employed, from time to time, by this or that structure of power, that is by the person-institution.

I would like to use an example that is historically more tangible to try to summarize what the concrete sense of the thing-institution is: a simple but significant passage by one of the many professors of "Cameralism" who populated German universities in the eighteenth century. In defining the leading discipline of that new university teaching, the author preferred an approach which seemed to be minimalistic when he spoke of the police as a *congeriem mediorum*, a complex of means.[19] Therefore, perhaps it is necessary to start from here, from a person-institution—embodied here by an *Anstalt* par excellence like the police—whose authority is deflagrated in the dispersion of the instruments with which this person-institution is equipped. The means, by definition, is not in the order of the principles or in that of the ends, but in the theater of the ever-changing strategic combinations, a condition that ensures a certain amount of sovereignty disguised behind a servile appearance. The institution in the classic sense thinks of the means as the articulation of one's will in the pursuit of a goal. The revisited institution is instead thought of as the result, though never definitive, of a tension of pre-existing means potentially capable of configuring different structures. Recognizing that "in the beginning lies the means" means to assert oneself with an ever-valid materialistic antidote to all personalist metaphysics and, ultimately, the idealism of the institution. For law, it means irrevocably moving the borders to the *forma fluens* of praxis.

19 P.C.G. Hohenthal, *Liber de politia* (Lipsiae: Hilscherum, 1776), § 2, p. 10.

Overcoming Law

Daniel Loick

"...as if it were a thing"

A Feminist Critique of Consent[1]

The international #MeToo campaign has been one of
the most successful feminist interventions in recent history. Not only has it brought down a number of powerful men who previously deemed themselves immune
against any allegations of misconduct, it also helped to
demonstrate the dramatic extent of the problem of sexual assault and harassment, to create solidarity among
women and empower them both in intimate encounters
and public discourse, and to raise men's awareness of
women's experiences with sexual violence. Besides challenging cultural norms of sexual behavior, in a number
of countries the campaign either already has or might
in the near future result in concrete policy changes and
new legislation, such as compulsory sexual harassment
trainings in companies, providing better support for
survivors of rape and abuse or creating better ways of
reporting cases of sexual violence.

At the center of the feminist agenda against sexual
violence and assault lies the category of *consent*. Lack
of consent provides the legal definition of assault and
rape; consent also works as a cultural norm within sexual encounters and as a central point of reference for
many feminist debates (paradigmatically expressed in
the slogan "No means no, yes means yes"). This centrality notwithstanding, there has been growing criticism

1   This paper was first published by *Constellations: An International
Journal of Critical and Democratic Theory*, July 12, 2019, online:
https://onlinelibrary.wiley.com/doi/abs/10.1111/1467–8675.12421.

of the category of consent within feminist philosophy. Feminist thinkers have argued that focusing on consent not only hinders the articulation of a more comprehensive understanding of sexual harm, it also leads to an oppressive, individualized and reified form of subjectivity and intersubjectivity that blocks women from deploying actual social, cultural and sexual power. In this paper, I understand the focus of consent as a paradigmatic case of what can be called *juridicism*, i.e. the problematic dominance of law within the ethical life of our society.[2] The concept of juridicism not only helps explain why the category of consent has come to play such a crucial role, it also provides a social-philosophical vocabulary to explicate its inherent normative problems. Critiquing consent as an instance of juridicism not only implies rejecting liberal feminism's reliance on the violence inherent in the judicial apparatus of the modern state (which some critics have coined "carceral feminism"[3]) but also puts into question liberalism's entire underlying normative grammar. Liberal juridicism tends to convert all human interaction into legal or quasi-legal matters and thus fails to acknowledge the specific normative structure of intimate interactions. Rather than reproducing this juridicism, I argue, femi-

---

[2] I have developed my critique of juridicism in more detail in Daniel Loick, *Juridismus. Konturen einer kritischen Theorie des Rechts* (Berlin: Suhrkamp, 2017).

[3] See for example, Victoria Law, "Against Carceral Feminism," *Jacobin*, October 17, 2014, online: https://www.jacobinmag.com/2014/10/against-carceral-feminism/; Nickie Phillips and Nicholas Chagnon, "'Six Months Is a Joke': Carceral Feminism and Penal Populism in the Wake of the Stanford Sexual Assault Case," 2018, *Feminist Criminology*, online: https://journals.sagepub.com/doi/abs/10.1177/1557085118789782?journalCode=fcxa; Mimi E. Kim, "From carceral feminism to transformative justice: Women-of-color feminism and alternatives to incarceration," *Journal of Ethnic & Cultural Diversity in Social Work* 27:1 (2018): pp. 1–15. For an explicit critique of the carceral implications of affirmative consent models, see Janet Halley, "The Move to Affirmative Consent," *Signs. Journal of Women in Culture and Society* (2018), online: http://signsjournal.org/currents-affirmative-consent/halley/ [all online sources consulted on the 01/02/20].

nism should reflect on its historical potential to develop post-juridical forms of political action.

In what follows, I will first introduce the recent debate on the case of the actor and comedian Aziz Ansari to raise some initial concerns about the usefulness of a juridical notion of consent to describe sexual harms. Utilizing a range of feminist legal and political theories, I will then go on to present a particularly clear example of a juridical understanding of intimate relationships, namely Immanuel Kant's theory of marriage. Kant's contractualism, its egalitarian grammar notwithstanding, is not only deeply connected with inequality and coercion, it is also based on a disembodied and reified view of human subjectivity. Such notions, I attempt to show, are not merely ideological views *about* sexuality, they are also operative *within* our sexual practices, reinforcing the problematic dichotomy between active men and passive women. In order to overcome this intimate juridicism, I will conclude by proposing a feminist *politics of forms of life,* i.e. a politics that enables women to meaningfully create and shape the conditions of sexuality.[4]

---

4   This criticism, to clarify this upfront, is sharply demarcated from the concerns recently raised by Slavoj Žižek, who in an article for *Russia Today*, entitled "Sign a contract before sex?," fears that "political correctness" would "destroy passion." In an ostentatiously taboo-breaking posture that has become typical for contemporary "anti-PC" approaches, Žižek bemoans that it would no longer be possible to speak the truth that it is women who willingly objectify themselves in order to be attractive to the male gaze. While Žižek also criticizes a legalistic notion of consent, his main worry is not the juridical domestication of the feminist struggle against toxic masculinity, but quite the contrary: he complains that "long bureaucratic negotiations" turn out to be a "mood killer." Žižek is thus just one more on the long list of men to accuse feminists of being killjoys. Slavoj Žižek, "Sign a contract before sex? Political correctness could destroy passion," *Russia Today*, December 25, 2017, online: https://www.rt.com/op-ed/414219-sex-political-correctness-relations/ [consulted on the 01/02/20].

The problem with consent

On January 13, 2018, in the wake of the #MeToo debate, the website babe.net published a detailed account from a young woman, referred to in the article as "Grace," about a night with the famous actor and comedian Aziz Ansari.[5] Grace describes how she met Ansari, whom she admired, at a party and bonded with him over a mutual interest in vintage cameras. After they exchanged a few texts in the following days, he asked her out for a date. Grace and Ansari ended up in his apartment and engaged in sexual activities. During this night, Ansari repeatedly pressured Grace into doing things she wasn't comfortable with, until she left his apartment in tears. Grace texted Ansari in the morning to tell him that his behavior had made her uneasy, to which he responded with an apology. In retrospect, Grace came to define the night not only as "the worst experience with a man I've ever had," but as a case of sexual assault. In a statement published the day after the babe.net piece, Ansari, on the other hand, wrote that he believed they had "engag[ed] in sexual activity, which by all indications was completely consensual."[6]

Grace's account of her night with Aziz Ansari has been a matter of controversy within the #MeToo movement. On the one hand, some commentators have drawn a clear line between Ansari's behavior and that of notorious rapists like Harvey Weinstein, who assaulted multiple women, mostly at the workplace. For Ansari's defenders, the encounter between him and Grace constitutes at best a case of "bad sex" or "a date gone wrong,"

5   Katie Way, "I went on a date with Aziz Ansari. It turned into the worst night of my life," January 13, 2018, online: https://babe.net/2018/01/13/aziz-ansari-28355 [consulted on the 01/02/20].
6   Katie Way, "Aziz Ansari issues statement denying sexual misconduct," January 15, 2018, online: https://babe.net/2018/01/15/aziz-ansari-statement-28407 [consulted on the 01/02/20].

but not of sexual assault[7]; according to *New York Times* columnist Bari Weiss for example, Ansari is only guilty "of not being a mind reader."[8] On the other hand, other feminists have insisted that Ansari's misconduct is part of a larger culture of misogyny and toxic masculinity that ultimately enables and engenders rape and sexual violence.[9] Incidents like these deserve scrutiny and critique precisely because they stem from cultural norms that are deeply embedded in our everyday routine, as for example *vox* writer Anna North has pointed out.[10]

Both sides of the debate have in common that they juxtapose violence and consent: the sexual encounter between Grace and Ansari was *either* consensual *or* violent. The problem with this dichotomy, however, is that cases like this one precisely prove that social interactions can be consensual *and* still be violent; in other words, that the category of (non-)consent is not adequate to describe the wrong that has been done here. The Ansari case indicates at least five initial problems with the concept of consent:[11] 1. Temporality: sometimes we initially

---

7   Caitlin Flanagan, "The Humiliation of Aziz Ansari," *The Atlantic*, January 14, 2018, online: https://www.theatlantic.com/entertainment/archive/2018/01/the-humiliation-of-aziz-ansari/550541/ [consulted on the 01/02/20].

8   Bari Weiss, "Aziz Ansari Is Guilty. Of Not Being a Mind Reader," *New York Times*, January 15, 2018, online: https://www.nytimes.com/2018/01/15/opinion/aziz-ansari-babe-sexual-harassment.html [consulted on the 01/02/20].

9   Lily Herman, "The Allegations Against Aziz Ansari Show That Consent Really Isn't Common Sense – When It Should Be," January 14, 2018, online: https://www.refinery29.com/en-us/2018/01/187840/aziz-ansari-sexual-misconduct-allegations [consulted on the 01/02/20].

10   Anna North, "The Aziz Ansari story is ordinary. That's why we have to talk about it," January 16, 2018, online: https://www.vox.com/identities/2018/1/16/16894722/aziz-ansari-grace-babe-me-too [consulted on the 01/02/20].

11   For a fascinating psychoanalytical reflection on the process of consenting see Judith Butler, "Sexual Consent. Some Thoughts on Psychoanalysis and Law," *Columbia Journal of Gender and Law* 22:1 (2011). For a reflection on some of the problems of such "grey areas," see "Introduction," in Linda Alcoff, *Rape and Resistance* (New York: Polity, 2018). As Alcoff points out, the feminist insistence that "rape is rape" is not always helpful or even feminist. Acknowledging the heterogeneity of survivors' experiences does not imply minimizing

agree to something but only later realize that we have been uncomfortable with it or that a boundary has been crossed. 2. Inconsistency: sometimes we want different or contradictory things at once and thus have to suppress parts of our own subjectivity in order to represent one single unified will. 3. Opacity: sometimes we don't have access to our desires or don't know what we want (and what we don't want). 4. Asymmetry: agreements take place under unequal conditions, where one party might accept a proposal out of fan admiration, pressure or fear of negative consequences. 5. Partiality: agreement often means accepting a given yes-or-no option, without being able to shape or co-determine the larger context of the interaction. None of these five problems curtail the *juridical* validity of a consent given, yet they can lead to a situation where even consensual interaction can still be experienced as violent.

Already a superficial description of the Ansari case shows the conceptual limitations of the category of consent. In addition, it is useful to investigate this scene using the tools provided by feminist political philosophy. The question of consent has been highly debated within feminist theory and activism at least since the 1990s, and it concerns a number of topics such as sexual violence and rape, pornography, human trafficking, and prostitution. The idea of consent has always played a crucial role for liberal theories, as the cornerstone of the political legitimacy of state power and as a justification of citizens' obligations. Liberal feminists have used the category in order to advocate for the expansion of choices for women and thus the strengthening of individual liberty and agency.[12] This implies not only

their harm or making excuses for the perpetrators. On the contrary, taking the complexity of experience—which includes the complexity of culpability—into account is necessary in order to develop more successful remedies.

12 For liberal feminist positions working within the contractarian model, see for example Susan Moller Okin, *Justice, Gender, and the Family* (New York: Basic Books, 1989); Alison Jaggar, "Taking Con-

the demand to delegitimize and criminalize all forms of *non-consensual* assault, but also the call to destigmatize and decriminalize all forms of *consensual* interaction.[13] Speaking with Heidi Hurd, consent works as "moral magic": for liberal theory, it is consent that "turns rape into love-making."[14]

Radical feminists, on the other hand, have questioned the usefulness of the category of consent by pointing out that women's choices take place in a situation pre-defined by patriarchal norms. One of the most prominent voices of this criticism is Catherine MacKinnon. Already in her important essay "Rape: On Coercion and Consent," MacKinnon exposes some of the implications of the consent model under conditions of male dominance: consent further entrenches an image of sexuality in which the man has the privilege of initiative which the woman can only accept or reject. The power supposedly exercised on consent, MacKinnon insists, is thus

sent Seriously: Feminist Practical Ethics and Actual Moral Dialogue," in Earl R. Winkler and Jerrold R. Coombs, eds., *The Applied Ethics Reader* (Oxford: Blackwell, 1993). Liberal positions vary on how explicit the consent has to be in order to constitute legitimate sex. For a negative consent model, see Susan Estrich, *Real Rape* (Cambridge MA: Harvard University Press, 1989); Donald Drips, "Beyond Rape: An Essay on the Difference Between the Presence of Force and the Absence of Consent," *Columbia Law Review* 92 (1992): pp. 1780–1806. For an affirmative consent model see Stephen Shulhofer, *Unwanted Sex: The Culture of Intimidation and the Failure of Law* (Cambridge MA: Harvard University Press, 1998); for a communicative model (in general critical of the category of consent), see Lois Pineau, "Date Rape: A Feminist Analysis," *Law and Philosophy* 8:217 (1989): pp. 217–243; Michelle Anderson, "Negotiating Sex," *Southern California Law Review* 78 (2005): pp. 1401–1438.

13 For a rather consent-affirming overview of this debate, see Robin West, "Sex, Law, and Consent," in Franklin G. Miller and Alan Wertheimer, eds., *The Ethics of Consent* (Oxford: Oxford University Press, 2009); for a rather consent-critical overview and a deep historical inquiry, see Maria Drakopulou, "Feminism and consent: a genealogical inquiry," in Rosemary Hunter and Sharon Cowan, eds., *Choice and Consent: Feminist Engagements in Law and Subjectivity* (London: Routledge, 2007), pp. 9–38.

14 Heidi M. Hurd, "The Moral Magic of Consent," *Legal Theory* 2, Special Issue: Sex and Consent (1996): pp. 89–112.

based on a more fundamental powerlessness.[15] Other radical feminists, too, have made the point that a woman's choice, if conceived of as a singular "signing off" of an unequal contract, does not indicate true freedom. Carole Pateman and others have invoked the parallel to the Marxist critique of the consent of the worker to the labor contract: Because the worker does not really have another choice, her consent cannot be regarded as an expression of free affirmation understood in a meaningful way.[16] The same is true for female consent to heterosexual sex: As long as men control the economic, political, cultural, and symbolic resources of society and as long as a gendered dichotomy of activity and passivity is reproduced in the socialization of girls and boys, the consent model ratifies rather than redresses patriarchal relationships.[17]

In addition, intersectional feminists have insisted that sexual harm cannot be properly understood without taking race and class dimensions into account. The "patri-

---

[15] Catherine MacKinnon, "Rape: On Coercion and Consent," in *Toward a Feminist Theory of the State* (Cambridge MA: Harvard University Press, 1989), p. 175.

[16] According to this analogy, the situation of women is similar to the one of workers in capitalist societies as Marx described it: they *appear* as formally free and equal when actually they have entered into the contract under unfree and unequal conditions. See Karl Marx, *Capital Vol 1*, trans. Ben Fowkes (London: Penguin Classics, 1992), pp. 270–271. For this analogy, see Carole Pateman, *The Sexual Contract* (Stanford CA: Stanford University Press, 1988); see also, Jeffrey Gauthier, "Consent, coercion and sexual autonomy," in Keith Burgess-Jackson, ed., *A Most Detestable Crime: New Philosophical Essays on Rape* (Oxford and New York: Oxford University Press, 1999), pp. 71–89.

[17] Interestingly, there is no consensus on the question of consent within queer feminist theory. Some queer theorists side with radical feminism in pointing out the heteronormative logic underlying the liberal contractualist framework; see for example, Wendy Brown, *States of Injury: Power and Freedom in Late Modernity* (Princeton NJ: Princeton University Press, 1992). Others insist that normalizing or conservative effects occur precisely as a result of curtailing deviant subjects' authority to consent; see for example Gayle Rubin, "Thinking Sex. Notes for a Radical Theory of the Politics of Sexuality," in Carole S. Vance, ed., *Pleasure and Danger: Exploring Female Sexuality* (London: Pandora, 1992), pp. 143–178.

archy" that shapes sexual relationships is not a mono-
lithic block but is itself highly differentiated. Women
of color, poor women, and transgender and non-binary
people are not only more vulnerable to (cis-) male acts of
sexual violence, they also have less access to state means
of enforcing their rights and are frequently confronted
with situations in which their accounts are devalued,
up to the point where survivors' testimonies are made
unintelligible.[18] In addition, these marginalized groups
often face the risk of becoming subject to victim blam-
ing and re-traumatization, often carried out by representatives of state and law. The ability and opportunity to
deploy the legal power of consent as well as the extent to
which life worlds are actually shaped by agreement and
affirmation are thus not only gendered but also stratified by race and class dimensions. Not only the analysis
of sexual violence, also the proposed remedies should
therefore be based on intersectional[19] and decolonial
concepts.[20]

Contract and coercion

Many feminist thinkers have thus rightly pointed out
that the notion of consent (or the lack thereof) does not
fully express women's experiences with sexual violence,
and further, that it might turn out to be an obstacle
to developing a more adequate model of sexual harm.
Drawing from these feminist critiques, I want to suggest that these problems stem from a notion of consent

18 Angela Davis, "The Color of Violence Against Women," Keynote Address at the *Color of Violence* Conference in Santa Cruz, published
in *Colorlines*, 3:3 (Fall 2000), online: http://www.hartford-hwp.
com/archives/45a/582.html [consulted on the 01/02/20]; Patricia
Hill Collins, *Black Sexual Politics: African Americans, Gender, and
the New Racism* (New York: Routledge, 2005).
19 INCITE! Women of Color Against Violence, eds., *Color of Violence*
(Boston MA: South End Press, 2006).
20 Alcoff, *Rape and Resistance*, ch. 4.

that essentially envisions sex as a *juridical* relationship. Understanding intimate encounters essentially as juridical interactions fails to provide safety (and pleasure) for everyone involved and limits our imagination about how to properly address and overcome experiences with sexual violence. Let me explain this claim by investigating the most famous example of a juridical view of sexuality in the history of political theory, namely Immanuel Kant's theory of marriage.[21] By taking this extreme case as an example, I hope to carve out the problematic effects of juridicism operative in our routines of intimacy in a particularly illustrative way.

In the "Doctrine of Right" chapter of his *Metaphysics of Morals*, Kant famously defines sexual intercourse as a "natural commercium," for which it is necessary to enter into the contract of marriage. This is the case, because during sex, one person takes the "sexual faculties" of the other into their possession. Giving up my bodily integrity, however, is only legitimate if I gain something equal in exchange. In other words, according to the law of universal reason, I can only give you my penis, if you give me your vagina in return (it goes without saying that for Kant, only heterosexual sex is permissible). In Kant's own words:

> For the natural use that one sex makes of the other's sexual organs is enjoyment, for which one gives itself up to the other. In this act a human being makes himself into a thing, which conflicts with the Right of humanity in his own person. There is only one condition under which this is possible: that while one person is acquired by the other as if it were a thing, the one who is acquired acquires the other in turn; for in this way each reclaims itself and restores its personality. But acquiring a member of a human being is

---

21 For a balanced collection of feminist engagements with Kant, see Robin Schott, ed., *Feminist Interpretations of Kant* (University Park: Pennsylvania State University Press, 1997); for a discussion of Kant's individualism see especially Annette Baier's essay in this volume.

at the same time acquiring the whole person, since a person is an absolute unity. Hence it is not only admissible for the sexes to surrender to and accept each other for enjoyment under the condition of marriage, but it is possible for them to do so only under this condition. That this right against a person is also akin to a right to a thing rests on the fact that if one of the partners in a marriage has left or given itself into someone else's possession, the other partner is justified, always and without question, in bringing its partner back under its control, just as it is justified in retrieving a thing.[22]

Although it is easy to dismiss Kant's argument right away—generations of philosophers have had their fun with it[23]—it is illuminative for our context in a number of ways. First of all, it is striking how much the idea of the contract is bound up with coercion. This is true both for the moment of contracting as well as for the outcome of the contract. For the moment of contracting because, unlike the contract to buy a new car, the contract to marry my lover is not a result of my free will; while I always have the option *not* to buy the car, I am not free not to marry, since, for Kant, this would put the natural end of procreation and thus the reproduction of the species at risk. Unlike the political theories of Hobbes and Locke, Kant's contractualism is not voluntaristic; the contract is not the result of will but of reason, i.e.

---

22 Immanuel Kant, *The Metaphysics of Morals*, trans. Mary J. Gregor (Cambridge: Cambridge University Press, 1991), pp. 96–97, §25.

23 For instance, Hegel succinctly called Kant's theory of marriage "disgraceful," G.W.F. Hegel, *Philosophy of Right*, trans. H.B. Nisbet (Cambridge: Cambridge University Press, 1991), p. 105, §75; and Bertolt Brecht spells out the consequences of Kant's theory for the delinquent party (more seriously than he might have thought): "To contemplate that contract more scrupulously. / If he doesn't give / it care, I fear very much / That the sheriff will have to appear." Bertolt Brecht, "On Kant's Definition of Marriage," trans. Scott Horton, online: https://harpers.org/blog/2009/05/brecht-on-kants-definition-of-marriage/ [consulted on the 01/02/20].

insight into necessity.[24] It is important to note that what is classified as "reason" here effectively limits rather than expands individual choices. For the outcome of the contract because, for Kant, this necessary, non-arbitrary agreement creates an actual obligation. According to a fundamental principle of Roman law, *pacta sunt servanda* (contracts must be kept). Once I have entered the contract, I am therefore legally required to fulfil my corresponding duties, in this case, conjugal cohabitation. As with every other contract, if one business partner is delinquent, the other has the right to enforce his claim. While Kant's argument is based on the principle from civil law *volenti non fit iniuria*—s/he who agrees cannot be wronged—"agreement" merely indicates the acceptance of a pre-established law of reason (which, unlike an actual contract, can never be changed by the parties involved). In Kant, consent thus serves precisely not as a category that secures free affirmation of an action; on the contrary, it operates as a legitimization of de facto coercion.

Second of all, treating sexual organs and, in the last instance, entire persons as "things" immediately seems odd, especially for a thinker who puts so much emphasis on human dignity and autonomy. This reified concept of the human body stems from Kant's project of applying the principles of private law to all forms of human interaction. As a result of this ultra-juridical concept of normativity, the body can only appear as *property* of persons. "Legitimately" "using" one's own or another's body becomes then a question of just property relations. Consequently, understanding sex as "commercium," a community of trade relationships, requires a double separation: a separation of the body from the mind and a separation of the sexual property owners from each other. The mind-body dualism introduces an instrumen-

---

24 Daniel Loick, *A Critique of Sovereignty*, trans. Amanda DeMarco (London and New York: Rowman and Littlefield, 2018), pp. 69–71.

tal relationship to the body: I have the same relationship to my body parts (and, when married, to the body parts of my spouse) as I have to other things in my possession; I can freely dispose of them and use or abuse them as I deem fit. The separation of the property owners from each other fabricates a highly individualistic orientation of action on the part of the sexual partners. Since sex is the result of a private contract, both parties will pursue their own goals in a solipsistic manner and develop a predominantly strategic relation to their own and the other's sexual resources. They recognize each other not in a comprehensive sense, as bodily and affectively bound human beings, but merely as property owners.

In her seminal work *The Sexual Contract*, Carole Pateman has pointed out that despite its formally reciprocal language, Kant's marriage contract is not based on egalitarian premises. For Kant, all women lack civil independence and the self-mastery necessary to participate in civic life. This incapability, however, miraculously does not impair the legal validity of the contracts they have agreed to. Just as we already noted with regard to the impossibility of rejecting the marriage contract, once again Kant uses the binding function of contractual relationships without basing them on any sort of voluntary affirmation. Women, for Kant, are thus persons and non-persons at the same time. Men, on the other hand, are endowed with civic independence and autonomy and are thus in charge of representing the unity of the family. While the woman is bound by the contract but can never invoke it, the man always has the possibility to bring his straying woman back into his possession, just as, to quote this remarkable formulation again, "it is justified in retrieving a thing." The sexual contract, although equal in the abstract, is unequal in the concrete. As a result, it is not a mutual agreement but the confirmation of the "the masculine sex right,"[25] in other

---

25 Pateman, *The Sexual Contract*, p. 168.

words, it is an instrument to secure the man's access to the woman's body.

Radicalizing Pateman's account, Nancy Hirschmann has shown that the sexism inherent in contractualism is not contingent, but structural.[26] This means that it is not enough to simply include women in the framework of liberal political theory, for example by overcoming formal exclusions, but that it is necessary to find a completely different political vocabulary. Consent theory, Hirschmann argues, fundamentally privileges men because of its inherent individualism. The notion that obligation results from consent presupposes independent, interest-oriented and self-sufficient subjects who can deliberately dispose of their bodies and freely choose if and how to act. Drawing on the psychological and psychoanalytical work of object relations theorists like Nancy Chodorow and moral development theorists like Carol Gilligan, Hirschmann demonstrates that such a notion of human subjectivity excludes women not only on a political, but already on an epistemological level.[27] In societies in which raising children (as well as care for the sick and elderly) are tasks almost exclusively assigned to women, women's norms and values significantly differ from the ones presupposed in consent theory. One of the reasons for this is that women in their everyday life frequently have the experience of binding obligations even though they never intentionally agreed to them: childrearing and care work, for example, require attention towards another person in need, even though this requirement is not the result of "consent."[28] Such everyday life experiences then form and inform moral and ethical orientations and viewpoints. Citing the findings of moral psychological

---

26 Nancy J. Hirschmann, *Rethinking Obligation: A Feminist Method for Political Theory* (Ithaca NY: Cornell University Press, 1992), p. 12.
27 Ibid., ch. 3.
28 Eva Kittay, *Love's Labor: Essays on Women, Equality and Dependency* (New York: Routledge, 1992), p. 201.

research, Hirschmann points out the differential structure of hegemonic normativity: rather than individualism, women seek to build connections; rather than independence, women seek to maintain relationships; rather than control and mastery over one's domain, women seek to nurture the conditions for human flourishing and healing. Hirschmann herself notices a certain danger of an essentialist romanticizing of women's moral orientations in these claims. But even under an anti-essentialist proviso, she insists, in patriarchal societies, normative attitudes and habitual dispositions are highly gendered, making it unjust to presuppose specifically male experiences as universal conditions for political legitimacy. Rather than on consent, Hirschman suggests, a more comprehensive understanding of practical obligations can be based on notions such as communication, trust, and participation, thus taking women's everyday experiences into account.[29]

While for Pateman and Hirschmann it is the social inequality of men and women and the resultant gendered division of everyday experiences that renders liberal concepts counterproductive to advancing the project of feminist emancipation, Linda Martín Alcoff, in her recent book *Rape and Resistance* (2018), identifies the specificity of the normative structure of sexual interactions to explain the inadequacy of juridical models. Contractualist categories, Alcoff argues, are "phenomenologically unsuited to the domain of sexuality": "Relations involving familial bonds, or any bonds of affect and friendship, are not usefully illuminated by the concept of a contract, given that contracts assume relations that are freely chosen and entirely volitional. Familial relations are not generally volitional, nor is the energy expended on children generally given with an expectation of fair compensation, but simply in the joy of the act itself, or out of a sense of duty." This phenomenological

---

29 Hirschmann, *Rethinking Obligation*, pp. 249–285.

description of the nature of intimate relationships has implications for the issue of consent. For Alcoff, the very notion of consent always draws from the contractualist imaginary. "The act of choice," she says, "implied in legal concepts of consent, implies a decision made prior to an act in which I contract with the other in order to make use of my body and his (or hers) in certain ways. But the nature of human sexuality belies this description."[30]

Following the line of theoretical positions from Pateman via Hirschmann to Alcoff, it becomes clearer and clearer that the problem with the sexism inherent in contractualist categories is not the result of the fact that they remain inauthentic or illusionary. The solution, therefore, cannot simply lie in creating conditions in which "authentic" or "actual" consent would be possible. If, as these feminists have argued, the concept of consent originates from a completely wrong normative register, inapplicable to the domain of intimate relationships, then an entirely different vocabulary is needed in order to describe (and overcome) the harms and violations done in this domain. Before I offer some suggestions for this vocabulary, I discuss some aspects of how consent is not only a wrong theoretical category, but also a problematic legal and cultural practice.

Creating the liberal legal subject

Criticizing Kant and other modern contractualist thinkers might seem both outdated and like attacking a straw man. What does all this have to do with the notion of consent in the Aziz Ansari case or, more broadly, as it is being used by the #MeToo movement? After having engaged with liberal political theory as an *ideology* of consent, I will now explore how this ideology operates

30 Alcoff, *Rape and Resistance*, p. 159.

within actual legal, social, political and sexual practice. The juridicism apparent in Kant's theory of marriage, I suggest, is not only an ideological perspective *about* sexual and intimate relationships, it also is a harmful and oppressive *practice of* intimacy.

In Kant, we have observed that the notion of consent is deeply amalgamated with coercion, both in the moment of contracting as well as in its outcome: women give their consent under highly unequal and unfree conditions, and this is then used to justify actions that enforce the man's access to their body. Legal theorist Nicola Lacey has diagnosed a very similar logic within contemporary criminal law regarding rape. In a patriarchal society, in which men have significantly more material and symbolic power than women, consenting to sex is similar to accepting the "terms and conditions"—it's a yes-or-no decision about a setting that is completely defined by somebody else. Under these circumstances, the very notion of consent reinforces the dichotomy between the active man and the passive woman: "men have sex: women permit men to have sex with them."[31] As Wendy Brown reminds us, the idea of consent marks the "presence of a power (...) that one does not oneself create but to which one submits."[32] In criminal law, focus on the question of consent not only completely concentrates attention on the survivor's behavior (and often her previous history) rather than the perpetrator's;[33] it also works as a justification of the pre-established unequal power relationships. "The victim's consent," Lacey explains, "responds to power by conferring legitimacy, rather than shaping power in its own terms: consent is currently understood not in terms

---

31 Nicola Lacey, "Unspeakable Subjects, Impossible Rights: Sexuality, Integrity, and Criminal Law," in Nicola Lacey, *Unspeakable Subjects: Feminist Essays in Social and Legal Theory* (Oxford: Hart, 1998), p. 103.

32 Brown, *States of Injury*, pp. 162–163.

33 Already discussed in MacKinnon, "Rape."

of mutuality but rather in relation to a set of arrangements initiated, by implication, by the defendant, in an asymmetric structure which reflects the stereotypes of active masculinity and passive femininity."[34] Taken to its logical conclusion, the legitimacy thus conferred on unequal power relations creates an actual obligation on the part of the consenting party. The most extreme consequence of this contractualist understanding is represented in North Carolina's currently still applicable sexual assault laws. According to a North Carolina Supreme Court ruling of 1979, it is impossible to revoke consent during a sexual act: if a woman has initially agreed to sex, the man is legally allowed to finish, even if the woman changes her mind.[35] Echoing Kant's doctrine of a husband's right to bring a runaway wife back into his possession ("just as it is justified in retrieving a thing"), North Carolina holds that one party's consent constitutes a legally enforceable right for the opposing party, which in this case amounts to a man's *right to cum*.

The reification of the body, as it results from a contractual notion of the self and of social relations, is also very much operative in our legal and cultural practices. Lacey traces the criminalization of rape back to a propertization of the female body.[36] Women were originally regarded as the property of men. Rape, accordingly, was considered not to be a violation of the woman's autonomy, but as a trespassing on another man's property

34 Lacey, "Unspeakable Subjects," p. 114.
35 Michelle Redden, "No doesn't really mean no: North Carolina law means women can't revoke consent for sex." *The Guardian,* June 24, 2017, online: https://www.theguardian.com/us-news/2017/jun/24/north-carolina-rape-legal-loophole-consent-state-v-way [consulted on the 01/02/20]. The state of California (along with countries like Sweden) is on the other end of the consent spectrum. A law passed in 2014 requires "affirmative consent," meaning a knowing and voluntary decision to engage in sexual activities ("yes means yes" model). While affirmative consent rules might actually help in educating men and women to mutually and actively agree on their shared activities, they are still part of the contractualist framework and thus might have the opposite effects.
36 Lacey, "Unspeakable Subjects," p. 112.

rights. Even after women formally gained political and legal rights equal to those of men, the mind-body dualism inherent in this proprietary understanding of sexual faculties remains intact. The concept of consent treats the body like a thing: a body part that can legitimately be used if the owner grants access to it. Rape, accordingly, is understood as an unauthorized appropriation of another person's sexual properties. (Bodily integrity is therefore understood in a territorial sense: "You crossed a line" means you crossed the fence of somebody's property.) This definition presupposes a disembodied subjectivity, in which the mind is separated from the body and has a merely instrumental relationship to it. Such a mentalist definition, Lacey points out, fails to acknowledge the affective and corporeal aspects of sexual harms: "violation of trust, infliction of shame and humiliation, objectification and exploitation find no expression in the legal framework."[37]

The impact of the contractualist concept of consent is neither merely ideological, nor limited to the sphere of law. Even beyond the law, consent is a crucial normative operator within contemporary sexual encounters (at least in Western liberal societies).[38] To be sure, the current legal situation is undoubtedly significantly advanced over Kant's conception of marriage, since under today's rule of law, women's consent is actually necessary for legitimate sexual or marital relationships, presupposing at least formally a reciprocal and symmetrical relationship and thus addressing women as equal

[37] Ibid., p. 105.
[38] A cultural symptom of the role consent plays in sexual encounters in Western liberal societies are consent apps like *Legalfling*, *WeConsent* or the now defunct *Good2Go*, all of which can serve as communication tools but also create actually legally binding contracts. It is to be assumed that such apps are mostly used by men who want to safeguard sexual actions from possible legal ramifications. See https://legalfling. io/, https://we-consent.org/. For the older Good2Go, see https://slate. com/human-interest/2014/09/good2go-a-new-app-for-consenting-to-sex.html [all online sources consulted on the 01/02/20].

and autonomous participants.[39] However, the structural features of a contractualist understanding of the body are still at work. In simulating free-floating and independent agents, a contractualist notion of consent as a cultural norm creates individualized realms of actions which are mutually repellent. It requires people engaging in sexual activities to abstract from their concrete, often contradictory or ambivalent emotions and affects and to reinterpret them in light of a disembodied proto-juridical normative framework. It thereby fosters a solipsistic pursuit of one's own sexual interests and thus a merely strategic relationship towards the other, rather than a dynamic communication about desires, needs, and fears. This individualization not only undermines the communicative substance of intimate relationships, it also tends to depoliticize sexuality by treating it as the result of private individuals voluntarily exchanging goods.

As feminist critics have shown, this general dynamic has highly gender-specific effects: It requires women to abandon the habitual dispositions formed through their everyday life experiences and to inhabit the domain of contractual reason,[40] while it contributes to the creation of a sense of entitlement in men, encouraging them to reject all forms of responsibilities towards others they have not voluntarily agreed to, thus denying any form of pre-established dependency and interconnectedness.[41] This gender difference also reinforces the dichot-

---

39 Acknowledging this difference is also important in order to understand the specificity of harm that lies in overriding a weaker partner's "no." See West, "Sex, Law, and Consent."
40 Brown, *States of Injury*, p. 184.
41 The most extreme and violent expression of this male culture of entitlement is the movement of "involuntary celibates," or incels. Incels have committed two mass shootings in North America in 2018, the shooting by Nikolas Cruz in Parkland, Florida in February, which killed seventeen people; and the shooting by Alek Minassian in Toronto in April, which killed ten people. Incels believe they have a right to sex, which—as this paper argues—stems from a contractual understanding of sexual encounters, denying the ontological fact that most of our ethical obligations as human beings are involuntary.

omy of the active man and the passive woman: men "get" consent, women "give (or withhold)" consent. In summary: Understanding sexual harm predominantly in terms of a lack of consent has denied women the possibility to meaningfully shape *the conditions* of sex—it has kept them from sexual power.[42]

Fuck like a feminist.
On the politics of forms of life

In this paper, I have shown how a widespread juridicism in Western societies undermines the possibility of sexuality between free and equal participants. The category of consent, as it stems from a contractual normative register, has not only *ideologically* obfuscated the specificity of the harm done in sexualized violence, it has also *practically* contributed to creating a culture that promotes a reified and asymmetrical notion of sexuality. I have argued that rather than reproducing the problematic effects of juridicism, feminist theory and activism should move beyond the consent model in order to find a more adequate and more comprehensive understanding of sexual harm / sexual flourishing. In conclusion, I should at least briefly address the question of alternatives. If not the category of consent, what other point of reference can ensure the free affirmation of sexual activities by all parties involved?

---

42 In this paper, I have not dealt with the role and significance of the concept of the contract in BDSM relationships and sexual encounters. Without going into too much detail, it can be said that the use of the contract in the BDSM scene often serves a parodic function; it *stages* rather than reproduces the contractual model operative in most heterosexist "vanilla" sexual encounters. On the specific non-heteronormative notion of consent in BDSM, see Jordana Greenblatt, "'Cruelty Is Uncivilized.' Consent, BDSM, and Legal Regulation of the Civil(ized) Subject," in Nikita Dhawan et al., eds., *Negotiating Normativity* (Basel: Springer, 2016), pp. 175–188; for an empirical study see Robin Bauer, *Queer BDSM Intimacies: Critical Consent and Pushing Boundaries* (London: Palgrave Macmillan, 2014).

In the history of philosophy, the most pointed critique of juridicism was penned by Hegel. For Hegel, conceiving of sex as a contract misses precisely what the physical communion is about, namely an inner, emotional bond. In sex, individuals follow their desire to form a non-violent unity with the other, thus expressing their primordial mutual interconnectedness. As such, marriage can become the manifestation of a deeper and constitutive sociality that Hegel calls ethical life. While Hegel can hardly be called a feminist, since he uncritically accepts the forms of patriarchal domination that continue to mark current forms of sociality, a feminist critique of consent can take up Hegel's insight that the creation of successful ethical relationships takes place not in the sphere of the law, but in the realm of the concrete social fabric of a society. Therefore, the transformation of the culture of toxic masculinity has itself to be not contractual, but cultural—it has to be situated in the respective social spheres and take their specific normative structure into account. This is exactly what Linda Alcoff's phenomenological approach accomplishes, by defining good sex not simply as consensual sex but as an "interactive, intersubjective engagement, in which each partner stays attuned to the emotional states and experiences of the other(s)."[43] Obviously, such an experience will also involve situations of asking for and expressing either affirmation or rejection of certain activities ("Is x okay?", "Do you want to do y?"), but unlike the proto-juridical consent model, it emphasizes communication, attention and reflexivity about the structures of power and domination surrounding the concrete sexual interaction.

In the January 17, 2018 episode of her show *Full Frontal*, fellow comedian Samantha Bee offered her perspective on the Aziz Ansari incident. In particular, Bee criticizes the notion that the incident wasn't "serious

43 Alcoff, *Rape and Resistance*, p. 129.

enough" to speak out about; it is precisely because it's ordinary (and thus an example of experiences many women have on an everyday basis) that Ansari should be held accountable for his actions. Bee especially takes issue with the fact that Ansari had in the past cast himself as a feminist ally, dealing with feminist topics both in his standup act as well as in his TV show. Even if what he did is not legally actionable, Ansari should be held accountable according to his own political standards: "If you say you're a feminist," Bee insists, "then fuck like a feminist."[44]

With this advice, Samantha Bee points at an alternative to a juridical understanding of consent. Her reference to feminism situates sexual encounters within a broader social framework and above all makes clear that sex has to be treated neither as a personal, nor as a legal, but first of all as a *political* question. To have sex in a feminist way, however, is not political in the conventional, state-centered way, but invokes a specific form of politics that can be called a *politics of forms of life.*[45] A politics of forms of life is located on the terrain of the life world itself and seeks to transform the conditions of personal relationships without detour through the state. Feminist movements have long championed this form of politics, be it through organizing anti-authoritarian child care, setting up rape crisis centers and women's shelters, reorganizing reproductive work, boycotting the proliferation of pornographic images or questioning hegemonic notions of beauty and sexuality. In this context, a feminist politics of forms of life might include

---

44 Caroline Framke, "Samantha Bee on sexual coercion, period," January 18, 2018, online: https://www.vox.com/culture/2018/1/18/16905372/samantha-bee-aziz-ansari-me-too [consulted on the 01/02/20].

45 Daniel Loick, "Juridification and politics: From the dilemma of juridification to the paradoxes of rights," *Philosophy & Social Criticism* 40:8 (2014): pp. 757–778; Daniel Loick, "On the Politics of Forms of Life," in Amy Allen and Eduardo Mendieta, eds., *From Alienation to Forms of Life: The Critical Theory of Rahel Jaeggi* (University Park: Pennsylvania State University Press, 2018).

a whole range of strategies, from methods of community accountability and transformative justice in cases of rape and sexual assault to trying to change attitudes, attentions, and behaviors on a more everyday level, for example by diminishing harmful male expectations and toxic masculinity. This approach situates sexual activities within a history of power, domination and abuse and aims at promoting a reflexivity regarding this history and cultivating a corresponding sexual ethics.

Besides the strategic advantages of a politics of forms of life—overcoming social domination directly on the terrain of the intimate rather than ratifying the state's power to (re-) program social life—such an account is sensitive to the specific normative structure of the respective social sphere, pointed out by Hegel and Alcoff. If the category of consent simply misses *what sex is about* (since it is not a contract but an intersubjective engagement under conditions of differential vulnerability), then an emancipatory politics cannot simply encourage more consent, but must focus on promoting and enabling circumstances under which the sphere-specific expectations and needs of women can be met. More than a legal question, this seems to be a question of changing cultural norms, images, and patterns of behavior in order to create conditions under which an increased intersubjective attention and attunement can evolve.

Instead of relying on a contractual model of affirmation, feminist theorists have therefore proposed to work towards a social and communicative model of individual autonomy.[46] Such a relational notion of autonomy implies a more sophisticated idea of the sexual experience and the wrongs that might come with it, and provides for a broader perspective on possible social action.

---

46 Catriona Mackenzie and Natalie Stoljar, eds., *Relational Autonomy: Feminist Perspectives on Autonomy, Agency, and the Social Self* (Oxford: Oxford University Press, 2000).

Rather than understanding the sexual partners as atomized, self-sufficient and strategic owners of their sexual faculties, it sees them as vulnerable, corporeal and dependent beings. Rather than giving women a yes-or-no option within a predefined situation, it aims at empowering them in such a way that they can equally co-create the general conditions of sexual encounters. Rather than authorizing the masculinist rejection of non-voluntary obligations, it encourages men to take responsibility and develop habits of caution and care. Rather than reproducing the juridicism operative in our intimate routines, learning to fuck like feminists combines social criticism with an ethics of nonviolence.

Franziska Dübgen

Rethinking the Law

Taking Clues from Ubuntu Philosophy

Critical criminology and Marxist theory have criticized the penal state for reinforcing social hierarchies and using the state's monopoly of violence to protect the current distribution of wealth and property. More recently, black feminists, social workers, LGBT activists as well as activists fighting for the rights of asylum seekers have joined in this critique. Under the banner of *transformative justice*, they are demanding new forms of dealing with social deviance and are struggling against the incarceration of refugees, minorities, and poor people. Transformative justice, so far, is a vague umbrella term demanding fundamental change of the legal and social system. Some activists argue for a stronger social state while others oppose the state as such. Some activists and scholars prefer community-driven solutions whereas others highlight the power differentials and possible violence within communities. There is hardly no academic literature clarifying this term. The scope of this essay is to explore how a transcultural comparative approach could contribute to defining a strategy of how to conceptually understand the term transformative justice and how to put it into practice.

1.
Transformative Justice and its Roots
in Restorative Justice

The debate about transformative justice mainly started in activist contexts in the Anglo-Saxon world, particularly the USA and Canada, from the 1990s onwards. Theoretically, it might be situated as both a critique and reform of restorative approaches to justice. Restorative justice has been advanced as an alternative to punishment-based retributive justice. Rather than adhering to a higher-order institution, it focuses on the relationship between victims and perpetrators. It understands crime not as a violation of a legal norm, but as a conflict between two or more parties.[1] Rather than demanding punishment by the state, restorative justice centers around healing through communication between all the parties involved, asking forgiveness and/or providing restitution for the experienced loss or harm. Mechanisms of restorative justice, such as group conferencing or reintegrative shaming, aim at strengthening empathy between the social members of a community and providing social control from below. In contradistinction to retributive justice, restorative justice is a vertical conception without a higher-order institution, such as the legal state, intervening in local conflicts. Hence, restorative approaches come to decisions *with* and not *over* the involved parties.

Ruth Morris, a Canadian sociologist, was one of the first scholars to prominently coin the term transformative justice. Belonging to the Quaker movement of prison abolitionists, she published in 2000 a monograph entitled *Stories of Transformative Justice*, wherein she demands a shift in the criminal justice system. Mor-

---

1 Gerry Johnstone, *Restorative Justice: Ideas, Values, Debates* (Abingdon and New York: Routledge, 2011).

ris pledges to move from restorative to transformative approaches:

> "So, many people today advocate moving from retributive to *restorative* justice. Restorative justice includes victims, and focuses on those healing questions. But even restorative justice does not go far enough. It still accepts the idea that one event now defines all that matters of right and wrong – it leaves out the past, and the social causes of all events. It's like one of those science fiction stories where time stops, and the whole world focuses on this one moment, without a past or future."[2]

She maintains that only if we understand the structural causes of why people commit certain acts, defined as *crime*, can we holistically start dealing with them. Restorative justice focuses on conflicts on an inter-subjective level. It does not, however take into account the overall power structures that produce identity positions in the first place, and that are oftentimes rooted in a history of domination of certain groups over others. In addition, Morris argues that both retributive and restorative justice neglect the distributive aspect of social inequality and economic exploitation that matters when talking about social violence and crime. Finally, the term *restorative* implies that the remedial process aims to return to a prior status quo which, however, oftentimes was not just in the first place: "Do we want to restore offenders to the marginalized, enraged, disempowered condition most were in just before the offence?"[3] Rather, transformative justice shall look to the future and transform the injustices of the presence.

---

2 Ruth Morris, *Stories of Transformative Justice* (Toronto: Canadian Scholars' Press, 2000), p. 4.
3 Ibid., p. 19.

1.1.
Transformative Justice as a Contested Strategy

There are different general ways of how to *transform* the justice system at hand. All of them are in need of specification. Generally, we can opt for institutional responses by seeking to intensify democracy on different levels, either on state or community level. Civil rights activist Angela Davis argues that thinking about the abolition of prisons needs to start by focusing on the social ills that set people on the track to crime. Therefore, we first need to find solutions for access to housing, the labor market, health insurance, and education for all citizens.[4] I call this strand of transformative justice the *structural-democratic* version that demands strong social institutions to battle the root causes of social conflict.[5]

Activists fighting sexual abuse and domestic violence in the USA have equally demanded "transformative justice". However, they challenge the monopoly of the state in dealing with social violence and criticize the repressive function of state institutions when intervening in local contexts. For example, if the penal state incarcerates a battering husband in order to punish his violent behavior towards his wife, this also means in practice that a potential breadwinner is taken from the family and that children grow up without their father. It might be better if the family members are not separated and the community works with both husband and wife to stop the entrenched violence. Another practical example entails that the victim of violence is an undocumented worker and that involving state institutions might cause the deportation of this person. Hence, for some very vulnerable social groups, involving the penal state might

4   Angela Y. Davis, *Abolition Democracy: Beyond Empire, Prisons, and Torture* (New York and London: Seven Stories, 2005).
5   Franziska Dübgen, "Rechtsbruch und Strafe. Gerechtigkeitstheoretische Erwägungen," *Ethik und Gesellschaft* 2 (2018): pp.1–21, p.14 http://www.ethik-und-gesellschaft.de/ojs/index.php/eug/article/view/2-2018-art-4/580 [consulted on the 14/06/20].

not be an option since it causes a series of other related problems whose negative aspects prevail.[6] Transformative justice therefore needs to look at a variety of patterns of domination: "A transformative practice challenges not only the state's monopoly on responses to crime, but also challenges racial and gender subordinating institutions, beliefs, and practices."[7] As a consequence, it needs not only to change the way we deal with social deviance, but also to tackle the structural racism and sexism inherent in many state institutions. A transformative approach should address the "complicated realities of individual incidents" and look at the specific "conditions impacting each individual."[8] This strategy hence entails opting for community-driven solutions to conflicts and norm transgressions. This version of transformative justice appropriates methods of restorative justice for the sake of "transforming" social power relations. In analytic contradistinction to the former structural-democratic approach, I have called this approach *anti-statist*.[9] Whereas the structural-democratic approach is rooted in socialism, the anti-statist approach might be associated with an anarchist critique of the legal state.

Both approaches link the criminal justice system to other spheres of justice, such as distributive, racial, or gender (in)justice and demand a fundamental rethinking of legal punishment. However, taking other spheres of justice into account contradicts some presuppositions entailed in Western legal philosophy: Liberal philosophy,

---

6 Margaret E. Martin, "From Criminal Justice to Transformative Justice: The Challenges of Social Control for Battered Women," *Contemporary Justice Review* 2 (1999): pp. 415–536; generationFIVE, *Ending Child Sexual Abuse: A Transformative Justice Handbook*, 2017, http://www.generationfive.org/wp-content/uploads/2017/06/Transformative-Justice-Handbook.pdf [consulted on the 22/05/20].

7 Donna Coker, "Transformative Justice: Anti-Subordination Processes in Cases of Domestic Violence," in Heather Strang and John Braithwaite, eds., *Restorative Justice and Family Violence* (Cambridge: Cambridge University Press, 2002), pp. 128–152.

8 generationFIVE, *Ending Child Sexual Abuse*, p. 28.

9 Dübgen, "Rechtsbruch und Strafe," p. 15.

which prevails in the twentieth and 21st century, presupposes everyone as *equal*. It construes the legal subject as an autonomous person whose deeds need to be considered as free acts that she consciously opts for. Punishment is based on this idea of a free will that is the condition for criminal responsibility. This disembedded vision of the liberal self abstracts from the complex power relations that shape a subject's identity in the first place. To transform the penal law, we might hence start by rethinking legal subjectivity. The postcolonial discourse on Ubuntu, rooted in sub-Saharan African culture, suggests an ontological vision of the subject as intrinsically interrelated with other subjects. In addition, it suggests an alternative way of dealing with crime. I therefore propose looking transculturally at Ubuntu for clues for how to rethink the present Western penal system.

2.
Ubuntu Philosophy from Sub-Saharan Africa

Ubuntu is a normative ideal rooted in many sub-Saharan African societies. The term, which is a postcolonial construction based on different linguistic sources, is generally translated with *humaneness*.[10] South African intellectuals

10 Ubuntu takes its legitimizing force from its rootedness in African (oral) culture, transmitted from generation to generation. Some authors also link Ubuntu ontology with the metaphysical realm: Ubuntu philosophy, according to this interpretation, takes its legitimation from the ancestors, the "living-dead" who serve as legislators and judges whenever the cosmic equilibrium has been disturbed. See Mogobe B. Ramose, *African Philosophy through Ubuntu* (Harare: Mond Books Publishers, 2005), p. 88. These metaphysical underpinnings make it difficult to provide a transcultural interpretation of Ubuntu, since to anyone who does not share the spiritual dimension, Ubuntu remains unintelligible. Oftentimes, Ubuntu is simply justified as distinct African *way of life*, ingrained in many local traditions, rituals, and proverbs, regulating communal life. For the scope of this essay, I assume, that we can discuss Ubuntu as an ethical ideal based on social praxis without necessarily subscribing to its metaphysical content.

revived Ubuntu as an African concept in the mid-1990s, in the process of rethinking law and politics in the post-apartheid era. The interim constitution of South Africa from 1993 made explicit reference to Ubuntu: "[...] there is a need for understanding, but not for vengeance, a need for reparation but not for retaliation, a need for Ubuntu but not for victimization."[11] This passage became part of the justificatory foundations for the Truth and Reconciliation Commission in South Africa. Ubuntu, however, was not included in the final draft of the constitution and is now a contested constitutional value, influencing a variety of legal case decisions.[12]

Ubuntu has been a source of reshaping African jurisprudence[13], debated as a new principle informing policy-making[14] and as a new ethical humanism informing law and social policy.[15] Judges made reference in their decisions to Ubuntu as demanding social peace and the well-being of all citizens in the new South Africa. These legal cases included matters of housing, basic socio-economic rights and the labor law.[16] In addition, constitutional lawyers argued for the abolition of the death penalty based on the values associated with Ubuntu.

According to the relational ontology of Ubuntu, it does not make sense to discuss penal law without looking at the social sphere. Therefore, this essay will sketch

11 Interim Constitution 1993, Section "National Unity and Reconciliation," www.gov.za/documents/constitution/constitution-republic-south-africa-act-200–1993 [consulted on the 27/06/20].
12 See Drucilla Cornell and Nyoko Muvangua, *Ubuntu and the Law* (New York: Fordham University Press, 2012), part I.
13 Yvonne Mokgoro, "Ubuntu and the Law in South Africa," 1998, http://www.puk.ac.za/opencms/export/PUK/html/fakulteite/regte/per/issues/98v1mokg.pdf [consulted on the 27/06/20].
14 Muxe Nkondo, "Ubuntu as Public Policy: Challenges and Opportunities," *UJCI Africa-China Occasional Paper* 2 (2017), http://confucius-institute.joburg/wp-content/uploads/2017/08/UJCI-africa-china-occ-paper-no-2-desktop.pdf [consulted on the 22/05/20].
15 Drucilla Cornell, *Law and Revolution in South Africa: Ubuntu, Dignity, and the Struggle for Constitutional Transformation* (New York: Fordham University Press, 2014).
16 Cornell and Muvangua, *Ubuntu and the Law*, part 1.

the most distinct characteristics of Ubuntu as both a juridical and social principle. It suggests that a critical engagement with Ubuntu as a principle from the global South can inspire legal philosophers in the global North to radically rethink penal justice in more holistic and contextualized terms, responding to some of the key demands of the transformative justice movement.

2.1.
Ubuntu Ontology: Being as Caring

According to the relational ontology of Ubuntu philosophy, human beings are intrinsically linked to one another. A proverb of the Nguni, oftentimes referred to when explaining what Ubuntu means, states: "A person is only a person through other persons" (*umuntu gnumuntu ngabantu*).[17] This implies that human beings are always socially constituted persons who cannot be considered apart from their embeddedness in society. This relational ontology is premised on a distinct anthropological vision: Persons, in their quality as *human* beings, need to care for each other. Accordingly, somebody's *humanness* depends on his or her capacity to care, to engage, and to give to others within one's community.[18]

Freedom, viewed from this angle, is always acting with others, not against them, because individual freedom is interdependent with the freedom of all other members of the community. On an ethical level, this implies that if a person is striving for a good life, she should do it in a way that will not make others suffer, since her own well-being is bound up with that of others. Its ontological perspective sets Ubuntu apart from assumptions prevailing in liberalism. The latter, based on Hobbesian con-

---

17 Christian Gade, "What is *Ubuntu*? Different Interpretations among South Africans of African Descent," *South African Journal of Philosophy* 31:2 (2012): pp. 484–503, p. 487.

18 Note that in most African theories of personhood, the status of a human person is a quality that is not given, but needs to be acquired. John S. Mbiti: *African Religions and Philosophies* (New York: Heinemann, 1970).

tract theory, presuppose that human beings are inherently self-interested and need to be tamed by a social contract in order to overcome the chaos and anarchy of the natural state.

2.2.
Ubuntu and Criminal Law: Overcoming Punishment

If we wish to consider Ubuntu as a legal principle ingrained in African law, we first need to distinguish between customary law, as it has been codified during the colonial era, and contemporary *living* African law, that is oral in nature and continually evolving.[19] Since the former customary law has been influenced and shaped by colonialism and might therefore be deemed "outdated and distorted,"[20] it seems more appropriate to focus on contemporary African living law. The latter, according to the Ubuntu expert Mogobe Ramose, is unformalized and dynamic.[21] As opposed to *Western* law, it has to be adapted according to the singularity of the particular case and social circumstances as well as changing norms and conventions. Ubuntu is hence always situated: "It is always a desideratum arising from concrete experience at a particular place and time."[22] It can therefore not be codified in a long-lasting manner, but is continually evolving.

In line with the ontology of interconnectedness, a crime is never a fault committed by a single individual. Rather, the whole community, family, or society carries co-responsibility for the wrong that occurred. Therefore, we must not consider the individual alone in a process of conflict resolution, but also her social circle that allowed

---

19 Ilze Keevy, "Ubuntu versus the Core Values of the South African Constitution," in Leonard Praeg and Siphokazi Magadla, eds., *Ubuntu: Curating the Archive* (Pietermaritzburg: KwaZulu-Natal Press, 2014), pp. 54–95, p. 61.
20 Mokgoro, "Ubuntu and the Law in South Africa," p. 8.
21 Ramose, *African Philosophy through Ubuntu*, pp. 79–80.
22 Ibid., p. 87.

her to become who she is and how she acts.[23] Criminal responsibility, from this angle, can never be thought of as purely individual. Since the "offender" is part of a social network, his or her actions must be considered in light of the social structures, milieu and norms that he or she inhabits. The overall aim of any criminal justice system according to Ubuntu is to restore a social equilibrium, which has been disturbed through a conflict between two or more parties.

Ubuntu averts punishment as the prime response to norm transgressions because punishment is destructive: It tends to recreate a circle of crime rather than providing solutions.[24] Imprisonment is therefore considered as senseless: If a person goes into jail, she might start a criminal career and her re-entry into mainstream community becomes more and more difficult.[25] Therefore, it is better to aim at reintegration of the offender in the community in the first place. African living law favors mechanisms other than punishment, such as asking for forgiveness, shaming, shunning, making someone pay reparations, or—in the worst case—excluding somebody from a community.[26] All these mechanisms are relational, in so far as they concern the relationship between the offender, the victim and their social networks. Like restorative approaches, Ubuntu conflict resolution mechanisms appeal to the moral conscience of a person and his or her status within a community.

The Kenyan philosopher Henry Odera Oruka stresses in line with this idea that a person can only be considered to act freely if she does not suffer from oppression: hunger, disease, social exclusion and the like. He names the conglomerate of factors leading to crime *criminal*

23 Ibid., p. 62.
24 Keevy, "Ubuntu versus the Core Values," p. 61.
25 Jacob Mugumbate and Andrew Nyanguru, "Exploring African Philosophy: The Value of Ubuntu in Social Work," *African Journal for Social Work* 3:1 (2013): pp. 82–100, p. 94.
26 Keevy, "Ubuntu versus the Core Values," p. 61.

forces, including the following: "[...] irresponsible parental care, belonging to a despised or poverty-stricken class, discrimination and suppression by the family or society, being a moral or social outcast, mental derangement, a bad education, etc."[27] According to him, not a decision taken based on free will, but the social structures—hence the *criminal forces*—make a person commit a crime. Through this lens, the individual criminal alone should not be held responsible for his or her deed; instead the criminal forces generated by the community call for correction. The primary addressee of corrective action is therefore the state or the society that does not deliver the services and the infrastructure to eliminate these primary causes. Rather than punishing the offender, a political context should aim at eradicating the social conditions that lead to crime.

Moreover, African law does not prohibit, but rather seeks to guide individual conduct.[28] Hence it operates through positive reinforcement rather than negative prevention. Instead of setting negative limits to individual freedoms, African law generally aims at setting up positive imperatives of how to act in light of the wellbeing of society.

To sum up, this essay suggests considering the following aspects as distinctive characteristics of a legal philosophy in line with Ubuntu:

• Legal norms need to evolve in the light of changing norms and legal decisions must be sensitive to the singularity of the case.

• There is no purely individual criminal responsibility; the social community bears co-responsibility for a crime.

---

27 Henry O. Oruka, *Punishment and Terrorism in Africa* (Kampala, Nairobi and Dar Es Salaam: East Africa Literature Bureau, 1976), p. 18.

28 Ramose, *African Philosophy through Ubuntu,* p. 85, cites Jack H. Driberg, "The African conception of law," *Journal of Comparative Legislation and International* Law XVI (1934): pp. 230–245, p. 231.

- Ubuntu justice prefers conflict resolution mechanisms other than punishment (such as reparation payments or discursive means to settle conflict).
- Law should be aimed at creating social peace.
- Legal decision-making should transform the social background conditions that frame individual behavior and preferences, where these have contributed to a crime.
- Legal justice as a regulative tool should operate through positive reinforcement rather than negative prevention.

Hence, according to Ubuntu discourse, we need to consider penal justice in co-relation to the general background conditions of a society. This article will therefore turn now to the field of social policy.

2.3.
Ubuntu as a Social Justice Philosophy: Solidarity and Sufficiency

The Ubuntu discourse can be said to articulate a communitarian social justice philosophy.[29] In line with its relational ontology, it strongly emphasizes solidarity amongst community members. A person is only free if the community is doing well and if her freedom does not result from diminishing somebody else's freedom.[30] Solidarity within a community relies on a sense of shared identity, since helping others is grounded in the insight that the others' identity is bound up with

---

29 Andreas Rauhut, "Expanding motivations for global justice: A dialogue between public Christian social ethics and Ubuntu ethics as Afro-communitarianism," *Journal of Global Ethics* 13:2 (2015): pp. 138–156. Thaddeus Metz, "An African Theory of Social Justice. Relationship as the Ground of Rights, Resources and Recognition," in Camilla Boisen and Matthew C. Murray, eds., *Distributive Justice Debates in Political and Social Thought: Perspectives on Finding a Fair Share* (New York and London: Routledge, 2017), pp. 171–190.
30 Drucilla Cornell and Karin van Marle, "Exploring uBuntu: Tentative Reflections," in Cornell and Muvangua, *Ubuntu and the Law*, pp. 344–366, p. 353.

the self.[31] However, this notion of solidarity can also be extended to foreigners, if they form part of a given society.[32] In a utopian vein, it could even include everybody who is *human*, considering mankind as brothers and sisters to whom solidarity is owed.

Poverty, according to Ubuntu, is not only a lack of money, but means the inability to participate in social life on an equal footing. The goal of social policy is to strengthen the relational capacities of its citizens to establish social ties, which constitute a prosperous society.[33] This includes allocating to citizens the time, self-esteem, and resources to engage with others.

The principle guiding social well-being in an economic sense is that of sufficiency. Economic policy in line with Ubuntu does not aim at constant growth and endless consumption.[34] Rather, it organizes the *oikos* in such a way that everybody has enough and can live well. The ideal polity exists in a state of social equity. In such a society, all citizens live under fairly equal material conditions. This prevents envy may between citizens, which is socially destructive. Conversely, material egalitarianism enhances feelings of interconnectedness and peace.

The question of who is the prime agent responsible for creating conditions of solidarity and sufficiency remains a contested issue in the debate about Ubuntu. Some theorists argue that social policy needs to come from below and find its prime expression in the family, social network and/or community. The immediate neighbor should provide care, if possible. Social policy, then, is not only a state's function, but also a common civil task.[35]

---

31 Metz, "African Theory of Social Justice," p. 177.
32 Cornell and van Merle, "Exploring uBuntu," pp. 360–361.
33 Thaddeus Metz, "An African Theory of Dignity and a Relational Conception of Poverty," in John W. De Gruchy, ed., *The Humanist Imperative in South Africa* (Stellenbosch: Sun Press, 2015), pp. 233–241, p. 236.
34 Murove, "Ubuntu," p. 40.
35 South African policy programs such as the *Masakhane Campaign* and the *Batho Pele* initiative speak to this idea: *Masakhane* means

Others demand a strong welfare state that organizes the economy, provides mechanisms of social redistribution and brings forward community-oriented political reforms to meet the basic needs of all citizens.[36] However, even if state-driven, social policy needs to be informed by the demands of the people, based on broad consultation and adapted to the changing needs of its subjects.

Hence, some of the most important aspects of the demands for social justice with reference to Ubuntu might be summarized as follows:

- Solidarity should be the guiding social norm of civic and state actions.
- The economy should be based on the principle of sufficiency.
- Redistribution mechanisms should aim at an egalitarian society.
- Social policy needs to rely on mechanisms of broad consultation.

3.
Tensions between Ubuntu and Contemporary Liberalism

So far, this essay has demonstrated that the ideas associated with Ubuntu demand connecting retributive justice to social justice based. This resonates with one of the

---

"mutual constructiveness" and was a campaign initiated to persuade people to pay their taxes in order to contribute to the socioeconomic transformation of the country. See Munyaradzi F. Murove, "Ubuntu," *Diogenes* 59:3–4 (2015): pp. 36–47, p. 43 and D. P. Ahluwalia and Paul Nursey-Bray, *The Post-Colonial Condition* (Commack NY: Nova Science Publishers, 1997), p. 151. *Batho Pele* can be translated as "People First." The South African government under President Mandela started this initiative in 1997 in order to counter distrust in public services—a remnant of the many years of apartheid. *Batho Pele* promoted better accountability and accessibility to state services for citizens, and demanded standards of courtesy, regular consultation, and transparency.

36 Nkondo, "Ubuntu as Public Policy."

key demands of the transformative justice movement. However, a transcultural translation of Ubuntu as a legal and social principle faces some fundamental challenges: There are strong differences between Ubuntu's philosophy based on a relational ontology and liberal philosophy centered on the autonomous subject. The following table will briefly point out some of the major differences in the fields of social ontology and morality, as introduced earlier:

Ubuntu Social Ontology, Morality, and Law	Liberal Social Ontology, Morality, and Law
Human beings are *caring*.	Human beings are *greedy* and guided by self-interest.
Human beings are *socialized* into morality.	Human beings affirm morality through *reason*.
Freedom is *action with others*.	Freedom is *rational autonomy*.
Civic *responsibility for the community* is foundational for the political.	Individual *rights against the state* is foundational for the political.
Law should be *situated* and flexible.	Law needs to be *rule-based*.
Corrective justice aims at creating a *social equilibrium* for everybody involved.	Retribution restores the *authority of the law* through punishment.

What implications do these differences entail when discussing penal law, and what are the contested issues at stake when *translating* key aspects of Ubuntu to a non-African context?

First, like Ubuntu, feminist care ethics[37] in the West has stressed the relational ontology of the subject: To think of individuals as fully independent and autonomous underestimates the ways in which a society relies on care and mutual support in order to function. The rational,

---

37 Carol Gilligan, *In a Different Voice: Psychological Theory and Women's Development* (Cambridge MA and London: Harvard University Press, 1993).

autonomous subject is a regulative idea that never exists in its pure form. To think of persons as interrelated is hence neither a purely African nor Western idea.[38]

What seems more problematic from a Western legal perspective is the demand for a flexible, situated law. This might negatively affect the impartiality and equal application of the law. Entrenched power structures threaten to distort the legal decision-making process. For example, a flexible justice system might disadvantage particular identities. According to Keevy, the conservatism of many African law systems has resulted in discrimination against social minorities: "Ubuntu jurisprudence ranks the status of homosexuals, lesbians and witches very low within its patriarchal hierarchy."[39] Such legal systems violate egalitarian norms, on which Ubuntu is said to rely. We might hence point out these self-contradictions and demand that the flexibility of the law must not violate moral egalitarianism, which means the equal worth of all human beings. The call for flexibility and singularity of the law might rather be understood as demanding the consideration of each case in its context, reflecting the specific circumstances of how it came about. This resonates with deconstructive approaches to the law that stress the incommensurable singularity of each event.[40]

Another issue that is likely to cause controversy is the communitarian orientation of Ubuntu philosophy, which seems difficult to fit into a nation-state or transnational, cosmopolitan context. The preference of one's own community might result in discrimination against outsiders. Ubuntu as a community-driven ethics might

38 Mechthild Nagel, "Ubuntu, Gender and Spirituality: Transformative Justice Considerations," *Kalagatos* 15:2 (2018): pp. 56–70.

39 Keevy, "Ubuntu versus the Core Values," p. 73.

40 Jacques Derrida, "Force of Law," trans. Mary Quaintance, in Drucilla Cornell, Michel Rosenfeld and David Gary Carlson, eds., *Deconstruction and the Possibility of Justice* (New York: Routledge, 1992), pp. 3–67; Christoph Menke, *Kritik der Rechte* (Berlin: Suhrkamp, 2015).

favor kinship over distant others. As a remedy, Justice Yvonne Mokgoro suggests that Ubuntuism might be used to create a new patriotism based on national unity and solidarity.[41] At least in theory, solidarity could be extended to a world community, regulated by a shared legal system.

Despite these great challenges, by way of conclusion, this essay will consider what clues we could take from Ubuntu philosophy to rethink the law in a transformative manner.

4.
Conclusion: Clues from Ubuntu Philosophy for Rethinking the Law

The transformative justice movement demands to rethink the legal system by minimizing the violence inherent in norm stabilization, protecting vulnerable groups, addressing the social structures that lead to violence and norm transgressions and finding new avenues of how to solve interpersonal conflict.

Ubuntu's relational ontology invites us to rethink the idea of a free autonomous that is fully responsible for his or her deeds. Most justifications of punishment are dependent on the idea of a free will that is foundational for criminal responsibility (at least in backward-looking, retributive accounts). However, socially constituted subjects are shaped by the social community they live in. Social circumstances inform decision-making processes and frame the range of available options that a person faces at a certain point in time. Therefore, legal decision-making should be knowledgeable about the social background of a legal case. This should not only inform the assessment of penalty, but the manner in which *social deviance* is dealt with in the first place. Instead

---

41 Mokgoro, "Ubuntu and the Law in South Africa."

of coming up with more or harsher punishments that mostly target poor and vulnerable subjects, Ubuntu calls for eliminating the criminal forces that lead to crime in the first place. The overall scope of the law should be to create social peace and well-being. Therefore, we should strive for implementing alternatives to punishment that create social peace, involving the affected communities. Finally, we should think of positive reinforcement measures to induce *social* behavior, by making people feel worthy and accepted members of society.

Ubuntu demands consideration of the humanity in each member of society and treating him or her in a caring, compassionate manner. By inducing feelings of respect and recognition, citizens will be less likely to resort to violence to sort out interpersonal conflict. Ubuntu hence combines elements of both versions of the transformative justice movement: first, by demanding community-driven solutions for social conflict and, second, by focusing on the criminal forces as structural causes for crime.

Turning back to the cases mentioned above, this might imply the following: In the case of domestic violence, legal mechanisms would need to restore the dignity of the victimized person and censure the violent behavior in an integrative manner. More profoundly, the society as such needs to start coping with sexist, masculinist cultural norms that lead to violent behavior towards women, homosexual, and transgender people. In the case of the violence against an undocumented worker, Ubuntu might call for creating mechanisms that enable this person to report the crime without allowing the involved institutions to forward this information to the migration office. It addition, it might call to reconsider a state's policy to criminalize migration and see the humanity of each person.

Some of these ideas can be raised irrespective of Ubuntu philosophy. However, the idea of a relational ontology as a foundation for a future legal system is particularly distinctive for the Ubuntu approach and therefore offers an attractive counter-model to most liberal approaches to the criminal justice system. Therefore, bringing debates about Ubuntu into the legal and social philosophical discussion in Western academia might provide fruitful grounds to rethink the law and legal subjectivity in a progressive manner.

Deconstructing Law

Peter Goodrich*

Specters of Critique

Hauntology and the Ghosts of Law

> *Everything that has wings is*
> *beyond the reach of the laws.*
> Joseph Joubert

We are a long way now from the campus drugs of Derridium and Lacanium, as François Cusset rather deftly termed the fashion for French theory in the heterotopic curricula of North American campuses.[1] The culture wars have come and gone, the generations have changed, critique in the law schools has collapsed and part of that demise, intellectually peripheral yet politically and structurally central, has been the dissipation of critical legal studies, the oppositional collectivity and leftist movement in the North American legal academy. The process, in anthropological terms, was one of anathematization, cursing of the name; or in the old terminology of Roman law, *damnatio memoriæ*. Continental theory, deconstruction, the fundamental contradiction between autonomy and private property as elaborated in critical legal studies were all to be banned from the law school and the proprieties of professional training for the high honors and substantial salaries of a legal career. The clinical displaced the critical, practice and pragma-

* Cardozo School of Law, New York. Many thanks to the irrepressible Adam Gearey, the inexhaustible Daniela Gandorfer, and also to Liza Mattutat and Heiko Stubenrauch for critical readings and suggestions.

1 François Cusset, *French Theory: How Foucault, Derrida, Deleuze & Co. Transformed the Intellectual Life of the United States* (Minneapolis: University of Minnesota Press, 2008), p. 7.

tism pushed out philosophy of law, the "Conservative Legal Movement," in essence law and market economics, drove out "Critical Legal Studies."[2] In the US, my field of study and comparative empirical example, the movement was killed but, as Nietzsche remarks, beware of killing your enemy because you thereby immortalize her. In Derrida's terms, you push the ghost out of time, beyond belonging, and such is the story, the specter that I will endeavor to locate and portray here.

Legal Hauntology

The figure that I intend to fashion is that of the ghost of critique, the specter of critical legal studies, the *revenant* of rights that haunts the most recent developments in texts that variously bear titles that indicate the introduction of novelties, new beginnings, contemporaneity, exception and divagation. There is an element, of course, of the cyclical, as there always is with the passage of time. Historical materialism morphoses as the "new materialism"; aesthetics becomes synaesthetics; rhetoric refigures into semiotics; architecture and law buttress a new spatial justice; law and literature now narrativize as digital humanities; feminism respires as post-feminism; queer theory or gay and lesbian studies transition to transgender sensibilities; psychoanalytic jurisprudence shapeshifts into the affective turn; ethnomethodology evaporates as atmospherics; the spirit becomes breath, West becomes East, and I could go on but the point is made that the trajectory of disciplines and sub-disciplines is that of accommodating social change and addressing technological innovation in the mode of inventing neologisms and displacing old forms in new vocabularies, changing modes of advocacy and

2 Steven Teles, *The Rise of the Conservative Legal Movement* (Princeton NJ: Princeton University Press, 2008) tells the story.

mutating practices. Nowhere more so, and here I make a beginning, than in relation to the concept of critique itself which, as the governing category of interdisciplinary anxieties and their radical projects, experiences a constant morphosis according to conjuncture and political necessity—and particularly so in law where, as adverted, critique cannot speak its name.

The protestation, profession, promulgation or pronouncement of critique as an abstract criterion of negation of opposing positions was termed "trashing" in the US legal academy and in essence argued directly and without ornament the superiority of the movement to the discourse critiqued. To trash is to wreck and not to build, not even the bricolage of the structuralists that promised at least a new combination or hybridization of rearranged elements. For the critical legal studies movement there was simply the phatic force of empathy for the similar mixed with denunciation, ridicule and attempted exclusion of the opposition. Critique, the child of crisis, operated according to a hermeneutics of suspicion, a cold, aggressive, distanced, oedipal attack upon structures that hid the truth, theorists who concealed their motives, texts that falsified their foundational assumptions; in sum, a parade of ideologies spelled out in terms of lies and inauthenticity masking a narcissism of interests and a thinly veiled lust for power.[3] The mood of critique was variously antinomian, playful, rebarbative and dismissive and, as Felski points out, critique mirrored the law in that "[m]odern legal systems are grounded in a generalized distrust, presuming that there are hidden forms of malfeasance to be uncovered: faked documents, deceptive testimony, concealed crimes. Suspicion permeates the practice of the law, molding its protocols,

---

3   Duncan Kennedy, "The Hermeneutic of Suspicion in Contemporary American Legal Thought," *Law and Critique* 25 (2014): pp. 91–139. On suspicion and authenticity there is also Duncan Kennedy, *Critique of Adjudication: Fin de Siècle* (Cambridge MA: Harvard University Press, 1997).

forms of reasoning, and bureaucratic processes, inspiring acts of surveillance, investigation, interrogation, and prosecution."[4] Critical legal studies in retrospect was the bearer of a very considerable undertow of legalism, both in a negative desire for law and in the less conscious mode of pronouncing verdicts, issuing judgments, proffering (symbolic) penalties—excommunicating, playing, toying, denouncing, litigating in abundance.[5] It was critical in what might be termed a literally reactive sense, proffering no positive program nor constructive institutional template, hence the success of the conservative counter movement, *critique écrasé*.

Death dissipates, disperses and disseminates and that metaphor pervades hauntology, which studies precisely that which, no longer living, lives on. *Plus d'un*—no more one, more than one—references the ambiguity of the anachronic, or in Marxian terms both the specters of futurity and the collectivity that constitutes the dead weight of tradition on the back of the present. Melancholy and hope, retention and aspiration, departed and not yet are the figures of the specular non-present that orients being. This is the initial point, namely that critique is where it is not. In one sense, it is an elsewhere or other, *alieni iuris* in the old language, a foreign will within that marks the memory and unstable incorporation of critique into the contemporary institutions of law. If critique is not there, not yet, then its role is one of haunting, of ghostly demarcation and continuing spectral presence in other forms, in images, in the collectivity of a tradition and what Derrida terms fidelity to the phantasmatic forms that inheritance must take.[6] Remaining with the other, being faithful to critique as

4   Rita Felski, *The Limits of Critique* (Chicago: Chicago University Press, 2015), p. 47.
5   Peter Goodrich, "The Critic's Love of the Law: Intimate Observations on an Insular Jurisdiction," *Law and Critique* 10 (1999): pp. 343–360.
6   Derrida, *Spectres of Marx: The State of Debt, the Work of Mourning, and the New International* (New York: Routledge, 1994), p. 86.

a movement, as a radical egalitarian project and insistence on rights to thought, to sight, to becoming visible requires an openness to otherness that allows non-being, the idea, the community of intellect that Hobbes viewed as the work of angels, of spirits as such, to have its place. The ghost opens up the space between life and death, being and nothingness, of sounding and speaking between.[7] Thus the recent and monumental collection, collect, aspiration that bears the title *Searching for Contemporary Legal Thought* in which, first word, opening for content, searching—looking outside, becoming suspicious all over again—is the operative mode.[8] The lost tribe of jurists variously laments, pursues, hunts; is in quest of an alternative space and mode of thought, new offices, an ability to influence, to change the course of the spectral, of ideas, and through ideas actions, borders, bodies.

The sense of the contemporary critic as one of doubt, of lacking a place, suspicious of being excluded, has tended to be backward looking and hence the reference to melancholia, to the sense of loss of power, place, purpose, project and trajectory. The critic looks back in nostalgia and sorrow, recounting in the form of powerlessness the failure and the falsity of what has gone before. Roberto Unger in a reprise of his founding text announces that the critical legal studies movement was "never intended to generate a permanent genre of legal writing ... it was a disruptive engagement in a particular circumstance" and aimed simply at intervening in the complacency and stasis of legal thought.[9] It required reorientation, and for Unger that meant the anticipation of a greater life, a freeing of the spirit of creativity and, to borrow his

7   On which, see Mark Fisher, *Ghosts of my Life: Writings on Depression, Hauntology and Lost Futures* (London: Zero Books, 2014).
8   Justin Desautels-Stein and Christopher Tomlins, eds., *Searching for Contemporary Legal Thought* (Cambridge and New York: Cambridge University Press, 2017).
9   Roberto Unger, *The Critical Legal Studies Movement: Another Time, a Greater Task* (London: Verso, 2015), p. 4.

slogan, everyone to become their own prophet.[10] The air
or mood of spiritualism that Unger tends to invoke in a
Christian vein should not distract from a key and original feature of his work, the openness to futurity, the recognition of the alternate space of the not yet, the democracy to come. There are many other iterations of the
degeneracy, death, limbo or lostness of critique and of
critics in law, and failure or demise are seen by some to
take a negative form as closure or post-ignition, the stut-
tering of a machine that has broken down. Thus the critics become the "walking dead," and their practice in one
locution a "zombie jurisprudence, in the sense that they
study a curious facet of Western legal consciousness: an
idea is (intellectually) dead, but nevertheless continues
to influence our thought."[11] The spirit of the father, the
ghost of the forebears, *nom du père*, pulls on the scholar's coat tail, forces her to look back. Hence the sense
and sensibility of death, the "After the End," the "Afterword," the "ruins," nostalgia, and ageing out.[12] There is
a strong sense of the nemesis complex, pleasure in seeing
something wasted, burned to ash, consumed by flame, in
the critic's wistful and reverie-driven propensity to remi-
niscence. On the other hand, and borrowing from Gas-
ton Bachelard, we can also invoke the desire to learn, the
drive of history, a forward looking lust for death with
which the philosopher approaches each morning the
stack of books on the desk in their study.

Derrida distinguishes hauntology as comprehending
a discourse of and about the end, from the spectral as

10 Ibid., p. 73.
11 Omri Ben Zvi, "Zombie Jurisprudence," in *Searching for Contemporary Legal Thought*, p. 417. On the "walking dead," see William Mac-
Neil, "The Litigating Dead: Zombie Jurisprudence in Contemporary
Popular Culture," in Delage et al., eds., *Law and New Media: West of
Everything* (Edinburgh: Edinburgh University Press, 2019).
12 Desautels-Stein, "After the End of Legal Thought"; Desautels-Stein
and Christopher Tomlins, "Afterword: Contemporary Legal Thought
As …"; Samuel Moyn, "Legal Theory among the Ruins"; all in *Searching for Contemporary Legal Thought*, ibid., and respectively, pp. 517,
533 and 99.

that which comes back, the *revenant* being defined as "a ghost whose expected return repeats itself, again and again ..." and indeed "*it begins by coming back.*"[13] It is that beginning, the optimism, the speaking of the spirit to engender a future, a shared proleptic state or communal imminence that potentially overcomes the malediction of history and the injustice of law. The ghost is anachronic and by analogy justice for Derrida, in the spirit of spirits, is exactly the recognition and putting into words, bringing to play the jointure that not only rectifies the law of history, and sets the juridical to rights but also resolves the anachronism of the past's disjunction from the future. The *revenant* joining with the *arrivant*, in other words, is a coming together, a jointure and accord that reconciles the time that is out of joint, that promises a spirit to come. This is the fissure of opportunity that seeks and succeeds in escaping the haunting of the past, the law of the fathers and the malediction and injustice of history through the apparition of the spectral yet to come. Here Derrida is very precise, critique manifests, it is an apparition, a specter but "also an appearance and finally an image; in the sense of phenomenon and in the sense of rhetorical figure."[14] Again, all speculation is of specters, fabricated from figures of thought, appearing and disappearing spirits which lead Derrida eventually to "a panoply of arguments but also of images" and then, the punctilio of the panoply is that "while it furnishes the rhetoric or the polemic with images or phantasms, perhaps [it] gives one to think that the figure of the ghost is not just one figure among others. It is perhaps the hidden figure of all figures."[15] The ghost is already a meta discourse, the emblem of intellection, the word before and after being made flesh.

---

13 Derrida, *Spectres*, pp. 10–11.
14 Ibid., p. 117.
15 Ibid., p. 119.

The Imaginal, the Sensible, the Spectral

All speculation, all thought, involves specters, the specularity of ideology, the institutions of the society of the spectacle that Debord critiqued, and Derrida's point, a forceful one, is that there is no escaping the specular character of thought, the speculum of intellection. We do not have to believe in ghosts but while law and tradition may be embodied in things, in monuments, buildings, statues and statutes, it is much more intimately and intellectively incorporated in the body as the spirit that moves, engages, pulses forward because of the images it harbors. The waking body, the oneiric form, the subject of reverie, are all sites of imagination and, in an argument made at length by Chiara Bottici, in the imaginal as the concept that recognizes the power of the image as suspended between epistemology and ontology, neither real nor unreal, but a motivating, driving, configuring form, an evanescent, chimerical body extant within as cerebration and as incarnadine sense. The imaginal takes the primary form of social relationships mediated through the constant flux and flow of images.[16] As Coccia puts it, touching upon the same theme in different words, "if the psychic is the embodied form of the medial, the medial (the imaginal) is able to exist beyond the psychical," and has its own supplementary and excessive space, beyond the body, the thing, in an "ontological interregnum," as image.[17] The sensible question is not that of entity or being as such, but rather and more radically that of movement, of being in flow, entities in flux.

What form then does the ghost of critique take in legal doctrine and philosophy of law? The initial answer is not the singular but the plural, the figures and fabrica-

16 Chiara Bottici, *Imaginal Politics: Images Beyond Imagination and the Imaginary* (New York: Columbia University Press, 2014), p. 198.

17 Emanuele Coccia, *Sensible Life: A Micro-ontology of Images* [2010] (New York: Fordham University Press, 2016), p. 36.

tions, the specters that live on, that transform, are multiple. The first point is simply, as adumbrated above, that critique lives on in a different mediological form, most obviously, which is to say obtrusively, in the material visual presence of images as the media of social relationships and institutional action in the videosphere or spectacularity of the contemporary political and juridical domain.[18] Change in the dominant media propels new modes of critical apprehension and specifically an apprehensive and haptic turn to sensibility, a shift towards aesthetic disciplines, even within law that cannot any longer evade a "twenty-first century characterized by a hyper—and even hysterical visuality that touches every aspect of our lives ... Yes, aesthetic modes are prime agents in the transmission of legal subjectivity."[19] What Débray, borrowing from the surrealist Louis Aragon, mobilizes as the stupefying image, the passionate and unruly entry of the visual into the social injects an active and transgressive element of affect—the Venusian, the amorous, lust—into the juridico-political realm.[20] The digital image, social media, omnipresent cameras generate our new collectivities, myths and divinities, if by the stupefying presence of the latter we mean emblems of extreme belonging, identification with the charisma of stars, the tumescence of nation, party, leader.[21] But it

18 The concept of mediology is developed by Régis Debray in a series of works, only small parts of which have been translated. The starting point is *Cours de médiologie générale* (Paris: Gallimard, 1991) and then *Vie et mort de l'image* (Paris: Gallimard, 1992), from which latter work I borrow the term videosphere. More recently there is *L'Image stupéfiante* (Paris: Gallimard, 2013).

19 Desmond Manderson, "Introduction: Imaginal Law," in Desmond Manderson, ed., *Law and the Visual* (Toronto: University of Toronto Press, 2018); Christian Delage, Peter Goodrich and Marco Wan, eds., *Law and New Media* (Edinburgh: Edinburgh University Press, 2019).

20 Débray, *L'Image stupéfiante*, p 19; Keston Sutherland, *Stupefaction: A Radical Anatomy of Phantoms* (London: Seagull Press, 2011) makes the important point that the phantom comes into the social also as satire and critique.

21 On which point, see Giorgio Agamben, *The Kingdom and the Glory: For a Theological Genealogy of Economy and Government* (Stanford CA: Stanford University Press, 2011), especially pp. 253–259 on the

is precisely in being unruly, in its capacity for stupefaction that the image and political aesthetic open possibilities for critique. In an age of what Debord termed "integrated spectacles," an era of pervasive falsification, the unruly has to take the form of experimental positivity, of acting "as if" the unthought has its own jurisdiction, the power to change the institution through change of the body, writing the self, reforming the immediate institutional environment, holding the eye of the other in the uneasy dance of decision. It is curation of the self, the abandonment of alienation in the frame of creative expression, utopian thought, or Debord's radical drinking, the space of reverie that needs to be reclaimed.[22]

Taking off from *New Critical Legal Thinking* of 2012, the theme of the future of the movement developed literary figurations of juristic analysis, meaning anarchic, novelistic and aesthetic reinventions or conjurations of scholarly intervention.[23] Thinking differently, exercising critique as a positive mode of relating and apprehending the social and legal in divergent literary forms expands with the haptic turn of new materialist aesthetics, the dominance of the specular, and takes to images, to the desire and stupefaction of the sensible. By the time that the great advocate of atmospheres Andreas Philippopoulos-Mihalopoulos published the *Routledge Handbook of Law and Theory* in 2019, a synaesthetics had come to dominate and ghosts, bodies, matter populate the collective intellection of dense struggle and

acclamatory character of the political. The theme is impressively developed in Marinos Diamantides, "A Postmodern Hetoimasia – Feigning Sovereignty during the State of Exception," in Peter Goodrich and Michel Rosenfeld, eds., *Administering Interpretation: Derrida, Agamben, and the Political Theology of Law* (New York: Fordham University Press, 2019), p. 189.

22 Guy Debord, *The Society of the Spectacle* [1967] (New York: Zone Books, 1994), pp. 112–116; and further, Guy Debord, *Comments on the Society of the Spectacle* [1988] (London: Verso, 1998), pp. 9–10.

23 Matthew Stone et al., eds., *New Critical Legal Thinking: Law and Politics* (London: Routledge, 2012), particularly Part III: Futures of Critical Legal Thinking.

critical artisans working through pictures because that is what the social offers.[24] Theory reattaches here to its etymological roots in seeing and in theatricality, as the mode, medium and modality of contemporary practices of thought relayed explicitly through shared modes of embodiment, through the ghosts of the pneuma and time and texts that are out of joint. Theory as seeing is also thought as breath, as insufflation, incorporation, the movement of being as inhabitation of body, space and objects.

The specter carries threat as well as potential. The image as ghost harbors the dead, the sense of loss, the feeling of injustice and what Luis Eslava terms "out-of-syncness – the out of whackness" of the global: "In this spectral turn that has accompanied the arrival of the twenty-first century, ghosts express the moment when your bearings in the world lose direction."[25] Driven by the sense of loss and of injustice, the ghost that wishes to be seen, the dead that want to be remembered, as Nietzsche remarks, are but phantoms and forerunners to the rose of the present. It is the inchoate character of both specter and theory that critique now seeks to address, even as thought becomes spectrally embodied, history a ghostly apparition of other presences, and now that unruly images rule. What theory as seeing, and critique as aesthetically informed apprehension of new forms emphasizes at the political level is the embedded, material and embodied site of the image, as portrayal of and embodied in the subject. To borrow, 500 pages on, from one version of a new jurisprudence: "the strange strength of critical jurisprudence is that it oscillates between the revelation of critique of/in this world, and a promise of understanding founded in an ontology

24 Andreas Philippopoulos-Mihalopouos, ed., *Routledge Handbook of Law and Theory* (London: Routledge, 2019).
25 Luis Eslava, "Dense Struggle: On Ghosts, Law and the Global Order," in Philippopoulos-Mihalopoulos, *Law and Theory*, pp. 17 and 19.

dependent upon a 'beyond', an outside of this world of space/time."[26]

The image brings reasons of which reason knows not. It carries an affective force, a lure, a depth and drive which, as populism has recently demonstrated, can unhinge. It is unruly in reactive and futuristic or anarchic senses and whichever is in play, the critic has to account for, apprehend, touch upon images. The image as haptic and affective relay and transmission is the exemplary medium of social relation and of political movement. So too, as Manderson notes, the imaginal opens up the law, it generates a novel jurisprudence precisely by virtue of its ghostly, imaginal form, the requirement and the desire to see anew, to see what is there, to see who lives on. As one commentator puts it, in a Derridean vein, the new media and their technologies trigger "moments of undecidability that spectrally hover into both law and regulation."[27] What is outside inevitably also inhabits the interior just as the oneiric occupies the diurnal, propelling new meanings, unleashing images, undoing theory and remaking it.

The specter of deconstructive theory, the threat of critique as the undoing of legal texts, haunts the law, internally as also externally. It represents the ghost, the past of critique, attached to the insensibility of lives lost, of relationships ruined, land grabbed and the whole phantasmagoria and seraglio of inequality. Theory, in other words, is inhabited by specters and endeavors to give expression to ghosts while simultaneously representing future potentials, bodies that do not become images before their time. This is the nowhere of theory that exists between the stupefaction of the past and *détournement*, the turning around of the turned around, the

---

26 Anne Bottomley and Nathan Moore, "On new model jurisprudence: The scholar/critic as (cosmic) artisan," in Philippopoulos-Mihalopoulos, *Law and Theory*, p 512.

27 Peter Kalulé, "On the Undecidability of Legal and Technological Regulation," *Law and Critique* 30 (2019): p. 139.

coming to terms with ghosts, with images, so as to live (finally) with the relationships we spectrally embody, so as to map potential and embark upon another art of law, one in which critique is an opening up not just to the past and injustice but to the comedy of future possibilities.

Openings: Unfurling Wings

There is by definition nothing conclusive about critique, just the endless travail of looking, apprehending, touching, enacting and thus embodying, moving on. The specter of theory and the hauntology that it prepares does have its figures, specific ghosts. Theorists are one such, souls searching and soul searching which is positively embraced and embodied in what Peter Gabel has coined as "spiritual legal practice" and to a lesser degree in therapeutic jurisprudence.[28] There is in this concatenation an inward turn, an attempt to turn the unhappy consciousness of the singular universal into a spiritual positivity and conscious relational awareness, into a practice, a love towards the world: "it is the fear of the other that causes the real power relations rather than the converse; and it is this fear, underlain by humiliation, that is the driving force in reproducing society's injustices and inequalities."[29] The various alternative registers of freedom also gain a species of reprise in postfeminist theory and in critical race studies, in black lives matter, where self-consciousness, working on the body and on immediate and intimate practices can act as orientation for political—which is to say collective—action,

---

28 See, for example, Peter Gabel, "Critical Legal Studies as Spiritual Practice," *Pepperdine Law Review* 36 (2009): p. 515; Peter Gabel, "The Spiritual Dimension of Social Practice," *Journal of Legal Education* 67 (2014): p. 673; and his magnum opus, Peter Gabel, *The Desire for Mutual Recognition: Social Movements and the Dissolution of the False Self* (New York: Routledge, 2018).

29 Gabel, *Desire for Mutual Recognition*, p. 69.

inter-subjective movement. Ratna Kapur concludes her expansive elaboration of what she terms freedom from the fishbowl of neo-liberalism with the observation that "I have not sought tidy outcomes and resolutions, but have focused on scrutinizing the horizon of epistemic possibilities and envisioning the insightful critique that might manifest once the solipsism and self-reflexiveness of the liberal episteme that is evident in human rights is exposed."[30] A political spirituality, a body politics implies a revisioning of relationships that moves outside of the normative distributions and binary oppositions that law imposes. As Davina Cooper formulates the project of critique from the ground up, it is everyday utopias, spontaneous and autonomous group activities—nudist communities, non-monetary trading collectives, locations for casual sex—which reflect the force of conceptual creativity and the multiplicity of spaces that such invention can create.

The theoretical starting point for this spectral critique, what I would term the haunting of radical projects by the desire for renewal of critique as located in the body, in the sensible, is best posed aesthetically in terms of respiration and of bringing to life. The art historian Georges Didi-Huberman, in a powerful essay on the opening of images, addresses precisely the sensory quality of the image through the body of the viewer. The specters without mirror those within, and thus his account starts by stating that "images open themselves, expand and contract, like the bodies of those who view them."[31] The metaphor is intended corporeally and synaesthetically. Artistic images unfold themselves only to our senses: "they open *to* us and they close on us to the

---

30 Ratna Kapur, *Gender, Alterity and Human Rights: Freedom in a Fishbowl* (Cheltenham: Elgar, 2018), p. 251. I became aware of this text by virtue of the fine discussion in Swethaa Ballakrishnen, "Book Review," *Feminist Legal Studies* 27:1 (2019): pp. 109–114.
31 Georges Didi-Huberman, *L'Image ouverte* (Paris: Gallimard, 2007), p. 25.

extent that they arouse in us something that one can name an interior experience."[32] They are windows opening out but also reflecting, unfolding what is within. "A hard science of the window," Gérard Wacjman articulates, has the goal "of making this object an object of thought, imagine an idea behind the head: that the window, in its very simplicity, is a machine for thinking the world. The window thinks the world, materially, as the work of artisans."[33]

It is necessary to release our specters, cease fearing ghosts and from a methodological perspective believe in the body and in what is within. Opening to the image, unshuttering the windows places theory back in its classical position of conceptual creativity, of imagining futures, and most significantly for an age of imaginal relays, recognizing that light is law, that seeing is the eminently contestable imposition of norms. The role of critique is here that of utopian thinking, of oceanic encounters that recognize the revenant, that are open to the spectral quality of conceptual invention. The specters of critique are those of the return of radical impulses that start with the body, as the radical, as the origin of creative processes and of imagining alternative modes of being together, bonded by interior experiences, viewing the other as a work of art, a living, expanding, searching and haptic being of thought.

Critical Jurisprudence begins with autobiographical narratives, literary forays introducing material themes, each chapter offering an anecdotal opening, early morning in Piraeus, but significant though this shift of style may be, it is rapidly abandoned.[34] Ratna Kapur opens by looking out of her family home at "the picturesque foothills of the Himalayas" and adds "my thoughts wander

32 Ibid., p. 25.
33 Gérard Wacjman, *Fenêtre: Chroniques du regard et de l'intime* (Paris: Verdier, 2004), p. 22.
34 Costas Douzinas and Adam Gearey, *Critical Jurisprudence* (Oxford: Hart, 2005), p. 3.

across the view of the Doon valley." She speaks of the aperture of her location, the atmosphere—the sights, sounds, colors, smells—in which she thinks, the freedom that she will put to use.[35] Davina Cooper heads for bathhouses and beaches, sex and nudism, alternative symbolic and locational forms, potentials, possibilities, openings both literal, metaphoric and metamorphosing. The ghosts of critique seek material forms, artisanal projects, creative forms of being and being together that are at their most effective when material and embodied, lived and expressed in the radical transformation of the interior in response to the commonality of alterity and exteriority.

The examples of openings, the desire for novel communities, for interiority and reorientation of experience, can be multiplied, new windows opened, a haunting of unforeseen specters released. What matters is that the sites of these openings are the body, experience, connection, and the specular quality of the spirit that drives critical desire. Didi-Huberman reinvokes the figure of the gay scientist and the ambiguities of atlases, of maps as sensible guides deconstructing the normative and closed character of tradition, history and law.[36] Bottici borrows from anarchism. We are open when we are equal and we are equal when we acknowledge and start from the "I" of experience, the who of theory, the here and now that signals the irreducibility of beginning with the body and the specters within.[37] It is as if the other, alterity, is the first ghost, the alien self within and it is that figure that prompts creative acts, critique as the writing of the body and the expression of its aesthetics and synaesthetics, its here and now, as troubled, wounded, hopeful artisan of the unfolding of the collectivity of thought.

---

35 Kapur, *Fish Bowl*, p. 9.
36 Georges Didi-Huberman, *Atlas, or the Anxious Gay Science* (Chicago: Chicago University Press, 2018), pp. 3–6.
37 Bottici, *Imaginal Politics*, pp. 182–183.

In a circuitous way, all of the critical theories adumbrated, or adverted to, express a coming to terms with ghosts. Critique is dead, meaning the old forms have died, but the impetus, the specter lives on. The figures, the ghosts, of Marx, Mackinnon, Martin Luther King, respectively of socialism, feminism, race theory continue to haunt but have taken now a bodily and transitional turn. The radical project of critique continues, and survives, in potential at least in law, in the mode of counter-memory and its bodily materializations. We live in trans times, and coming now to the radical and mutating sense of what is corporeally possible deconstructs old laws, physical strictures and normative constraints alike. We can choose our sex, change our gender, challenge the primary and structural category of legal persons as male or female in favor of radical self-expression, in a spirit of indefinition as the new mode of intellection and as the creative minor gesture of critique.[38] In recognizing and expressing the choices of habitus and inhabitation, of body and movement, we materialize and enact our incorporation in its interiority and viscerality, but also in its sensibility, its immaterial and spectral forms. Acknowledging the body, here and now, writing this, also recognizes that I am a ghost, that even for myself I am and I am not. I carry the images of critique, unleash specters, live and live on, wings inchoate on my back, soon enough to be no more one, more than one in the collectivity of thought to come.

[38] On which theme, in a legal context, see Peter Goodrich, *Schreber's Law: Jurisprudence and Judgment in Transition* (Edinburgh: Edinburgh University Press, 2018).

Manuela Klaut

On the Run from the Law

Alexander Kluge's *Yesterday Girl* as Cinematic Institution of Subsumption

Before Alexander Kluge's first feature film *Yesterday Girl* (*Abschied von gestern*, 1966) begins, the audience is presented with a message on screen: "What separates us from yesterday is not a rift, but a changed position."[1] *Yesterday Girl* is, in terms of film history, the first German feature to emerge from the Oberhausen Manifesto, that is, the first film about a changed situation, a changed outlook.

In 1962, as the Oberhausen Manifesto was speaking of film's potential for "freedom from standard industry conventions"[2] and marking the beginning of the New German Cinema in film history, Alexander Kluge and Edgar Reitz founded the independent *Institut für Filmgestaltung Ulm* (Ulm Institute for Film Design) and, in the following year, 1963, the production company *Kairos-Film*. A major approach of the Ulm Institute is the differentiation between an *official* history of New German Cinema focused on successful films, and another, *subterranean* history.[3]

This history, as told along two differentiating lines, is Alexander Kluge's concept of cinema, which, on the one hand, produced new forms of film language and, on the

---

1 Unless otherwise indicated translations are those of the author.
2 http://www.edgar-reitz.de/das-oberhausener-manifest.html [consulted on the 13/03/20].
3 Compare Alexander Kluge and Klaus Eder, *Ulmer Dramaturgien. Reibungsverluste* (Munich and Vienna: Carl Hanser Verlag, 1980), p. 5.

other, provided a method for New German Cinema to branch out into short forms and documentary content, in order not only to transform film pictures, but also to design new narrative styles. In this process of transforming cinema as it had been to date, a new non-literary linguistic form of cinema was developed, which established the connection of legal, official and administrative language and cinema as a form of *New Objectivity*.

The *Ulmer Dramaturgien* (Ulm dramaturgies) discuss the differences between cinematic and literary methods of expression and their relation to the organisation of language, and finally their necessary reorganisation in cinema, which, following a breakup of syntactic and grammatical structures, is rearranged in order to overcome the forced sense of historical derivation and the traditional prominence of language: "Language in cinema is permitted to be blind."[4]

It could be said that Alexander Kluge, who first worked as a lawyer in Berlin and Munich in 1958 after his state exams, and in the same year as an assistant to Fritz Lang for film and literary writing, established two essentials of the New German Cinema: Kluge's films are cinematographic institutions that undertake legal tasks. Kluge not only enacts the legislative, the executive and the judicative in his films, literary texts and television reports. His cinema also subsumes and interprets the law, and as such becomes an instance which explores the narrative limits of law as well as those of cinema. This thesis is the subject of the following study, using *Yesterday Girl's* protagonist Anita G. (played by the director's sister, Alexandra Kluge) as an example.

---

4   Ibid., p. 21.

The Case of Anita G. as an Institutional Puzzle

Anita G. sits in court and is accused of theft. We hear in the reading of her indictment of her willful act to acquire "a foreign, movable object, with the intention of appropriating it unlawfully, and taking it away."[5] From the stolen cardigan, the subject of her indictment, we learn nothing more. There is no picture of the deed in question; the act only exists as a construct of judicial directives and in Anita's compliance with them. In order to form a mental image of the deed, the viewer must also engage in the appropriation of something foreign and movable. Thus, the viewer is introduced to Alexander Kluge's approach to the film, in which sparse intertitles, the use of non-actors and improvised dialogues are leveraged to reformulate the procedures of cinematic history. When asked by the judge, "Are you saying that something you could not have been aware of until 1943–44 at the earliest has anything to do with your current situation?" Anita answers simply with "No." In this simple statement, *Yesterday Girl* illustrates one of its central themes: new beginnings and their impossibility. Kluge's film presents his vision for New German Cinema, which eschews the normal immutable dogma that follows new schools or movements in order instead to focus on the uncertainties of film making, the precariousness of method and subject.[6]

5 Alexander Kluge, *Abschied von gestern* (Frankfurt am Main: Verlag Filmkritik, 1967), p. 9, scene: courtroom. The numeration of the scenes, minutes and the texts were cited from the protocol recorded by Enno Patalas from the screenplay of the film *Yesterday Girl*.
6 Ibid., p. 77. In the scene 376, Manfred Pichota (Oberministerialrat and the married lover of Anita G.) is reading a story from Bertolt Brecht, *If Mr. K loved someone*. "What do you do," Mr. K. was asked, "if you love someone?" "I make a sketch of the person," said Mr. K., "and make sure that one comes to resemble the other." "Which? The sketch?" "No," said Mr. K., "the person." Subsequently Anita G. and Pichota are discussing whether the sketch should resemble the person (Anita), or the person has to become similar to the sketch (Pichota).

The texts from which Alexander Kluge develops his films are subject to various transformations—they arise in the case of Anita G. from cases that Kluge worked with in 1956, during his legal traineeship in juvenile detention. These experiences turned into literature, became actions and, finally, in cinema, again became actual legal analysis when in *Yesterday Girl* Kluge interviewed the Attorney General Fritz Bauer, and in his later film, *The Patriotic Woman* (1979), questioned the lawyer and educational researcher Hans Heckel as a fairy-tale researcher.

My study of Kluge's case of Anita G. is meant to demonstrate in what way the existing institutions shown in the 1966 film are failing. It is not just Anita G. who, in the film *Yesterday Girl* (the correct translation of the German title is actually *Farewell to Yesterday*), remains difficult to grasp, because she is on the run from the law. It is also the problem of subsumption—because the situation which Anita G. finds herself in cannot be clearly classified in a legal sense, again and again leading Anita G. to defeat in the face of the institutions: there is the unavailable university entrance qualification, despite the fact that Anita is studying, the unavailable cheque for the landlord, which makes it impossible for Anita to settle down and find a secure base, and also the probation officer, who, although she verbally helps Anita to orient herself towards a good life, fails her in a practical sense. The university also leads Anita to fail because of its didactic and disciplinary guidelines. And yet it is the interesting perspective of Alexander Kluge that allows us to feel that it is not Anita who is failing, but the institutions, and the determination of life situations according to certain legal concepts or according to the logic of custom. Kluge transfers these situations into indefinite legal concepts: malicious deception, suitability, common good and reliability— and giving this elasticity of interpretation back to these fixed concepts is endlessly beautiful.

During the exchange in the court room, the film succeeds in reducing Anita G.'s whole life to become the

short summary of a legal defendant, and in doing so
it offers the viewer a perspective on the dysfunction of
institutions, the distortion of the border between judicative and legislative operations and on the court case as
a reflection of Anita's living conditions. When the court
judge questions Anita G. as to why she moved to West
Germany from East Germany (then separated from the
West as the GDR), she responds:

> Anita: I worked in Zerbst as a telephone operator. I wanted
> to study something.
> Judge: Why did you give that up?
> Anita: I got scared and went to the West.
> Judge: Fear of what? Because of certain incidents?
> Anita: Because of prior incidents.
> Judge: Oh, you mean those from 1943–44? I do not believe
> that. In my experience they do not affect young people.
> Anita: I felt unsafe.[7]

The film *Yesterday Girl* is a carousel on which law
enforcement officials, senior ministry councilors, judges,
landlords, education officers and Anita G. all revolve.
One could in a way describe Anita as being like the
law—very vague and open to interpretation. It is difficult to determine what she really is: delinquent, cool
and calculating, emotional, emancipated, dangerous,
harmless, lazy, committed, hardworking, happy or sad,
and she would remain undefined in a way, were it not
for her arrest and placement in detention at the end of
the film. Therein lies the dichotomy of the legal relationships within which Anita must act: she has no clear
sense of right or wrong, of lawful or unlawful. If one
were to consider her deeds purely from a legal standpoint, one might conclude that Anita is guilty of theft,
fraud or the falsification of facts, but that doesn't tell the
whole story. The case must be brought to justice in order

7   Ibid., p. 10, scene: courtroom.

for Anita's story to be told, and for this, Kluge develops his own cinematic legal system. Within this system, the singular incident of Anita's crime becomes relevant only insofar as it can be categorized as a starting point, a circumstance, a result, or as a consequence. But here Kluge again highlights the gap of uncertainty between the incident of Anita's crime and the realities of her life. Into this gap the legal system continually intervenes, trying to perform its institutional duty of establishing a clear line of events through which to serve its judgment.

The case of Anita G. begins in the original book *Lebensläufe* (published in the GDR in 1981 under the title *Der Pädagoge von Klopau*, and in English in 1988 with the title *Case Stories*), not in court, as in the 1966 film, but with a displacement—Anita's escape through the cities of Wiesbaden, Karlsruhe, Fulda, Kassel, Frankfurt, Hanover and Mainz. "Why does she repeatedly commit offenses on her travels? She is continually the subject of police inquiries under multiple names. Why doesn't this intelligent person keep their affairs in better order? Why can't she keep her feet on the ground?"[8]

The case of Anita G. demonstrates that Kluge's form of criticism consists of deconstructing the legal texts—he uses them in his texts and scenographies to show how imprecisely they are able to capture the individual case. The failure of subsumption and, at the same time, the interpretive power that emerges from the words of the legal text are of interest to Kluge: thus, his protagonists remain in the case and move at the limits of judgment.

---

8   Alexander Kluge, *Lebensläufe*, in *Chronik der Gefühle* (Frankfurt am Main: Suhrkamp, 2004), p. 734.

Responsibilities and Non-acting
Institutions of Cinema

In one key scene, which Cornelia Vismann accurately analyzes in her book *Medien der Rechtsprechung (Judiciary Media)*, Anita G. searches for Attorney General and well-known judicial reformist Fritz Bauer. Bauer does not engage in conversation with Anita or take on her case, but instead appears in the film to provide an important parallel to Anita's judicial treatment, expressing critical opinions on the organisation of the German courts and in particular on the right of defendants to sit rather than stand in the court room. As Vismann writes:

> The question of the legality of standing in court, he puts in a "court film", which is made by another lawyer. Alexander Kluge's 1965/66 film "Yesterday Girl" puts this pressing question into the film image. Here you see the well-known liberalism of "Dr. Bauer", as he is referred to in the film. A standing defendant did not fit into the ideals of the new criminal law reforms of the time, as this left the defendant exposed. The defendant should be re-socialized, reintegrated into society. In order to take account of this goal within the court hearing, the authoritarian gap between those allowed to sit and those made to stand in court should no longer be allowed to exist.[9]

Interestingly in this scene, Anita G. not only functions as a character in a story, but also acts in the service of the filmmaker, namely to seek out the person who, via judicial process, can help reform German legal practice. Although Dr. Bauer is not responsible for representing Anita, as her case does not fall under his jurisdiction as Attorney General and would more appropriately require

9   Cornelia Vismann, *Medien der Rechtsprechung,* ed. Alexandra Kemmerer and Markus Krajewski (Frankfurt am Main: S. Fischer, 2011), p. 170.

a civil defense lawyer, he can represent for Kluge's film. In Kluge's original book version of the story, the figure of the famous defense lawyer Dr. Sch. is introduced, but here too Anita is deprived of direct contact with him: "But how should the defendant penetrate through the protective ring of celebrity, assessors, co-workers, office workers, this complicated organization, to the great defender himself?"[10]

Dr. Sch. is described very precisely, and special attention is given to describing how he operates during court proceedings: "Part of his popularity was based on his alleged character. He would approach the defendant's table with ambivalence, talk to all present before finally arriving at his bench and turning back to offer the defendant a greeting."[11]

As it appears that Anita G. will not be helped by Dr. Bauer in her case, and since Kluge does not immediately choose to investigate more concretely into her past as part of his main narrative, Anita is instead left awkwardly in the story to deal with her legal circumstances alone. All those that could potentially help her are somehow prevented from doing so: "Narrator (spoken by Kluge): A university professor who occasionally dealt with amnesty issues knew of the case of Anita G. He planned to talk to the Attorney General, but had to leave for Chicago. Two members of the socialist students' association wanted to inform Dr. Bauer, but they were soon to be sitting for their examinations."[12]

The gap between the portrayal of Anita G.'s life as presented in court through her biographical reports versus what we are shown of her life in the film illustrates the essential difference between the procedural jurisdiction of the legal system and that of Kluge's own cinematic system. Both systems are however ultimately inconclu-

---

10 Alexander Kluge, *Lebensläufe*, in *Chronik der Gefühle*, p. 742.
11 Ibid.
12 Alexander Kluge, *Abschied von gestern*, p. 74.

sive in delivering an accurate or complete judgment of Anita G.'s case—she remains an insoluble question to the two institutions, which in the end cannot help but arrest her, as they know not what else to do with her. As academic Michael Niehaus writes: "In this respect, however, one must distinguish between the pure question of the facts (quaestio facti) and the question of legal evaluation (quaestio juris). The distinction between quaestio facti and quaestio juris is problematic. However, the film always references this distinction because it is the medium that seems to be able to answer the question of the facts by showing the truth."[13]

One can say then for *Yesterday Girl* that it is not concerned with the determination of truth, or of guilt or innocence, but instead focuses on the court case and its circumstances, the way in which control of Anita's environment appears to be in the hands of others, such that she is diminished to the life of a vagabond between law and non-law, and that no other way out remains for her.

In another scene which occurs in the middle of the film, titled *Imaginary*[14] in the screenplay, Anita G. is pursued in almost comic fashion by police motorcycles, theatrical characters, toy soldiers in battle, and Nazi prosecutors. Then the intertitle follows: "Truth, if it occurs seriously, will be killed." It is in the comedy of this chase that Anita G. succeeds in temporarily escaping her situation and fleeing into her imagination. Then, after a journey in the paternoster elevator of the University of Frankfurt, (which in the film's transcript is listed as the staircase of the Ministry of Culture) follows a scene that could not be more bizarre: ministerial councilor Pichota takes Anita to an event at a dog training club. Here the pair play audience to a display of rehearsed canine rescue routines. The scene ends in

---

13 Michael Niehaus, "Evidenz. Die Wahrheit des Films und die Wahrheit des Verfahrens," in *Recht im Film*, ed. Stefan Machura (Baden-Baden: Nomos, 2002), p. 20.
14 Alexander Kluge, *Abschied von gestern*, p. 55.

the rain: "324. Long Shot: the flooded terrain. The man who 'attacked' the girl takes refuge in the background of the frame; the dog pursues him and bites into the man's protected arm."[15]

When in *Lebensläufe* Anita G.'s case is punctuated by the question "Don't you have a more pleasant story?" this certainly also refers to the history of the German authorities and their attempt to resolve grief, shock and trauma through administrative procedure. Anita G. would have experienced the air raids of 1945 just as Alexander Kluge did and has since written about. As Adorno writes in *Minima Moralia*, "There is no right life in the wrong one,"[16] so Kluge's work is an opportunity to reformulate this as, "There is no right justice in the wrong one."

Kluge's texts and screenplays blur the boundaries between law and literature: the law becomes a narrative, which must in turn be subject to the law. This fundamental criticism of the law consists in Kluge placing fictitious cases in a legal context in order to make them testify against the law and its determinations; a law that has gaps and thus keeps the solutions open in order to always problematize its fixed definitions.

The scattered histories of the characters in Kluge's texts and films are received through reports and records. He uses a common procedure of investigation in his work, a juridical method that attaches little importance to the limits of its medium or legal responsibility. The way in which a case is fragmented or reconstituted through the medium of its investigation (i.e. through TV, radio, film) remains secondary to Kluge's casuistic process and the way in which it circumnavigates mediality whilst still retaining a coherent media form. Anita G.'s case is undermined by her flight not only from the law, but also from Kluge's thought process, which ultimately dis-

15 Ibid., p. 67.
16 Theodor W. Adorno, *Minima Moralia: Reflexionen aus dem beschädigten Leben* (Frankfurt am Main: Suhrkamp, 1962), p. 42.

solves the empirical procedures of the case into theories on legal processes and political transformation.

The crucial thing about Kluge's cases is that they reach the limits of what can be assessed in legal terms and thus become legal impossibilities. They refer back to the empirical values of legal history—the legislative comment.

Court Speech and Commentary as Cinematic Means of the Case

The scene in the courtroom ends with the following dialogue:

Anita: It was all very emotional.
Judge, irritated: Yes, well, that can't be conclusively established.
He delves into his file.[17]

This is followed by the judge's reading of a long legal commentary to the German Criminal Code. It becomes clear that he is unsure whether the removal of the cardigan by Anita G. is a theft or simply a transference of custody. He continues reading from the text, stating, "This is to be judged according to the principles of experience of daily life, not according to the civil code, as this knows ownership without rule... Daily life will establish whether rule over an item is applicable."

In January 2006, Cornelia Vismann and Thomas Henne hosted a workshop entitled "The Comment as a Medium of Communication on Law," which opened with the statement: "The success of the selected commentaries [...] implies that they became important structural features of contemporary communication on law, offering the establishment of an independent, easily comprehensible system for the processing of literature

---

17 Alexander Kluge, *Abschied von gestern*, p.13, scene: courtroom.

and jurisprudence, a user-friendly overview and a unified style for commentary."[18]

The film scholar Susanne Marten comments in her text "Leinwand und Richtertisch" ("The Screen and The Judges' Table") on the visual architecture and spaces of negotiation in *Yesterday Girl*. Marten positions the character of the judge not as undetermined, but as staged state authority:

> The empty wall behind the judge must not be misinterpreted as a lack of state authority. [...] In Kluge's film, the spatiality of the judicial apparatus is staged as a social arrangement primarily by means of image and language, and not according to the principle of elevation. The court sequence concludes with a seemingly endless reading of a commentary from the penal code on the subject of ownership. Now, towards the end of the trial, the judge's body fills the visual space on screen. Does this discourse come from the judge's body? Only a part of his face and hands can be seen, the rest is almost black. Here, as though placed in a bluebox, parts of his body are dematerialized. [19]

One could say that the film is Kluge's legislative comment, his own legal annotation, with which he displaces of the judge—a comment perhaps on the part of the penal code which states that questioning of the accused in court is to be opened by informing them of what acts they are accused and which penal provisions will be considered. In Section 136 of the German Code of Criminal Procedure, paragraph 2 states: "The questioning shall give the accused the opportunity to elimi-

18 https://www.rg.mpg.de/976055/Programm.pdf [consulted on the 13/03/20].

19 Susanne Marten "Leinwand und Richtertisch. Räumlichkeit und Theatralität im Film und vor Gericht in Alexander Kluges Abschied von gestern (Anita G.)," in Jörg Dünne, ed., *Theatralität und Räumlichkeit* (Würzburg: Königshausen & Neumann, 2009), p. 182.

nate the grounds for suspicion against him and to assert the facts in his favour."[20]

Here Kluge's cinematic courtroom becomes a space of possibility that can change the line of inquiry of the law, allowing it to drift away from the question of Anita's guilt or innocence, and towards the possible alteration of legal process. Only in the course of the court proceedings does the judge describe the criminal act Anita G. may potentially be incarcerated for. The film deliberately does not show the final outcome of the courtroom scene, and thus does not finally decide about her guilt. Perhaps Anita G. is not in prison because of the theft of the cardigan—perhaps it is only cut that way in the film, the court scene being directly followed by the image of Anita G. in prison. At this intersection, Kluge reads the poem "Good morning (The mammoth)" by Heinrich Hoffmann.

Can one really argue a connection between the trial and the incarceration of Anita G. solely on the basis of this visual montage?

The judge in *Yesterday Girl* interprets the law in the case as being against Anita G., but then, on further inspection of legislative criteria, he appears to exclude "theft" as a possible ruling. In doing so he demonstrates that interpretation of the law is by no means a mechanical process, but is instead essentially determined by the person interpreting it.

In his 2004 book *Gerichtsrede* (*Court Address*), Thomas-Michael Seibert writes:

> The legal case is constituted via sentences, through which the judgment can be described meaningfully. The basic question, "what is the case?" is strongly constrained in the legal context. A wide range of procedures and circumstances, which would be considered noteworthy in the course of everyday life, become disposable in practiced

20 Björn Gercke and Karl-Peter Julius, *Die Strafprozessordnung* (Heidelberg: C.F. Müller, 2019).

judiciary. They are "immaterial."' In the same way, generous allowance is made for the accused. The questioning of
the accused should give them the opportunity to eliminate
any grounds for suspicion against them [...]. But caution is
required here. Those who know that, in the judicial system,
it is necessary to integrate everyday truths, but who also
know how little everyday truth flows into official investigations will likely conclude that the best tactic is to remain
silent. Silence as an effective mode of address is the style of
public speaking easiest to teach. All officials know this. [21]

As Kluge is director of the film and not a court official,
the characters must always talk in court—and everything
is admissible, including their silences, which one must
be able to see in order to know they are taking place:

Perpetual re-examination and investigation are the conditions for dialogism as procedure, in which through the continuous adoption of new perspectives on the singularity of
a situation, new decisions are reached at every moment,
which in turn can invalidate the finality of all previous
decisions and thus the finality of any decision at all. Just
like Fritz Bauer's utopian ideas for courtroom reform, the
indeterminacy of the accused, nestled in the medium of
language, suspends judgment here. [22]

In Kluge's literary and cinematic cases, we learn what
one can cling to as a property of the law: it abstracts and
dematerializes the circumstances of life; it must be able
to systematically think along with initially insignificant
information (such as silence) and to resolve the vague-
ness of language. This failure of the legal text as a linguistic institution, however, makes it possible to prove

21 Thomas-Michael Seibert, *Gerichtsrede: Wirklichkeit und Möglichkeit
im forensischen Diskurs* (Berlin: Duncker & Humblot, 2004).
22 Valentin Mertes, "Dialogizität als medienästhetisches Verfahren," in
Formenwelt des Dialogs, ed. Christian Schulte and Winfried Siebers
(Göttingen: V & R unipress, 2016), p. 168.

ON THE RUN FROM THE LAW

the specific poetics of the case, which—unlike in literary texts—in the law do not hark back to a poetic intention. The poetics of the case are rather an expression of
the basic dilemma of justice between a singular event
and general law. It is this incompatibility between the
individual case and general law that makes the description of the thing to be dealt with in court directly —
which becomes particularly obvious when the case itself
becomes part of a literary work, which is "the case" in
the book, film and television productions by Kluge.

The Legal Jurisdiction of the University
versus Unauthorised People

But Anita G. continues to progress through institutions,
and the dialogue with them remains quite one-sided.
The integration of everyday truths, which the law can
suspend in legislation, but not in the actual application
of the law, determines the case:

> Close up: Anita, half from the front.
> Anita: Advice!
> Professor: Well, that depends. Sometimes no advice is bet-
> ter than bad advice. Of course good advice would be better
> than none, but you can't generalize.[23]

Even the university cannot help Anita G. In the secretar-
iat ("Open 9–12") she is instructed that she needs a university entrance qualification to study. In her consultation with the assistant professor (played by Alfred Edel),
she is asked how she ever came to the idea of studying
political science without being able to speak French.

In their text "Die Sprechstunde. Universität und Kooperation bei Alexander Kluge" ("The Consultation. University and Cooperation with Alexander Kluge"), Ursula

---

23 Alexander Kluge, *Abschied von gestern*, p. 55.

Geitner and Georg Stanitzek parallel Kluge's 1961 book *Kulturpolitik und Ausgabenkontrolle* (*Cultural Politics and Financial Control*), written in collaboration with lawyer Hellmut Becker, with an analysis of *Yesterday Girl*, showing ultimately that there is an inherent connection between the cases that Kluge and Becker devise for university law and the consultation that Alfred Edel holds as assistant professor: "Alfred Edel was an assistant professor for political science at the Johann Wolfgang Goethe University in Frankfurt am Main. He had his first film appearance in *Yesterday Girl*, where he plays a university assistant who assesses Anita G."[24] On this role of the university assistant, as Edel is so described in the text that accompanied the release of the film, Geitner and Stanitzek raise the following point:

> The secondary literature, the text from the DVD release, all assume that Edel is playing a university assistant here, but is that true? "A public prosecutor plays the public prosecutor, and it seems to be professors who play professors," a peculiar correspondence in *Yesterday Girl*, as noted by Peter Bichsel. After Alfred Edel moved from Munich to Frankfurt University in 1963, he was employed by political scientist Thomas Ellwein for a time as an assistant sinecure for the seminar on political education. It is more probable then, that the actor in the consultation scene is by no means playing an assistant professor corresponding to his own experience, but that instead he falls out of the role here: that Edel apes a vain professor at this point. [...] his behavior being purely ironic.[25]

24 Martin Weinmann and Alexander Kluge, *Neonröhren des Himmels* (Frankfurt am Main: Zweitausendeins, 2008), p. 9.
25 Ursula Geitner and Georg Stanitzek, "Die Sprechstunde. Universität und Kooperation bei Alexander Kluge," in *Chronik/Gefühle: Sieben Beiträge zu Alexander Kluge*, ed. Jürgen Fohrmann and Alexander Kluge (Bielefeld: Aisthesis Verlag, 2017), p. 149.

What Alfred Edel performs here in the case of Anita G. is of course not only the role of the professor, but also the formal assessor of Anita in her position as academically interested citizen. This scene is like something out of *Kulturpolitik und Ausgabenkontrolle* (*Cultural Politics and Financial Control*), yet somehow differentiated from the case study examples given by Kluge and Becker. The execution of the case in the film is much more categorical, less concerned with the question of costs of public administration, and more focused on the legal precedents for use of university facilities, not only in the sense of research and teaching, but in the sense of interest in education. Kluge's character Roswitha Bronski (also played by Alexandra Kluge) in his film *Part-Time Work of a Domestic Slave* (1973) issues a concrete challenge: Give me a place outside the family and outside existential coercion and I can change the world.

A board of auditors complains that university facilities are being used by unauthorized individuals, for example someone who is not a member of the university is conducting a scientific study using an institute and various libraries. Another board of auditors criticizes the fact that university members give concerts in the rooms of a physics institute. They point to the increased risk of accidents at such evening events.[26]

The lawyers Becker and Kluge comment on this case: "The university cannot be hermetic. It has a vibrancy that appeals beyond staff and students in the narrow sense. It is no misuse of the university for it to be open to private individuals involved in academic pursuits.

26 Hellmut Becker and Alexander Kluge, *Kulturpolitik und Ausgaben-kontrolle: zur Theorie und Praxis der Rechnungsprüfung* (Frankfurt am Main: Klostermann, 1961), p. 87.

It is not the task of the audit to limit the scope of the university."[27]

"The Klugean 'Kritik des Zusammenhangs' (Critique of Context)"[28]

Kluge explores the limits of what can be legally grasped. The institutions let Anita G. down, but they release her case into a new context that allows for decision, which transfers Kluge's film *Yesterday Girl* into a public decision-making process. The preface to Alexander Kluge's book *Das Labyrinth der zärtlichen Kraft* (*The Labyrinth of Tender Power*) begins with the sentence: "No matter what one says about a romantic relationship, its natural wealth of casuistry refutes it."[29]

Casuistry is therefore the power of refutation. The individual case is not only able to disprove the normative approach in general, by occurring as an incident that counters expectation—the case also refutes the wearing out of legal mechanisms of interpretation. And that is also where Alexander Kluge's work rebels against a general ability to be talked of in precise terms, against securing methodologies in secure methodological contexts, such as literary theory, didactics, jurisprudence, or historical scholarship—and thus also against a purely academic treatment of cases and objects in general. Because if the cases in Kluge's texts, films, streams, interviews and stories often take place within these institutions, then it is obviously, above all, in order to secretly undermine them. For even the case in the legal setting succeeds at that: it can be misplaced, falsely filed

---

27 Ibid.
28 I borrow this expression from Philipp Ekart, *Toward Fewer Images: The Work of Alexander Kluge* (Boston MA: The MIT Press, 2018), p. 154.
29 Alexander Kluge, *Das Labyrinth der zärtlichen Kraft: 166 Liebesgeschichten*, ed. Thomas Combrink (Frankfurt am Main: Suhrkamp, 2009), Preface.

away, forever in the darkest recesses of the collection, or get lost in the post. Cornelia Vismann writes this story in her book *Files*: "These acts—transmitting, storing, canceling, manipulating, and destroying—write the history of the law."[30]

---

30 Cornelia Vismann, *Files – Law and Media Technology*, trans. Geoffrey Winthrop-Young (Stanford CA: Stanford University Press, 2008), p. 14.

Transforming Law

Christoph Menke

Genealogy, Paradox, Transformation

Basic Elements of a Critique of Rights[1]

Why rights? Why are there rights, what's their mode of existence and what arises from the fact that (or if) they exist? These questions necessitate a response that is contradictory in itself. The response has to determine the form of rights in a way that both refutes and affirms, and thus defends it. For if we are to answer these questions by looking at the currently existing form of rights—that is, "subjective" rights within "bourgeois" law[2]—we will be led to a fundamental defect within this form: the bourgeois form of subjective rights is founded on a defect. From this defect results the fact that, within bourgeois law, rights are designed and practiced as rights of (or

---

1   First published in German in Andreas Fischer-Lescano, Hannah Franzki and Johan Horst, eds., *Gegenrechte* (Tübingen: Mohr Siebeck, 2018), pp. 13–31. The ideas presented in this essay are a first attempt at reacting to objections and questions that have been raised after I published my *Critique of Rights*; see Christoph Menke, *Kritik der Rechte* (Berlin: Suhrkamp, 2015); English translation Polity Press, 2020, forthcoming). I would like to thank the participants of a conference in Bremen in February 2017, to whom this essay owes a great deal. My thanks also go to the participants of workshops in Leipzig, Berlin, Frankfurt, Vienna and Bonn. See also Christoph Menke, Christian Schmidt and Benno Zabel, "Gespräch über die Möglichkeiten, Grenzen und Gefahren einer Politisierung der subjektiven Rechte," *Rechtsphilosophie. Zeitschrift für Grundlagen des Rechts* 1 (2017): pp. 54–79; as well as my responses to questions posed by Peter Moser relating to the transformation of rights in *Information Philosophie* (June 2017): pp. 88–90.
2   Bourgeois law meaning: the law of bourgeois society.

to) one's own [*Eigenrechte*³]. Yet by displaying the defect of the existing form of subjective rights, the possibility of another form of rights and thereby also the correct answer to the question "Why rights?" appears. This other determination of the form of rights is the determination of a new or "other law."

I would like to pick up this program of a critical discrimination of two opposing interpretations of rights (which, at the same time, are two opposing forms of politics) by explicating two lines of thought. The first line is concerned with the concept of critique. The task of critique is to discriminate, even decide between right and wrong; the critical approach is "discriminating and decisive."⁴ How does this critical discrimination between the two ways of interpreting the idea of rights—the bourgeois and the other law—operate? What is the criterion of this discrimination and how does it determine the relationship of these two forms of law? The second line, then, tries to elaborate a new determination of rights as a concept of an "other" law [*eines "anderen" Rechts*]. This new determination is a consequence of the critique of subjective rights: By displaying the defects of subjective rights, the critique works out the conditions of understanding them correctly. The critique of the form of subjective rights transforms the rights into the—completely altered—rights of the other law. The critique of rights thus opens up a space for a different, transformative politics of rights.

3   See *Kritik der Rechte*, chapter 9, for further details on this concept. The German term "Eigenrechte" is adopted from Robert Esposito, who speaks of "ius proprium." See Roberto Esposito, *Immunitas* (Cambridge: Polity Press, 1991), pp. 21–28.
4   Walter Benjamin, "Critique of Violence," in Walter Benjamin, *Selected Writings. Volume I, 1913–1926*, ed. Marcus Bullock and Michael W. Jennings (Cambridge MA: Harvard University Press, 1996), pp. 236–252, p. 251.

I.
1. The Genealogy of Form

The critique of rights methodologically pursues Marx's model of the critique of political economy as it is outlined in the first volume of *Capital*: "Political economy has indeed analysed value and its magnitude, however incompletely, and has uncovered the content concealed within these forms. But it has never once asked the question why this content has assumed that particular form, that is to say, why labour is expressed [*dargestellt*] in value [...]."[5] To say that the critique of rights pursues this model means that it proceeds *by analogy* with the critique of political economy; the critique of political economy is not the foundation of the critique of rights—it is thus not trying to trace back the rights to political economy and to explain their form by means of political economy.[6] Instead, the critique of rights has to do the same thing for (bourgeois) law that Marx did for (bourgeois) political economy. This analogy has three aspects.

(i) Marx's critique aims at political economy as a certain mode of analyzing the exchange value of a commodity in relation to other commodities. In like manner, the critique of subjective rights is a critique of a certain mode of analyzing the rights one person has in relation to another. The object of critique therefore is a certain mode of thinking: the predominant, bourgeois mode of grasping one person's rights in relation to other people's rights. This mode of thinking, as it is criticized here, is that of liberalism. The critique of political economy is the critique of economic liberalism, and the critique of subjective rights is the critique of juridical (so-called "political") liberalism.

---

5 Karl Marx, *Capital. A Critique of Political Economy. Volume One* (London: Penguin Books, 1976), pp. 173–174.
6 See Menke, *Kritik der Rechte*, pp. 266–270.

(ii) Bourgeois political economy, the object of Marx's critique, analyzes the exchange value of a commodity as a form that contains (or "hides") a certain content. This substance of exchange value is labor, a discovery Marx attributes to political economy. Similarly, the critique of rights criticizes juridical liberalism as a mode of analyzing the subjective rights of a person as a form containing a certain content. This content is the legal status of each individual, or, more precisely: The content of one person's rights in relation to another person's rights is the normative status of equality.

(iii) According to Marx, the critique of the analysis of value within the predominant, bourgeois political economy starts by posing a question "it [political economy, C.M.] has never once asked."[7] It is the question "why this content has assumed that particular form, why labour is expressed [*dargestellt*] in value."[8] The critique therefore targets a relation of presentation (and interrogates its procedure, effects and foundations) that has not even once been noticed by political economy. The question of form thus becomes vital: Exchange value is a specific form of the presentation of labor (which is its content). The critique of juridical liberalism proceeds accordingly: It all boils down to posing the question never once posed by liberalism, namely, why the status of equality is presented as the subjective right of a person. Why has this content assumed that particular form? Why even talk about (subjective) rights when talking about equality?

These three aspects of the critique of rights constitute a sequence of three consecutive steps, understood correctly only in conjunction with each other. The critique (i) opposes a certain mode of thinking, an ideology: It opposes the presentation of legal actuality within the predominant bourgeois, i.e. liberal thought. But then it

7   Marx, *Capital*, p. 174.
8   Ibid.

turns out (ii) that the legal actuality itself has to be conceived as presentation: It is not a mere fact, but a form containing a hidden content that, in turn, is presented (the content of the subjective rights of one person is his or her legal status of equality). "Critique" means reading presentations, or, to be more precise: In its process of reading, critique transforms that which appears to be merely given into something that is being presented. The concept of presentation not only serves the purpose of differentiating between (hidden) content and (appearing) figure, but inserts a second discrimination into this relation: the discrimination between, on the one hand, the content which appears as a certain figure and, on the other hand, the mode of this appearance. It is therefore a discrimination between the content and the mode of presentation.[9] By reading existence as a presentation, critique extrapolates *how* exactly—in which form—it is that content is presented. According to Marx, only this second discrimination between content and form is the critical discrimination (the bourgeois political economy had already discovered labor to be the hidden content of value).

To read what is given as something that is presented also means understanding presentation as an act of giving form, as formation. Reading what is given as a form of presentation thus means reading it as a presentation of a presentation—a presentation of the mode of presentation. Critique reads form as its self-presentation. We thus (iii) open up a field of questions that concern the generation of the predominant form of presentation. Where, when and how does the genesis of the form of subjective rights as the form of normative equality take place? Which act gave birth to this form? Which presuppositions allowed for the highly unlikely conversion of the idea of equality into the form of subjective rights to

9   Marx uses the concept of form (in the passage quoted above) ambiguously: both for the figure and the mode of appearance of the content.

occur? Why is this content—equality—presented in *this* form—the form of subjective rights? The critical interrogation of form therefore opens up a possibility of either not carrying out this type of presentation at all or carrying it out differently. This possibility, at first, is logical, but it might become practical, as well. It is the possibility of *not* presenting the content of equality in the form of subjective rights, but in a different way.

The critical examination of form crucially relies on the ability to conceive actuality as a presentation, to conceive reality as a representation and thus call it into question. Like the critique of political economy, the critique of the liberalism of subjective rights does not challenge an ideology, a false presentation of legal actuality. Instead, it consists of nothing but displaying the operation of presentation that is constitutive of legal actuality. The critique reads the form of subjective rights as the mode in which the status of equality presents itself within the given actuality, that is, within bourgeois law. (Conversely, bourgeois political economy and legal liberalism are ideology and actuality *at once*: Ideology and actuality have the same structure.) The critique of liberalism does not suggest that it distorts the legal actuality. On the contrary: It proposes to conceive of liberalism as—merely—repeating legal actuality; i.e. to conceive of liberalism as performing the *same* operation of presentation *again* that has brought about the legal actuality in the form of subjective rights. Liberalism thus obscures its mode of presentation—as a presentation of a content in a specific form. By merely repeating the presentation brought about by the form of subjective rights within legal actuality, liberalism transforms the presentation into something that is simply given. This is the "uncritical positivism"[10] of liberalism.

10 As Marx remarks with regard to "Hegel's later works"—especially the *Elements of the Philosophy of Right*—it is exactly this "uncritical positivism" that, at the same time, is an "uncritical idealism," because it transforms the given order into something that is self-evident and in-

2. Critique and Paradox

The critique of bourgeois or subjective rights is an examination of the formation processes which produce them. Or, to be more precise, it is an examination of the processes that give a specific form of presentation to the "content" of equality. In doing so, the method of the critique of rights resembles Marx's understanding of "true criticism" in contrast to "vulgar criticism."[11] According to Marx, vulgar criticism "struggles with its object."[12] By judging it from outside, vulgar critique opposes its object and sets itself against it. In doing so, vulgar criticism takes its object as a mere given, as positively existing. Vulgar criticism is as positivistic as the liberalism it criticizes. True criticism, on the other hand, tries to comprehend the "inner genesis" of subjective rights: "It [true criticism, C.M.] describes the act of its birth. Thus, true philosophical criticism [...] not only shows the contradictions as existing, but explains them, conceives their genesis and necessity."[13] The genesis of subjective rights lies in the fact and the way that they generate themselves as presentation (of the content of equality)—while simultaneously obscuring their being as presentation, which is the process of their formation. By problematizing existence, "true criticism" is, according to Marx, the genealogical explanation of its emergence (understood as the act of formation of a content). This definition though leads us to a next question, namely: How it is that a genealogical explanation of existence—what Marx calls the explanation of its "necessity"—is supposed to be its critique, rejecting it as false?

disputable. See Karl Marx, "Economic and Philosophic Manuscripts of 1844," in Karl Marx and Friedrich Engels, *Economic and Philosophic Manuscripts of 1844 and the Communist Manifesto* (New York: Prometheus Books, 1988), pp. 13–168, p. 148.

11 Karl Marx, *Critique of Hegel's 'Philosophy of Right'* (Cambridge: Cambridge University Press, 2009), p. 92. Translation altered.

12 Ibid.

13 Ibid., translation altered.

A first response to this question locates the critical power of genealogical explanations in dissolving the appearance of givenness [*Gegebenheitsschein*] of existence, whereas vulgar critique merely reproduces this appearance. The genealogical interpretation of the processes of formation consequently is critical in an ontological way: it is anti-positivistic (because it, to quote Adorno, reads the things in being as being-in-becoming—as something that has become and thus is becoming).[14] This leads us to the conclusion that things could possibly be much different. Genealogy ascertains the contingency of existence: Equality doesn't have to appear in the form of subjective rights. It could, in principle, be presented differently. But if Luhmann is right and it does not at all follow from the possibility that everything could be different that it also can be judged as wrong and changed, this is not enough for a critique of subjective rights.[15] The critique of subjective rights is not simply anti-positivistic and conscious of contingency. Rather, we can only speak of a genealogical examination, if it reasserts something that vulgar critique was only able to achieve in a "dogmatic" way: a militant opposition to the existing order, i.e. if it judges between what is right and what is wrong. This critical opposition is "vulgar," if it separates right from wrong externally, judging what is wrong by relying on a presupposed concept of what is right. If the genealogical examination is to be critical or even "true criticism" (as Marx understood it), it has to determine the concept of falsehood—the falsehood of subjective rights—differently, in a non-vulgar manner.

14 Theodor W. Adorno, *Negative Dialectics* (London and New York: Routledge, 2004), p. 52: "It is when things in being are read as a text of their becoming."
15 "Everything could be different – but I can change almost nothing"—this is how Luhmann puts the insight into the contingency of existence. See Niklas Luhmann, "Komplexität und Demokratie," in Niklas Luhmann, *Politische Planung. Aufsätze zur Soziologie von Politik und Planung* (Opladen: Westdeutscher Verlag, 1971), p. 44; translation Aaron Zielinski.

If we think of genealogy as the discovery of contingency, then the falsehood of the existing order is the appearance of its positivity, that is, the appearance of its necessity: that equality can only be presented in the form of subjective rights; that subjective rights are not a *specific* form of the presentation of equality. That it can or could be different, though, does not mean that it *should* be different. Yet this is exactly what the critique of subjective rights claims. But at the same time—and if we follow Marx's differentiation of vulgar and true, dogmatic and genealogical critique—the critique of the form of subjective rights can*not* take the approach of criticizing the form in the name of a presupposed norm of rightness. The genealogical approach of critique thus faces a dilemma: As a mode of critique, it wants to refute subjective rights on grounds of their falsehood. Yet it can't refute them dogmatically by juxtaposing a right form in opposition to the wrong form.[16] This dilemma is solved by criticizing positivism more fundamentally than the genealogical conscience of contingency is able to, leading to a fundamentally different interpretation of the critical concept of falsehood.[17]

For the positivism of rights does not simply consist in the fact that it appears as the only possible way to present the content of equality. Rather, it consists in the way this form implements the basic operation that is constitutive of the modern concept of law. This is the operation of its self-reflection; modern law is self-reflective law. The self-reflection constitutive of modern law is its mode of developing procedures and forms that

16 To put this in other terms, this means that the critique of rights itself cannot proceed in a legal form [*rechtsförmig*]. Law is the original model of critique, that is, of the normative decision between right and wrong. The critique of rights cannot pursue this legal model of critique: Critique does not, as does a judge, stand above the conflicting parties, deciding between right and wrong. The critique of rights thus has to be a critique of law as well as its practice of critique—a critique of the (legality [*Rechtsförmigkeit*] of) critique.

17 For the following, see Menke, *Kritik der Rechte*, chapters 5–7 and 9.

present law as being different from the non-legal [*Nicht-rechtliches*] within law. To put it differently, these procedures and forms within law refer to the violence of law, because law cannot act normatively on the non-legal. Law is related to its exterior, to the non-legal, not in the form of law, but in a form of external efficacy: in the mode of violence.[18] When we talk about the form of subjective rights being positivistic, this basically refers to the operation of self-reflection of modern law: Its form is positivistic in the way it carries out the modern self-reflection of law and represents the non-legal within law. For the form of subjective rights represents the non-legal within law, *as if* it were a given; it produces the "myth of the given" (Wilfrid Sellars) that Adorno called "positivism." The bourgeois form of law is *practicing* this myth of the given: Subjective rights are representations of the non-legal—interests, needs, identities etc.—within law, taking that which is represented to be pre-existing instead of being changed by being represented by the law. The form of subjective rights produces the appearance of givenness, of its immutability, of that which they entitle to. Subjective rights exist *in order to* prevent what they entitle to from ever changing; they immunize against critique and against a transformative practice.

According to this conception, the positivism of subjective rights runs much deeper than the critique of its obliviousness of contingency [*Kontingenzvergessenheit*] suggested. Their positivism consists in giving an illusionary status to that which they entitle to: the positivism of subjective rights is an effect of the relationship

18 See Christoph Menke, *Recht und Gewalt* (Berlin: August Verlag, 2011), and the critical debate in Christoph Menke, *Law and Violence. Christoph Menke in Dialogue* (Manchester: Manchester University Press, 2018).

of this form to its matter.[19] This relationship is determined by the way subjective rights carry out the act of
self-reflection that defines modern law: The subjective
rights carry out the self-reflection of law by representing that which is different from law within law, while
simultaneously treating that which is represented as
being predetermined and immutable. The form of subjective rights is thus positivistic *by* being self-reflective,
or in being self-reflective, it is naturalizing at the same
time (since "nature" is that which is presupposed by the
legal norm as being immutable).[20] This is exactly what
marks the falsehood of the form of subjective rights. The
form is wrong because it contradicts or disguises itself.
It carries out its self-reflection—representing the non-
legal within law—and it doesn't carry out (or even disguises) the self-reflection; for by treating the non-legal
as a given, it covers up that it's only given for and within
the self-reflection of law—and that it therefore is, in fact,
not pre-existing. The positivism of the subjective rights
is the implementation of the self-reflection of law that
denies this same self-reflection (and therefore: itself).

Yet the critical concept of falsehood—the way of calling the form of subjective rights wrong—we have hereby
developed, still seems to be a "vulgar" concept. For it
seems to compare subjective rights with the norm of
non-contradiction (in the way Marx described "vulgar

19 The *content* of the subjective rights is the normative status of equality. Its *matter*, on the other hand, is that to which they entitle: the
interests or needs or freedom, or, more generally, the performances
(ordinarily acts or omissions) in which they are realized.

20 This is not supposed to mean that the matter of subjective rights—
that to which they entitle—is immutable *per se*: That which subjective rights reify by presupposing it (as being given quasi-naturally)
does alter *itself*. It alters in the way nature changes; it alters itself
through evolution. Subjective rights are a dynamic form that display [*abbilden*] social, cultural and economic alterations within the
law. But they presuppose these alterations, naturalize them and thus
withdraw them from conscious (and thus political) control through
the law.

criticism"[21]): The norm of the critique of subjective rights seems to be that the self-reflection of modern law has to be realized in a non-contradictory way. But it only seems that way when the concept of self-reflection is defined insufficiently. The operation of self-reflection does not consist in going back to a foundation [*Grund*] of law and thus restoring the identity of law with itself. Rather, it consists in presenting and unfolding the way in which law differs from the non-legal—within the law. The operation of self-reflection is carrying out a paradox: the difference *between* law and the non-legal *within* law.

If the form of subjective rights thus is wrong because it both disguises and denies the self-reflection of this form (interrupting the self-reflection and depriving it of its transforming power); and if the self-reflection of law is nothing but the process of the paradox (which is the presentation of the difference of law and the non-legal within law) then the form of subjective rights is wrong, because it disguises the paradox that both defines and constitutes it. The positivistic falsehood of the form of subjective rights is the denial of its paradox. This is the critical judgement of the genealogical analysis of its processes of formation. "True critique" judges the form of subjective rights; critique finds the form to be wrong. But this judgement states that the form of subjective rights neither expresses nor performs the paradox that constitutes and generates this form. *That's why* it is wrong. The norm of true critique is the paradox at the foundation of the criticized: it criticizes in the name of the paradox.

---

21 Marx's example of a vulgar critique is the critique of the bourgeois constitution: "Thus, for example, it criticizes the constitution, drawing attention to the opposition of the powers etc. It finds contradictions everywhere. But criticism that struggles with its opposite remains dogmatic criticism, as for example in earlier times, when the dogma of the Blessed Trinity was set aside by appealing to the contradiction between 1 and 3." (Marx, *Critique of Hegel's 'Philosophy of Right'*, p. 92) Vulgar critique, by refuting the dogma on the grounds of self-contradiction, operates in the name of a dogma itself: the norm of non-contradiction that is externally set against that which it criticizes.

II.
1. An Other Law

The bourgeois, liberal political economy "discovered" labor to be the "hidden content" of exchange value. The critique of political economy only begins after this discovery has been made. The critical insight does not consist in revealing hidden contents, but in posing "the question why this content has assumed that particular form, that is to say, why labour is expressed [*dargestellt*] in value."[22] The critical question of the form thus surpasses the question of the content. Yet it simultaneously presupposes the determination of the content. The insight of the bourgeois political economy—that labor is presented as value—persists. Similarly, when the critique of subjective rights poses the critical question of their form, it presupposes the liberal insight that equality is the content of this form.

The critique of subjective rights thus recognizes that they have a twofold foundation: a contentual and a formal foundation. The contentual foundation is the equality of everyone; as to their content, subjective rights are egalitarian. The formal foundation of subjective rights is the positivistic self-distortion of the paradox of the self-reflection of law. In their form, subjective rights are naturalizing. The critique discovers, by analyzing the "inner genesis" of this form, that subjective rights are both egalitarian *and* naturalizing. The "discriminating and decisive approach" (Benjamin) of critique refers to the twofold foundation of subjective rights. It judges them by tracing them back to their foundation, which is in itself divided.

---

22 See above. The (true) critic is no "secret agent in a higher service," whose "art" it is to "expose what is hidden." See Søren Kierkegaard, "Repetition," in Søren Kierkegaard, *Fear and Trembling. Repetition. Kierkegaard's Writings*, VI, ed. Howard V. Hong and Edna H. Hong (Princeton NJ: Princeton University Press, 1983), p. 135.

But *how* does the critical decision relate to the doubling at the foundation of law? This critical reference can be understood in two very different ways. According to the first approach, the discriminating operation of critique consists in separating the two sides of the foundation; firstly showing how subjective rights on the one hand have an egalitarian content, whilst having naturalizing effects of the form on the other—and then taking a stand *for* the egalitarian content and *against* the naturalizing form of law. According to the first approach, it is thus possible to liberate the egalitarian content of the subjective rights from this form and to realize it without the form.

According to the second view, the critical decision proceeds differently: It doesn't decide between content and form of the subjective rights. Rather, the decision takes place *within* their form. It discriminates between the paradox of the self-reflection of law and the self-distortion as the positivism of subjective rights. The first approach of the critique of subjective rights abandons the self-reflection constitutive of modern law by abandoning their form. It wants to attain equality without self-reflection, without the paradox of self-reflective law. In its second approach, however, critique liberates both the egalitarian content *and* the self-reflection of law from the depoliticized naturalization with which the subjective rights immobilize both of them.[23] The program of this second figure of critique thus demands the equality of everyone to be realized in a way that simultaneously realizes the fact that everyone is different from the law, by being the non-legal. While, in its first approach, the critique of subjective rights tries to elimi-

23 See Christoph Menke, "Subjektive Rechte: Zur Paradoxie der Form," in Gunther Teubner, ed., *Nach Jacques Derrida und Niklas Luhmann. Zur (Un-)Möglichkeit einer Gesellschaftstheorie der Gerechtigkeit* (Stuttgart: Lucius & Lucius, 2008), pp. 101–102. For a shortened and revised translation of this essay see Christoph Menke, "The Self-Reflection of Law and the Politics of Rights," in *Constellations*, 2 (June 2011): pp. 124–134.

nate the form of law to liberate its egalitarian content, in its second approach it wants to attain a radically different form of law. This form of law is the presentation of the self-reflection of law. This presentation can either distort that which it presents, or express and unfold it. This is the alternative, the decision the critique of rights proposes: It can either immobilize the paradox of self-reflective law by naturalizing it, or it can perform it *as* paradox. The critical decision against the naturalizing distortion or even repression of the self-reflection of law thus demands that the form of law should not be abandoned, but be thought of differently. This has to be done by redefining rights as "counterrights" [*Gegenrechte*].

The method of critical analysis guides us away from the predominant, bourgeois form of subjective rights and towards their doubly redoubled foundation [*doppelt gedoppelter Grund*]. The foundation of subjective rights is, on the one hand, the content of equality and, on the other hand, its presentation in a form that contradicts itself by both presupposing and disguising its constitutive and paradoxical act. The critique thus shows in what way subjective rights are wrong. They contradict their own concept—by disguising the paradox that is constitutive of them. In doing so, the critique of subjective rights proposes a counter-program that combines the egalitarian content and the self-reflective paradox of modern law, conceiving them as being unabridged and unaltered; this is the program of an other law. Yet equality and self-reflection cannot be conceived of as being integrated in one form. Rather, an other law is required that asymmetrically combines two very different forms. The other law is not homogeneous; it consists of the tension between two opposed types of law: constitutionalizing laws [*Verfassungsgesetze*] and counterrights.[24]

---

24 See Menke, *Kritik der Rechte*, chapter 15.

(i) *Constitutionalizing laws*—more precisely: rules and norms that are constitutional and constitutionaliz-ing[25]—define and organize the order of practices, if they are to be successful. Constitutionalizing laws define the good and the success of a practice by determining the roles by which practices and institutions are realized. In doing so, they ensure the equality of every partici-pant, which is realized precisely in the difference of their practical and institutional roles, if this difference evolves from nothing but the structure of successful practice (i.e. corresponds with the factual difference of the division of labor). The two normative aspects of the equality of social participants and of the success of a social practice thus coincide in constitutionalizing laws. These laws deter-mine the structure of a social practice in a way that every participant is regarded as equal (considered or counted as an equal), in so far as he or she is not subjected to anyone—that is: to no one but *the* Other, the success of the social practice. What these laws achieve is that they address each and every one *as* "part" (Marx) and thus ensure their participation. This necessarily implies the participation in the political processes in which the form of the practice itself is up for decision. At the same time, the legal constitutionalization of social practices has to be the constitutionalization of political (meta-)practices with which the social practices govern themselves.

(ii) *Counterrights* vest the power of objecting against the social participation that is organized in an egalitar-ian way by laws, which are constitutional of practice, and that is thus secured for each and every one. More precisely, counterrights authorize non-participation in the social practice, that is, they protect the capacity and will not to participate, they authorize the impuissance of those who don't participate. This authorization of the

---

25 See Gunther Teubner, *Constitutional Fragments: Societal Constitu-tionalism and Globalization* (Oxford: Oxford University Press, 2012).

antisocial by means of counterrights is the operation of self-reflection that is constitutive of the form of modern law. Counterrights are supposed to assert—within the normative order or practices through law—that each and every one is not only an equal social participant, but also radically unequal, a non-participant. The constitutionalizing laws organize a social practice and ensure equal participation; the counterrights open up and ensure spaces (or times) of non-participation.

2. Other Rights

Both elements of the other law—and especially their double relation of opposition and coincidence—require a much more precise definition, which I can't provide here.[26] Instead, I would like to elaborate on the way this

26 One aspect of this more precise definition is the clarification of the difference and the overlapping of two dialectics of participation and non-participation:
1. The success of the political decision to constitutionalize a social practice through laws requires the equal participation of every one. At the same time, each decision produces an asymmetric discrimination between those who approve of it and those who reject it. For every political decision is disputed, and thus established against the will of a disputing minority party. Since the political decision about the legal constitution of a practice is binding for everyone, it has to be binding for the defeated party that rejected it and that now can't participate fully in the constituted order, as well. Regulating the social through means of constitutionalizing laws always produces semi- or non-participants. The liberty of the political government of the social cannot presuppose that everyone approves of its current order. Rather, it has to be constitutionalized by laws that empower everyone to question the decision and by reopening the decision process—thus proceeding to a position of social participation from the position of social semi- or non-participation.
2. Different from this first dialectic is the possibility of non-participation ensured by the counterrights. This possibility, again, is dialectically related to participation: it doesn't relate to it externally, but is produced by it. Yet in this second relationship of participation and non-participation, this doesn't happen in the mode of necessity or force, but in the mode of freedom. The non-participation ensured by counterrights is not enforced, but desired for the sake of a successful practice. While constitutionalizing laws produce non-participation by organizing social participation that is revisable through the

concept of an other law implicates a different concept of rights. In order to understand this different concept of rights, it is crucial to look at the relationship between the two fundamental meanings of the term "law"—in Hobbes's terms: between *"jus* and *lex*, *right* and *law*."[27] This discrimination, even contraposition, is the starting point of modern law.

The other law can be presented in two different ways. The first mode of presentation is negative; it determines the other law to be the opposite of the bourgeois form of subjective rights. This opposition consists in the fact that subjective rights are based on that which is one's own [*das Eigene der Einzelnen*], while the other law is based on the success of social practice. The second mode of presentation is positive; it describes the other law to be the adequate realization of the modern idea of rights (that has been exposed at the foundation of subjective rights by critical genealogy).[28] The modern idea of rights connects the content of equality with the self-reflection of law and the egalitarian empowerment of everyone with the recognition of the non-legal in each and every one. According to the second (positive) presentation, the other law is the redemption of this program: The other law realizes the idea of rights; it is the true law of rights.

processualization of political participation, counterrights are supposed to empower non-participation and deprive the political self-governance of the practice from access to non-participation.

Conceptually these two cases can be distinguished, empirically they merge.

27 Thomas Hobbes, *Leviathan* (Oxford: Oxford University Press, 2008), p. 86. Right and law are opposed to each other "because RIGHT, consisteth in liberty to do, or to forbear: whereas LAW, determineth, and bindeth to one of them." (ibid.) For a further discussion, see Menke, *Kritik der Rechte*, pp. 19–22.

28 Critique thus is the unity of negative and positive presentation: Since the other law originates from the critique of bourgeois law and since the critique of bourgeois law exposes the antagonism—and the antagonism with its antagonism [*Widerstreit mit seinem Widerstreit*]— at its foundation, it also leads to a form of an other law that doesn't dissolve this antagonism, but fulfills it. The fact that there are both a negative and a positive presentation of the other law follows from the previously outlined program of critique.

I will now make two brief statements concerning the positive presentation of the other law. At the center of these remarks lies the thesis that the other law is the true redemption of the modern idea of rights. The new or other form of rights that emerges can be characterized by two traits. The other form of rights (i) is doubled within itself: it only consists of the tension, the antagonism of two opposed types of form or logic. The other form of rights (ii) is determined by its status as being derived: Rights within the other law are not primary, but secondary—they have their meaning and their foundation in contributing to the lawful facilitation of successful social practices.

(i) The modern idea of laws consists in connecting the equality of law with the self-reflection of law. Equality is the content of rights. The self-reflection of law refers to its matter, which is recognized by the law as not being law and which is thus liberated from the normativity of law.[29] Subjective rights want to realize the double claim of equality and self-reflection in *one* stroke, in one and the same form. That's why bourgeois law defines rights as proper rights: They are rights to that which is one's own. In bourgeois law, every legal claim is understood as a claim for being able to realize—like everyone else, that is, in an egalitarian way—what one wants and what determines and constitutes one as an individual—that which thus is one's own. An equal entitlement is understood as an entitlement to realize that which is one's own, which thus is withdrawn from every common, normative and reasonable decision (that is, it is naturalized).

The conception of an other law conceives the individual entitlements that are both egalitarian and reflexively liberating in a different way. It understands them to be solely realizable as a discrimination of two opposing forms of entitlement. On the one hand, they are rights

---

29 See footnote 18 for the concepts of "content" and "matter."

to equally participate. They are generated by the laws which constitute practice [*praxisverfassende Gesetze*] and lie at the heart of the other law. The laws that constitutionalize social practices determine the forms of conduct, the implementation of which realize these practices. The facilitation of actions that lead to a successful practice is thus the entitlement of each individual to participate in this practice. Organizing practices through law means empowering [*ermächtigen*] and entitling [*berechtigen*] each individual.[30] This entitlement is extensive: It cannot lie in being the empowerment to assume a (pre-)determined role in a practice. Instead, it necessarily includes the freedom of every individual to (co-)determine his or her participation; since only the

---

30 This would indicate the objection that the other law—which is based on the social practice and its success—can only provide for the empowerment or justification of those who are already participants in a particular social practice. The equality of participation warranted by the other law would thus be limited: It would be the same right of the participants, but not the same right *to* participate. Therefore, the objection is that the other law cannot perceive of the "right to have rights" which, according to Hannah Arendt, is the "only human right." See Hannah Arendt, "'The Rights of Man': What Are They?," *Modern Review* 3:1 (1949): pp. 24–36. In order to reject this objection, we have to justify the thesis that the right of each and every one to participate in a social practice does *not* have its basis in a natural interest in or in a desire of every human being for social participation. If that were the case, the right to have rights would indeed be a subjective right or a proper right. A positive thesis corresponds to this negative thesis, namely that the definition of humans, which underlies the right to have rights, can only be won from the perspective that is from *within* the social practice. This is the definition of human beings as social beings: Every human always already *is* a social participant. This is the basis of his or her right to *become* a participant in a social practice, in which to participate he or she is denied. See Christoph Menke, "Die 'Aporien der Menschenrechte' und das 'einzige Menschenrecht'. Zur Einheit von Hannah Arendts Argumentation," in Eva Geulen et al., eds., *Hannah Arendt und Giorgio Agamben. Parallelen, Perspektiven, Kontroversen* (Munich: Fink, 2008), pp. 131–148; as well as "Zurück zu Hannah Arendt – die Flüchtlinge und die Krise der Menschenrechte," *Merkur* 7 (July 2016): pp. 49–58.By thinking of the rights of individuals in the context of the success of a social practice, the other law necessarily includes the right (of every human being) to have rights (of socially participating): This (sole) human right is a consequence of the concept of human beings that is based on the idea of a successful practice.

participants of a practice can determine what counts as its success. Constitutionalizing laws generate rights of participation that are both rights to participate in social practices as well as rights to participate in the political practices that regulate social participation.

The second form of rights of the other law are counter-rights. They realize the self-reflective recognition of the non-legal within law by empowering individuals to not participate in the social practice. In doing so, they take up a determination that is fundamental to the concept of rights. This is the moment of antagonism, of adver-sation: Rights are addressed at or against (*adversus*) an addressee. This thought derives from the origins of rights in proper rights. Here rights are claims of one per-son against another (or multiple others). With the con-cept of subjective rights, the antagonism is transferred to the relationship of the individual and the community it belongs to. The bourgeois concept of subjective rights can only understand this as a matter of that which is one's own, something that is prior or even external to the law and thus natural. The concept of counterrights conceives legal adversation differently: counterrights restrict the participation of the individual in a social practice, but they do so in the name of the social prac-tice. Just like the rights to participate, counterrights—that secure the non-participation in a social practice—serve the success of a social practice. For the success of the practice not only requires the participation of the individuals, but also its interruption and suspension by means of non-participation. Empowering the individual and liberating it of the social practice is nothing but the self-limitation of this practice.

(ii) What is at stake in the modern idea of rights is both the egalitarian and the liberating empowerment of the individual. Within the bourgeois concept of sub-jective rights, this empowerment is conceived of from the standpoint of the individual: subjective rights are based in what the individual is and wants prior to the law, i.e. naturally. In the other law, the rights of the individual have a different foundation and a different form. Like subjective rights, they are the entitlement *of* individuals[31], but not *due to* that which is their own. The rights of the other law much rather empower the individual based on the success of a social practice.

This opposition at the foundation and thus in the meaning and the form of rights—between the rights of the other law and the subjective rights of bourgeois law—can be summarized as follows:

- Subjective rights are the answer to the following question: How can the individual realize that which is his or her own? Which possibilities—spaces and opportunities—have to be ensured so that the individual can do so? The fact *that* it is his or her own is presupposed; it is the natural starting point of law.
- The other law starts with a different question: How can the success of social practices be organized by the laws that constitutionalize them? Which actions (and spaces of non-action) are necessary and how are they to be determined, limited and combined so that practices succeed? To which actions (and non-actions) must individuals be empowered—and which rights do they therefore need?

The rights of the individual, which are generated by the other law, thus have a different kind of foundation and a different kind of purpose: They are *derived* from the success of the social practice (and not from that which is the one's own). They *serve* the purpose of rendering the suc-

---

31 Can entitled and empowered individuals only be conceived of as able subjects? Is the legal concept of a person tied to the concept of a subject and its capacity to act? Or is this conjunction of (legal) person and (capable) subject a relic of the conception of subjective rights and should it thus be discarded, as well, once we redraft the status of the individual? The cost could be too high: It could mean that we depoliticize the law. See Christoph Menke, "Warum Rechte? Eine Bemerkung zu Malte-Christian Gruper," *Zeitschrift für Medien und Kommunikation* 7 (2016): pp. 71–76.

cess of a social practice possible (and they don't ensure or secure that which is one's own). This is what the rights of the individual are committed to in their justification and their execution. In the other law, the rights—the entitlement or empowerment of the individual or individuals—are neither constitutionalizing, nor are they unconditional. Referring to a right someone "has," will, in the other law, mean nothing else but referring to the condition of the success of a social practice. Whoever might say: This is my right, will actually say: This is the condition of a successful practice. The other law does not dispose of the rights of the individual. What it does is that it pushes them to the margins: They are neither center nor foundation of the law, but its effect. This is precisely how the other law ensures and secures them.

3. Outlines of a Transformative Politics of Rights

The genealogical critique of subjective rights shows that they have a doubly doubled foundation. Their substantial foundation is equality, the foundation of their form is the naturalizing distortion of the self-reflection of law. This doubling of the foundation is in accordance with the fundamental, inextricable ambiguity of their relation with politics, which Marx has described as the "puzzle"[32] of the bourgeois form of rights and which Wendy Brown has called their "paradox."[33] Politically, the form of subjective rights is determined by a self-contradiction: Because of their egalitarian content,

---

[32] See Karl Marx, "On the Jewish Question," in Karl Marx and Friedrich Engels, *Collected Works, Volume 3* (London: Lawrence & Wishart, 2010), pp. 146–174, p. 164.

[33] See Wendy Brown, "Suffering Rights as Paradoxes," *Constellations* 2 (2000): pp. 208–229. The paradox Wendy Brown describes is *not* the same paradox that I have described as the effect of the modern self-reflection of law. The paradox, as described by Wendy Brown, is a consequence of the defect of subjective rights that is rooted in the positivistic disguise of the self-reflection of law.

subjective rights are politicizing. They are a powerful instrument to transform society in an egalitarian way. For demanding rights (to something and for someone) means demanding equal rights. Demands for rights are demands for an empowerment in the name of equality. However, subjective rights are depoliticizing because of their form, which derives from the naturalizing and positivistic self-distortion of the self-reflection of law. For this is how they extract the political determination and transformation from the matter—what they entitle to— of law. It is that which is one's own that one can dispose of at one's convenience.

Due to this self-contradiction of the bourgeois form of rights, it is not sufficient to determine the politics of equality (or the politics of emancipation) as a "responsibility" of "inventing new laws."[34] Yet this determination is not only insufficient, because they "always remain inadequate for what I [Jacques Derrida, C.M.] call justice (which is not the same thing as law, even if it has to guide the history and progress of law)."[35] Rather, determining the politics of egalitarian emancipation through the invention of new rights is insufficient, because this determination leaves open in what way these rights are new. Are they rights with a new matter and with new bearers—e.g. rights to access for those who had hitherto been excluded—but in an old form? The emancipatory strategy of inventing new rights will then just relive the old experience of all the bourgeois revolutions that have established subjective rights as the basic form of the normative order: Namely, that they have a depoliticizing effect due to the legal form in which they have made their emancipatory demands, because this legal form generates zones within the social order that are withdrawn from

34 Jacques Derrida, "Not Utopia, the Im-possible," in Jacques Derrida, *Paper Machine* (Stanford CA: Stanford University Press, 2005), pp. 121–135, p. 124.
35 Ibid.

political determination and transformation. Due to this political self-contradiction of subjective rights, it is not sufficient to define the politics of egalitarian emancipation as yet another invention of new rights. One has to question the form of these rights.

But can the politics of inventing new rights not also be understood in a way that it not only generates new matters and new bearers of rights, but that it rather generates a new form? And thus as a politics of altering or transforming the form of rights? The politics of inventing new rights would then neither be the mere articulation of new contents in an old form, nor would it already be instituting an other law. The politics of inventing new rights would neither be a mere reform of what is given, nor would it already be the revolutionary introduction of an other law. Rather, the politics of inventing new rights would be understood as a politics *between* two forms, as a politics not of a transition from one form to another, but of an active transformation of one into the other. The politics of inventing new rights would be the start of a politics of the transformation of form: a politics of transforming the legal form.

Such a politics of altering the form can only work with what's already there. And what's there is subjective rights. Transformative politics thus applies and thereby inverts subjective rights against the logic of their own form. It is a politics of applying the existing form of subjective rights in an argumentative and strategic way *as if* we already were dealing with the rights of a new form, the rights of an other law. Transformative politics then is a politics of anticipation. It counterfactually anticipates the other law within the existing law. It is a politics of fiction (or of imagination).[36]

36 See the analyses of political strategies of litigation by Malte-C. Gruber, Johan Horst, Kolja Möller, Hannah Franzki and Tatjana Sheplyakova, in Fischer-Lescano, Franzki and Horst, eds., *Gegenrechte*, pp. 205–324.

The strategic application of subjective rights against the logic of their own form can obviously not be understood as separating the two contradictory sides that are combined by the form of subjective rights, holding on to the one side—the egalitarian politicization—while disposing of the other—the naturalizing depoliticization. The political self-contradiction of subjective rights cannot be dissolved within this form, for it consists of the intentions of egalitarian politicization changing into the opposite (namely: only due to the form of subjective rights, in which this wants to realize itself). This reversal into positivism and the ensuing depoliticization takes place exactly at the point where the newly obtained egalitarian empowerment functions (and is used) in a way that it entitles the individual to claim that something is its own and thus withdrawing it from political judgement and transformation. This reversal always takes place in the form of subjective rights; no use of this form, however reflected it might be, can prevent this from happening. But it can occur sooner or later. The transformative politics, which can start its work by using the existing form of subjective rights, tries to postpone or delay this reversal. It produces a gap between the two paradoxically entangled characteristics of egalitarian politicization and naturalizing depoliticization that are constitutive of subjective rights. This gap is a free space, where the fiction—that we already have obtained the other law—can evolve. Only those legal strategies can contribute to generating the other law, which, against every realism, assume that it's already here.

Translated by Aaron Zielinski

Benno Zabel

The Anarchy of Rights

On the Dialectic of Freedom and Authority

1. Reality and Ideology

The idea of legal *critique* is closely connected to the diagnosis of a *crisis*, namely, the crisis of political liberalism. This crisis is manifest in the relation between state and society, right and politics, subject and power. The implication of this crisis is the increasing juridification of social relations, the alienation of the individual from self-determined interests and needs, and at the same time a loss of every ethical perspective on human coexistence.[1] According to Christoph Menke's thesis, liberal thought does not ensure the realization of freedom; quite the contrary, it is an obstacle to it.[2] Contrasting with Menke's view is a different (thoroughly emancipatory) interpretation of liberal modernity. This interpretation takes as given that, in the relations of state and society and their related legal order, structures can appear that jeopardize concrete guarantees of freedom. This applies especially to authoritarian constraints on fundamental rights. Nonetheless, as Jürgen Habermas puts it, right is taken as *the* medium by which freedom is granted in a way that is universally recognized. Subjugation of right to democratic-procedural rules not only guarantees the containment of social pathologies in the

---

[1] Daniel Loick, *Juridismus: Konturen einer kritischen Theorie des Rechts* (Berlin: Suhrkamp, 2017).
[2] Christoph Menke, *Kritik der Rechte* (Berlin: Suhrkamp, 2015).

shape of authoritarian techniques and institutions; it also strengthens the opportunities for participation of *equal legal subjects*.[3] Thus, despite their common emancipatory orientation, we are dealing with two fundamentally diverging views of right. The difference between the diagnosis of crisis, on the one hand, and the justification of a democratized law, on the other, could only result from the fact that conceptions of how to realize equal freedom and with it the success of human life *in the form of right* are based on radically different presuppositions. What presuppositions are we, then, dealing with?

First consider the form of right. From the perspective of the critique of right that will be discussed here (the following reflections will draw primarily on Menke's conception), it is a matter of revealing how the form of subjective rights that represents equality is false (flawed). This means that the critique of liberal right "consists of nothing but displaying the operation of presentation that is constitutive of legal actuality. The critique reads the form of subjective rights as the mode in which the status of equality presents itself."[4] In this respect it becomes clear, however, that liberalism reconstructs the reality of right only in the shape of an ideology:

> The critique of liberalism [...] proposes to conceive of liberalism as [...] performing the *same* operation of presentation *again* that has brought about the legal actuality in the form of subjective rights. [...] By merely repeating the presentation brought about by the form of subjective rights within legal actuality, liberalism transforms the pre-

3   Jürgen Habermas, *Faktizität und Geltung* (Frankfurt am Main: Suhrkamp, 1992). Thus, in his discourse theory of right, Habermas for the most part withdrew the critical analysis of right that he had presented in his *Theory of Communicative Action*.

4   Christoph Menke, "Genealogy, Paradox, Transformation: Basic Elements of a Critique of Rights" in ed. Liza Matuttat and Roberto Nigro and Nadine Schiel and Heiko Stubenrauch, *What's Legit? Critiques of Law and Strategies of Rights* (Zurich, Berlin: diaphanes, 2020), pp. 219–244, see p. 224 in the present volume.

sentation into something that is simply given. This is the "uncritical positivism" of liberalism.[5]

Now consider the administration of freedom. The other side of this "uncritical positivism" concerns the unique character of the *administration of right*. According to the critique, the form of right and of rights generates at the same time a false approach to dealing with freedom, to dealing with the political foundations of modern communities. At issue is, on the one hand, the *principle of organization* of rights: Menke claims that subjective rights in the shape of basic rights and human rights safeguard the individual self-will, the co-government of those legally subjugated, consequently enabling political empowerment, whereby "the political co-government of the legal subjects is here *tied to the form of the subjective rights*. It is [...] participation in the government through subjective rights."[6] The false approach to dealing with freedom arises as rights socialize the practices of political acting and judging, no longer oriented to a common good (in disagreement with the theory of equal origin, of co-evolution of private and public autonomy that one finds in Habermas's texts). The administration of freedom thus designates a structural ambivalence: it empowers and subjugates, emancipates and disciplines. "The self-will of the subjects is the basis of validity for the modern state. But the subjects do not escape its power; on the contrary, they are the object and the aim of its relentless governing action."[7]

This construal of rights and right is not only in opposition to the project of political and democratic liberalism that is dominant today. It also distances itself from classical and alternative positions of critique of right and society—one need merely think of the post-Nietzschean

5   Ibid., p. 224.
6   Menke, *Kritik der Rechte*, p. 199.
7   Ibid., p. 205.

or Marxist, left-Hegelian or queer-feminist traditions.[8] We are evidently involved in a controversial debate on the capacity for transformation, on the self-reflective potential of modern right, as the promise of freedom and the claim of legitimacy of right is viewed increasingly as fragile. In particular, three fields of questions emerge, which this essay will consider. Firstly, questions arise on the methodological level concerning what critique can achieve in general, perhaps also what it must achieve in order to mobilize the self-reflective potential of right, and where the borders of the *divestment of right* run. Secondly, questions arise on the normative level concerning how self-reflectivity and authority (and with them violence) in right can be conceived and linked in a way that is *non-authoritarian*. And thirdly, with a view to the political dimension of modern communities, one may ask how a *post-liberal* conception of just right may be developed from the critical structural analysis of the present.

2. The Anarchy of Rights

a) Freedom and Critique

"Rights are grounded in the anarchic incentive to not be governed."[9] Shifting right and rights within proximity to anarchy, a space without ground or authority, must appear to liberal thought as a provocation. According to liberal thought, right and rights are precisely the result

8 Gilles Deleuze, *Essays: Critical and Clinical* (Minneapolis: University of Minnesota Press, 1997); Miguel Abensour, *Democracy against the State: Marx and the Machiavellian Moment* (Cambridge: Polity Press, 2011); Axel Honneth, *Das Recht der Freiheit* (Berlin: Suhrkamp, 2011); Judith Butler, *The Psychic Life of Power: Theories in Subjection* (Stanford CA: Stanford University Press, 1997); Wendy Brown, "Die Paradoxien der Rechte ertragen," in Christoph Menke and Francesca Raimondi, eds., *Revolution der Menschenrechte* (Berlin: Suhrkamp, 2013), pp. 454–473.
9 Christoph Menke, "Der Traum der Rechte," *Kritische Justiz* 51 (2018): pp. 475–478, here p. 478.

of a complex network of self-government and authority through laws, of guarantees for a co-existence characterized by freedom. (In classical political semantics we speak of a constitution.)[10] When Menke nonetheless emphasizes the "anarchic claim at the base of rights,"[11] then it is something that has, in liberal thought and in the modern consciousness of the constitutional state and the welfare state, been repressed and is in danger of being forgotten; it is a sensitivity to the processual, to the coming and passing of political orders and with it the contingency of what persists. This critique of the consciousness of freedom and authority insists on a *self-enlightenment* of right. Critique is thus not something imposed on right from outside. (In this sense liberal right has been called upon time and again to defend itself against every kind of totalitarianism, or harnessed precisely for this purpose.) Rather, critique in the sense of critique of ideology insists on the "inner genesis," the genealogy of subjective rights. This genealogical account is supposed to track down and above all deconstruct the above-mentioned procedures of representation and the legal reality. Representation means two things: (1) rights enable equality or equal freedom of the subjects to be exerted as the content and goal of liberal regimes; (2) in return, rights also define the hegemonic principle, the de-politicized and legal form, by means of which the interests, needs and identities of the subjects (the non-legal, as Menke formulates it) are to be represented.[12] The gist of this critique consists precisely in decisively objecting to the liberal regime of entitlements, the legitimation of subjective basic rights and human

---

10 Christoph Möllers, *Die drei Gewalten* (Weilerswist: Velbrück Verlag, 2008); Philip Pettit, *Gerechte Freiheit: in moralischer Kompass für eine komplexe Welt* (Frankfurt am Main: Suhrkamp, 2015), p. 155; Quentin Skinner, *Visions of Politics* (Cambridge: Cambridge University Press, 2002).

11 Menke, "Der Traum," p. 478.

12 Menke, see p. 229 in the present volume, there making reference to Marx and the *Kritik des Hegelschen Staatsrechts*.

rights—that is, it objects to this being *the* just regime of granting individual freedom. The representation of equality in the shape of rights purports to assert a merely natural fact, a *seeming necessity* of our social world. "The form of subjective rights," writes Menke, "produces the appearance of givenness, of the immutability of what they entitle one to." And further: "Subjective rights are *there to* withdraw what they entitle and to what they entitle; they immunize one from critique and changing practice."[13] Taking the place of a conception of right that immunizes itself against critique and change must be one that, "through the development of a common judgment about the good,"[14] integrates *collective self-government* (and in this respect also the self-reflectivity of freedom) into its own form—a conception of right that frees itself from political self-satisfaction. What has been gained, though, with this politicization of right? Is it not at the expense of the achievements of the model of the constitutional state and the welfare state? Is not right divested of its right?

It is not only political philosophy (we have already referred to Habermas), but also contemporary constitutional theory that is opposed to such a construal. The anarchic impulse of rights, the dismissal of the legal form in the traditional sense, is taken especially as a threat to the modern promise of freedom. The status of the individual is to be secured through the liberal-democratic model of order (though how the liberal and the democratic elements relate to one another is rarely explained). This only seemed possible, however, so long as the diverse spheres of power and interests, politics, morality, economy and religion, were marked off from one another. Modern communities are functionally differentiated, which is requisite in order to ensure stable

13 Ibid., p. 228 and *Kritik der Rechte*, p. 19.
14 Menke, "Der Traum," p. 478.

legal relations.[15] Now one can hardly deny the positive results of the liberal project. These include the normative delimitation of the state authorities (legislation, administration, jurisdiction) and the transformation of economic *laissez faire* into a social market economy— including the living conditions of the individual that often, however, first need to be earned. But are we also dealing, in Hegel's words, with a *progress in the consciousness of freedom*? The matter is by no means so clear. As we know, numerous pathologies and regressive tendencies are tied to liberal legal relations (to the corresponding political economy) and the constitutional state. It is sufficient here to recall neoliberalism as a paradigm of economic and political regulation and intervention and the accompanying social dislocations.[16] The liberal-democratic legal and constitutional theory strives mostly to reveal pathologies and regressive tendencies as problematic yet corrigible effects of an essentially welcome development. According to the conventional construal, the hegemony of right over politics is based on a *self-referential normativity*. It can perpetuate a state of peace and neutralize non-legal forces (which is why the conception of the right to resist is rejected, and also in part the figure of civil disobedience).[17]

Walter Benjamin and Hannah Arendt, Carl Schmitt and Franz Neumann highlighted that this construal of right as a hegemonic social guiding medium has a downside. It mediatizes the *emancipatory side* of the non-legal, especially political acting and judging (and

15 Ernst-Wolfgang Böckenförde, "Demokratie als Verfassungsprinzip," in *Staat, Verfassung, Demokratie* (Frankfurt am Main: Suhrkamp, 1991), pp. 289–378; John Rawls, *A Theory of Justice* (Cambridge MA: Harvard University Press, 1971).

16 Wendy Brown, *Undoing the Demos: Neoliberalism's Stealth Revolution* (New York: Zone Books, 2015); Michel Foucault, *Analytik der Macht* (Frankfurt am Main: Suhrkamp, 2005); Albert O. Hirschmann, *Leidenschaften und Interessen: Politische Begründungen des Kapitalismus vor seinem Sieg* (Frankfurt am Main: Suhrkamp, 1980).

17 Hans Kelsen, *Die reine Rechtslehre* (Vienna: F. Deuticke, 1960).

thereby creates the difference between politics and the political).[18] The formal analysis of the critique of right aims to convince us that de-politicized liberal right can generate freedom *from within itself* only by bringing forth at the same time pathologies and regressions, and that therefore other forms and practices of right need to be realized. To put it succinctly: the politicized right is not fragile right or right that has been divested of right, but rather the non-authoritarian and liberating right, i.e. the right of counterrights.

b) The Question of Violence or the Double Ground of Rights

If the other law of critique is the non-authoritarian right, then what makes liberal right authoritarian and defined by authority or, as Benjamin calls it, by violence? Liberal right is violent, according to the thesis of the critique, because it forces a false way of dealing with the non-legal, with the needs, interests and beliefs of subjects, because the form of rights registers a flawed operation of self-reflection in social practice. Self-reflection that constitutes modern right consists, according to Menke, in "developing procedures and forms that present law as being different from the non-legal [*Nichtrechtliches*] [...]. Law is related to its exterior, to the non-legal, not in the form of law, but in a form of external efficacy: in the mode of violence."[19] Right is accordingly a normative medium that has to struggle with two structurally dependent problems. On the one hand, it can grasp the non-legal, i.e. needs and interests, only as a presup-

---

18 Walter Benjamin, "Zur Kritik der Gewalt," in *Gesammelte Schriften*, vol. 2.1, ed. R. Tiedemann (Frankfurt am Main: Suhrkamp, 1999), pp. 179–204; Hannah Arendt, *Was ist Politik? Fragmente aus dem Nachlaß*, ed. Ursula Ludz (Munich: Piper, 1993), p. 9; Carl Schmitt, *Verfassungsrechtliche Aufsätze* (Berlin: Duncker & Humblot, *1958*), pp. 386–429; Franz Neumann, *Die Herrschaft des Gesetzes* (Frankfurt am Main: Suhrkamp, 1980); on the current debate, see Oliver Marchart, *Die politische Differenz* (Berlin: Suhrkamp, 2010), pp. 13–84.
19 Menke, see p. 227–228 in the present volume.

posed status, which empowers the individual and commits the individual on the side of right. Yet this dependence of right brings forth a latent *need for regulation* and with it a *power of regulation* belonging to right and the state. Empowering the subject in the form of basic rights and human rights leads, on the other hand, to far-reaching techniques of disciplining and subjugation. One need merely think of the new regime of visibility or the problematic approach to dealing with the needy in the context of basic security of the state. In this respect, the welfare state too remains "indebted to the logic of release from precisely the normativity that it wants to assert: it updates the aporia that it opposes. And at the same time the welfare state makes clear what the political self-disempowerment through rights consists in."[20] Talk of legal violence, of the aporias in which right and state get entangled, should in other words make clear the alienation and the illusionary elements with which liberalism is tied *genetically*.

Yet the concept of violence is itself unclear and ambiguous. One can indeed, with the semantics of violence, draw attention to the aporia of freedom of the dominating legal and constitutional theory. However, a critique of right would also have to show how to deal with violence and conflicts that can arise from human coexistence and that need not necessarily be tied to the ideology of liberal right. Shouldn't the resolution of social conflicts—concretely, the securing of a functional society—be possible by means of an intrinsically justified (non-authoritarian) monopoly of violence, that is, by means of an institution that subjects the individual to a universally recognized procedure and thus recalls the autonomy project of right? And in what relation does the *suspension of right* (Benjamin's *Entsetzung des*

---

20 Menke, "Der Traum," p. 477.

Rechts[21]), the abstaining from violence, stand to the responsibility of freedom of the other law?

The answer of the critique leads back to the idea of the form of self-reflectivity of right, for self-reflectivity of the other law re-defines the form and function of rights. Decisive here is that the approach to depicting the reality of right (which is criticized in reference to liberal right) is reconstructed differently. Menke calls this the positive depiction of right. This positive depiction of right marks, *firstly*, the double ground of rights. That is, the form "only consists of the tension, the antagonism of two opposed types of form or logic. The other form of rights [, *secondly*,] is determined by its status as being derived: Rights within the other law are not primary, but secondary—they have their meaning and their foundation in contributing to the lawful facilitation of successful social practices."[22] While the liberal form of rights looks to realize equality and non-legal interests, i.e. the egalitarian and reflectively freeing entitlement of individuals, in one move in a unified form, the new right entails the *division* or *doubling* of the form, that is, recognizing the anarchy in right as a liberating power. What is meant here is not the endorsement of conditions that are void of right. Rather, what is meant is the realization of collective self-government, a form of acting and judging that does not take one's own, the subject's own will as its point of departure but rather the cooperative shaping of the political. This radically changes the function of rights: rights now have a serving function, as a constituent of social practices, but they are "neither constitutionalizing, nor are they unconditional."[23] This means in turn: "The other law does not dispose of the rights of the individual. What it does is that it pushes them to the margins: They are neither center nor foun-

---

21 Benjamin, "Zur Kritik der Gewalt," p. 202.
22 Menke, see p. 237 in the present volume.
23 Ibid., see p. 241 in the present volume.

dation of the law, but its effect. This is precisely how the other law ensures and secures them."[24]

This definition of rights also allows one to draw conclusions concerning the treatment of violence in the other law. Violence grasped as state authority may lose its outstanding status. In the same way that rights acquire an ancillary character, the conception of violence is now likewise conceded only a secondary function. The consequence is that the conditions of success of social practices cannot be brought about by means of violence. It must nonetheless be possible to resolve disturbances through communication with the subjects. How else might the lasting maintenance of social co-existence look? We will not have a clearer view until we apply ourselves somewhat more closely to the relation of rights to the other law (and to the accompanying conception of justice).

3. Right and Justice

"Critique thus is the unity of negative and positive presentation: Since the other law originates from the critique of bourgeois law and since the critique of bourgeois law exposes the antagonism—and the antagonism with its antagonism [...]—at its foundation, it also leads to a form of an other law that doesn't dissolve this antagonism, but fulfills it."[25] Menke's recapitulation shows the path that critique has traveled in its deconstruction of liberal right. The other law thus designates the attempt to carry out the new form and the new function of rights self-reflectively (and as a paradox). The radicalization in determining the form (its division and doubling) results in the asymmetric connection of two, in Menke's words, "opposed types of law," the

---

24 Ibid.
25 Ibid., see p. 236 (fn. 26) in the present volume.

"constitutionalizing laws and counterrights."[26] Its contrast to liberal right, also to liberal constitutional right,
consists precisely in that the other law incorporates the
political as a meaning-giving or antagonistic force in its
normative structure. Constitutionalizing laws outline
the universally recognized context in which the free acting and judging of the actors is realized. They "define the
good and the success of a practice by determining the
roles by which practices and institutions are realized."
Thereby they safeguard "the equality of every participant, which is realized precisely in the difference of their
practical and institutional roles."[27] Menke has nothing
more to say on the institutional arrangement, on the differentiation of the social roles as a division of labor. That
this institutional arrangement is particularly important
for liberal legal and constitutional theories goes without
saying, for they must govern the presupposed entitlements (the non-legal) and adapt to the social needs of
freedom.[28] But also a right that incorporates the political in its normative structure cannot dispense with an
elaborate theory of the institutional networks and social
infrastructures, especially a theory of the *administration of justice*, albeit an administration of justice that is
appropriate to the other law and the form and function
of rights. It applies, too, for the other law to establish
procedures that regulate the production and application
of constitutionalizing laws (and thus also to guarantee
the success of social practices). Moreover, the other law
must make procedures available to judge controversial
interpretations of the political, and also to remedy violations of rights (for even when rights take a back seat to
the political, we should not forget that subjects in society have needs and may pursue egoistic interests.) For

26 Ibid., see p. 233 in the present volume.
27 Ibid., see p. 234 in the present volume, with recourse to Gunther Teub-
    ner, *Verfassungsfragmente. Gesellschaftlicher Konstitutionalismus in
    der Globalisierung* (Berlin: Suhrkamp, 2012).
28 Böckenförde, *Staat, Verfassung, Demokratie*, pp. 289–378.

this reason, violence as constitutional-legal violence is legitimate and able to claim its right only where it aims to restore social practices or promote them.

The second, contrary type of right, namely counter-rights, refers directly to the collective self-government connected to social practices. Precisely because the other law views the political as the defining force of human coexistence, counterrights ought to mediate the possibility of objecting to social participation. Counterrights are not, then, rights of defense in disguise or another title for what in the liberal tradition is called negative freedom. Rather, counterrights themselves exhibit the paradox of form, i.e. they guarantee non-participation, the empowerment of the individual to be different, the *entitlement of the asocial* in social practice. "Counterrights are supposed to assert—within the normative order or practices through law—that each and every one is not only an equal social participant, but also radically unequal, a non-participant."[29] Counterrights are barely graspable with the interpretative scheme of liberal right, primarily because the decision for passivity or power-lessness is not made on the basis of an individualism that is taken as given. Non-participation is the objection to the active claim of the political to shape society.

One would still have to investigate how the concept of counterrights relates to traditional conceptions of private and public rights, whether and how they take effect in the diverse practices of one's environment—one need think merely of friendships, love relations and families—or how counterrights re-codify these semantics and spheres. These questions cannot be pursued here. Instead we will turn to a different, equally important point. The critique of right itself does not clarify how the relation between constitutionalizing laws and counterrights (which Menke refers to as being a "double relation of opposition and coincidence") must be

29 Menke, see p. 235 in the present volume.

conceived.[30] What seems clear from the above is simply that the other law joins together two fundamentally different types of right asymmetrically, so that right is not something unified; instead it "produces" a tension. How this tension is moderated, however, and what forces are in effect remains more or less open. Menke addresses the problem itself in his talk of an "overlapping of two dialects." What is meant are the "dialectics of participation and non-participation." Accordingly, constitutionalizing laws not only enable social practices, for they are also connected with (democratically grounded) majority and minority positions.[31] These minority positions have the status of counterrights and are, in a remarkable way, *dependent* on the constitutionalizing laws. Menke claims that "[r]egulating the social through means of constitutionalizing laws always produces semi- or non-participants."[32] These laws must guarantee time and again political empowerment, i.e. political participation. Yet, if Menke does not want to reconstruct a classical model of liberal democracy and if he wants at the same time to grant counterrights (which indeed represent a contrary type of right) an emancipatory power, then a critique of right must show how this power of counterrights itself can become a counter power in right and how it can claim to also raise, from *its own power*, an objection against the legally drafted practices. Whether Menke's appeal to a "dialectic of judging," which relates particular and universal, passivity and emancipation, sense and sensibility to one another is sufficient, is something one would have to examine in more detail.[33] One thing at least should be clear: the mobilization of the political in and through right always harbors the danger of hegemonic effects that do not arise from the government of the (liberal) right, but rather from a sociality that unifies

30 Ibid.
31 Ibid. (fn 26).
32 Ibid.
33 Menke, *Kritik der Rechte*, p. 373.

THE ANARCHY OF RIGHTS

the justification and practices of the good with the free judgment of the subject. To be sure, this danger can be averted only by means of a *self-reflectivity of the political*, which, following Hannah Arendt or Paul Ricœur, for instance, keeps in view the fragility of every project of freedom and the concrete responsibility for human co-existence.

The other law is a post-liberal right. As a post-liberal right, it can only be grasped and developed, however, from out of the existing right of civil society, if it is not to get caught in the undertow of utopian notions. The other law thus finds its starting ground in the structures of liberal civil society and reflects in turn its difference. "The new right is at the same time like the right of civil society and contrary to it; it breaks with the right of civil society and falls back in it."[34] The decisive step beyond this critical distinction lies in a "politics of altering or transforming the form of rights."[35] This politics "thus is a politics of applying [...] subjective rights against the logic of their own form."[36] It is a politics that employs the existing form of subjective rights argumentatively and strategically in such a way "*as if* we already were dealing with the rights of a new form, the rights of an other law. Transformative politics then is a politics of anticipation. It counterfactually anticipates the other law within the existing law. It is a politics of fiction."[37] But is this really the case? In conclusion we will attempt a critique of the critique of right. It is clear that Menke's politics of fiction (which is not supposed to provide anything other than the precondition for the post-liberal constellation) is based on an idea of individual or collective *self-transgression*.[38] This idea is familiar to us from

34 Ibid., p. 401.
35 Menke, see p. 243 in the present volume.
36 Ibid.
37 Ibid.
38 Christoph Menke, *Autonomie und Befreiung. Studien zu Hegel* (Berlin: Suhrkamp, 2018), pp. 179–212.

Adorno's texts, but above all from Foucault's.[39] Foucault connects the idea of self-transgression with a standpoint of critique and care for the self that ought to enable a different, *aesthetic* form of life.[40] "What strikes me," says Foucault, "is the fact that in our society, art has become something which is related only to objects and not to individuals, or to life. That art is something which is specialized or which is done by experts who are artists. But couldn't everyone's life become a work of art?"[41] The aesthetic form of life (not the aestheticization of life in Baudelaire's, Mallarmé's or Nietzsche's sense) is the attitude of opposing opportunism and the persistence of what already exists. It is an attitude of defiance and creative appropriation of the world. Menke appears to fully endorse this aesthetic interpretation of the ethical.[42] But the decisive point is that he transfers it to the domain of right, thereby changing the appearance and the scope of the critique. The politics of the *as if* becomes the placeholder for the freedom of self-government that anticipates, indeed must anticipate, the justice of a new right in an emancipatory self-fashioning act. But doesn't this mean a promise is made of the potential to shape and create meaning, situated essentially—and here the artist comes again into play—outside of every right? Isn't

---

39 Theodor W. Adorno, *Minima Moralia. Reflexionen aus dem beschädigten Leben* (Frankfurt am Main: Suhrkamp, 2003); *Kritik*, in Theodor W. Adorno, *Gesammelte Schriften*, vol. 10.2. (Frankfurt am Main: Suhrkamp 2003), pp. 785–793; Michel Foucault, *Was ist Kritik?* (Berlin: Merve, 1992), pp. 8–9.

40 Michel Foucault, "Die Ethik der Sorge um sich als Praxis der Freiheit," in Michel Foucault, *Schriften*, vol. 4 (Frankfurt am Main: Suhrkamp, 2005), pp. 875–903.

41 Michel Foucault, "On the Genealogy of Ethics: An Overview of Work in Progress," in *Michel Foucault: Beyond Structuralism and Hermeneutics*, ed. Hubert L. Dreyfus and Paul Rabinow (Chicago: University of Chicago Press, 1982), p. 236.

42 Christoph Menke, *Kraft. Ein Grundbegriff ästhetischer Anthropologie* (Frankfurt am Main: Suhrkamp, 2008), pp. 58–63; idem, "Zweierlei Übung. Zum Verhältnis von sozialer Disziplinierung und ästhetischer Existenz," in *Michel Foucault. Zwischenbilanz einer Rezeption*, ed. Axel Honneth and Martin Saar (Frankfurt am Main: Suhrkamp, 2003), pp. 199–210.

right now used solely as a means to an end and thereby radically divested of right? In other words, does Menke in the end dissolve the tension between the legal and the political, between constitutionalizing laws and counter-rights, in favor of a *fiction of the political*?

Perhaps we ought not to over-dramatize it, and may nonetheless take note of the dynamic and the ambivalence that accompanies the project of politicization (and that for this reason also requires the self-reflection of the political). Contrary to Menke, we should at any rate retain the fact that each form of free self-government has developed out of a history of liberation and a crisis of right and rights, and that in this respect there is a consciousness of shaping the social that is motivated equally by political and legal practices. It will then become evident that this politics of *as if* must be embedded in a consciousness of emancipation and contingency that *already exists*. We must embrace a capacity of subjects for political judgment that grants efficacy to the will to bring about change in the society of the *here and now*, in a society that knows the aporetic, the confrontational, just as well as the diverse forms of successful life. Post-liberal right is a right that reflects its made nature, its ideology, and which, as something processual, recognizes its capacity and the necessity to shape politics, while at the same time remaining aware of its function and strength. This also means, however, that transformative politics cannot be realized without the *sense for justice* of existing legal forms and forms of life.

Translated by Aaron Shoichet

Jonas Heller

Deforming Rights

Arendt's Theory of a Claim to Law

According to Arendt's critical approach to modern law, the order of modern nation states and the idea of human rights are strongly connected. It is this connection which leads to the "aporia of human rights."[1] The aporia consists of the fact that human rights have been invented and established by modern nation states,[2] but it is, at the same time, the framework of nation states which hinders the fundamental protection of all human beings as such, and thus obstructs that at which human rights aim.

Arendt's point, however, is not that human rights, in their connection with modern nation states, have no effect and just remain a powerless idea. Then, human rights would not only be useless, but also harmless. Arendt's criticism is rather that human rights entail disastrous negative effects when incorporated in the heart of nation states. She argues that it was the institution of human rights as "the basis of the constitutions of all civilized countries"[3] which made possible that a vast number of people in the twentieth century—for the first

---

1   Hannah Arendt, "Die Aporien der Menschenrechte," in Hannah Arendt, *Elemente und Ursprünge totaler Herrschaft. Antisemitismus, Imperialismus, totale Herrschaft* (Munich and Zurich: Piper, 2011), pp. 601–625. Arendt's book *The Origins of Totalitarianism* was first published 1951 in English. The book appeared in 1955 in her German translation, which includes several new passages. Since they differ in many respects, I refer to both versions.
2   Compare Lynn Hunt, *Inventing Human Rights: A History* (New York and London: Norton & Company, 2007).
3   Arendt, *Elemente und Ursprünge*, p. 603, my translation.

time in history—lost any protection that human rights were originally supposed to provide.

At the heart of this problem there is, as I will show, a division between two kinds of rights: between human rights as citizen rights and human rights as such (1). The main difference between these two kinds of rights lies, according to Arendt, not in their form but in their content (2). The fatal consequences of this difference become evident when citizen rights are lost (3). This loss of citizen rights is not just the end of human rights, but involves the realization of a problematic aspect of their idea (4). Contrary to expectations, this realization takes place as a killing of the juridical person, that is, of legal capacity (5). As opposed to this effect of human rights, Arendt develops, as I will outline, the "right to have rights" as a right to being judged (6). In the last step, I will show what transformation of the idea of rights this involves, which problems this transformation answers and what problems it raises (7).

1. Two kinds of rights

The fact that human rights are nationally established "as the basis of the constitutions"[4] leads to their division into two kinds of rights. This division, induced by their national establishment, is the division between the *implementation* and the *idea* of human rights. As *implemented*, human rights are (only) the rights of the citizens, that is, the members of a nation state; they are incorporated in "the different laws of the citizens"[5] and realized through them. On the other side, and separated from these national implementations, there is "the inalienable Right of Man"[6] as the *idea* of human

4   Ibid., my translation.
5   Ibid., my translation.
6   Ibid., my translation.

rights. This idea of human rights is "as such indepen-dent from citizenship and national difference."[7] It is the idea that all human beings, regardless of where they come from and where they belong to, are in possession of these rights. In contrast to citizen rights, however, these human rights "as such" do not guarantee effective protection; they are rather "a kind of additional law, a right of exception necessary for those who had nothing better to fall back upon."[8]

This division between the idea and the implementa-tion of human rights involves two unequal subjects of rights. Whereas the subjects of implemented rights are the members of nation states, the subjects of the idea of rights are those who are more or less excluded from equal membership and thus excluded from enforceable rights. Although the idea of human rights as such is that they apply to human beings as such, they prove to be inapplicable: "The Rights of Man, after all, had been defined as 'inalienable' because they were supposed to be independent of all governments; but it turned out that the moment human beings lacked their own gov-ernment and had to fall back upon their minimum rights, no authority was left to protect them and no institution was willing to guarantee them."[9] Whoever becomes a subject of the idea of human rights, is "sig-nificantly deprived of all rights"; human rights as such are the "rights" of those without rights.[10]

The division between the rights of citizens and the rights of those without rights could be understood as follows. There is one side, the side of citizen rights, on which the idea of human rights is realized; and there is another side, the side of human rights "as such," on

7   Ibid., my translation.
8   Hannah Arendt, *The Origins of Totalitarianism. New edition with added prefaces* (San Diego, New York and London: Harcourt Brace & Company, 1976), p. 293.
9   Ibid., pp. 291–292.
10 Arendt, *Elemente und Ursprünge*, p. 602, my translation.

which this idea remains a mere idea, lacking all reality. In this perspective, human rights as such, independent of citizenship, appear to be a delusion: whoever believes that individuals as such can be the subject of human rights ignores that, under the conditions of the modern nation state, not the individual, but "the people" has become the "image of man."[11] Under such national conditions, human rights are nothing else than citizen rights. In line with this, Arendt speaks of the "identification of the rights of man with the rights of peoples"— and records, as the "full implication" of this identification, the absolute vulnerability of those without (citizen) rights.[12] According to this view, the idea of human rights—the idea that every human being as an individual *has* rights—is a delusion because human rights "as such" have no force: "The Rights of Man, supposedly inalienable, proved to be unenforceable—even in countries whose constitutions were based upon them— whenever people appeared who were no longer citizens of any sovereign state."[13] Against this background, citizen rights appear to be the only realization of the idea of human rights; and beyond citizen rights, the idea of human rights appears unreal, a mere fiction.

However, the difference between the idea of human rights and the implementation of human rights is not the difference between a realized and an unrealized idea. Rather, what is implemented as citizen rights is *not* the idea of human rights; and the idea of human rights as such is not something unreal, but becomes reality in a specific sense. Idea and implementation of human rights are not divided due to a difference in realization, but because of the fact that the implementation of rights has nothing to do with the idea. In other words, implemented (citizen) rights and the idea of human rights

11 Arendt, *Origins*, p. 291.
12 Ibid., pp. 291–292.
13 Ibid., p. 293.

are not just distinct in terms of their form, but also in terms of their content. By "form," I mean the question of juridical implementation and political weight, that is, the question of enforceability. By "content," I mean the conception of a human existence, which is implicated by human rights as citizen rights and human rights as such, respectively: the two kinds of rights do not imply the same "image of man." Whereas citizen rights are based on the image of man as a people,[14] the idea of human rights rests upon the image of man as "man as such." It is important to note that when the division between the two kinds of rights becomes apparent (in the moment when a significant amount of people lose their citizen rights and so fall into the domain of human rights as such), *both* conceptions of human existence are realized. Therefore, the content of human rights as such is not a mere and desirable idea, but proves to be a material and undesirable reality.

2. The content of rights

The idea of human rights as such—the idea of their inalienability—rests on the conviction that they express a timeless normative standard for a life appertaining to the human being as such. In other words, the claim of the inalienability of human rights entails the assertion that these rights correspond to human nature.[15] As derived from nature, these "natural" rights are prior to the invention of the juridical form of rights within political communities. Arendt opposes this perspective in two regards. Firstly, the content of human rights as

---

14 Compare ibid., p. 291.
15 This is a heritage of the natural law tradition. Compare Wolfgang Schild, "Person, IV. Recht. Rechtsperson; Rechtspersönlichkeit," in Joachim Ritter and Karlfried Gründer, eds., *Historisches Wörterbuch der Philosophie*, vol. 7 (Darmstadt: Wissenschaftliche Buchgesellschaft, 1989), pp. 322–335, here p. 325.

such does not correspond to a supposed human nature; it is rather opposed to what is good for human beings. Secondly, the content of human rights as such could not be realized in a hypothetical state of nature before the age of society; it could rather only be realized in the age of modern society, under the political condition of nation states and as a product of the exclusion they involve. It is, as Arendt argues, not the content of human rights as such, but the content of citizen rights, which precedes the life within the order of nation states and which therefore is prior to the juridical form of rights. This last aspect of the precedence of the content of citizen rights over the form of rights is the most crucial for Arendt. It is one of her central arguments that the transformation of this content into the form of rights is a modern occurrence, which took place in the second half of the eighteenth century when the order of nation states was established. The consequences of this transformation, however, have only become evident in the twentieth century, in the context of the deprivation of rights. Arendt speaks about this transformation and its consequences in her famous chapter on "The Decline of the Nation-State and the End of the Rights of Man," in her book *The Origins of Totalitarianism*. Here she writes:

> [W]hat we must call a "human right" today would have been—before the age of nation states—thought of as a general characteristic of the human condition which no tyrant could take away. Its loss entails the loss of the relevance of speech (and man, since Aristotle, has been defined as a being commanding the power of speech and thought), and the loss of all human relationship (and man, again since Aristotle, has been thought of as the "political animal," that is one who by definition lives in a community), the loss, in other words, of some of the most essential characteristics of human life. This was to a certain extent the

plight of slaves, whom Aristotle therefore did not count among human beings.[16]

Arendt not only changes the chronology, but also the normative evaluation of the two kinds of rights: regarding their content, human rights not as such (i.e. independent of membership and national difference), but as the rights of and within a community, correspond to a life fit for human beings. To live a life as a part of a community was, before the age of nation states, not only regarded as a desirable standard which could be met or not. It was not a question of normativity, but a fact of normality; of how it is—and not just how it should be— to live a life as a human being. For this reason, before its juridical transformation, the content of citizen rights was considered to be a "general characteristic"[17] of the human condition. Arendt does not positively define this characteristic, but only describes what its loss entails: that we no longer participate as equals in the relationships of a community, and that our speech is no longer regarded as relevant by others. These two deprivations are not distinct from each other; the irrelevance of speech is the means of exclusion, since being included as an equal part means, according to Arendt, that what one says makes a difference. What we call a human right today relates, in its content, to this way of being included.

This content, however, is not that of specific human rights claims—for example, of the claim for unemployment compensation or the claim for old-age insurance.[18] The content at stake here has nothing to do with particular rights themselves, but with the position of *having*

16 Arendt, *Origins*, p. 297.
17 Ibid.
18 Arendt mentions these two claims in order to illustrate that it is absurd to declare unrealizable human rights as "inalienable." See Hannah Arendt, "Es gibt nur ein einziges Menschenrecht," *Die Wandlung. Eine Monatsschrift* 4/6 (1949): pp. 754–770, here p. 765.

such rights. Arendt's question is not about the specific content of rights, but about what having rights contains. She asks about the loss of this position, since it entails more than the specific content of any particular rights. This additional loss, for those who are deprived of their rights, is usually ignored: "no one seems to know which rights they lost when they lost these human rights."[19] The issue Arendt becomes aware of is that the loss of these rights is associated with a "situation of absolute rightlessness,"[20] which exceeds the loss of rights.

3. What is lost with the loss of rights

Arendt emphasizes that something "much more fundamental than the citizen rights of freedom and justice is at stake"[21] when the deprivation of these rights occurs. This deprivation revokes any "position in the world."[22] Losing citizen rights means to fall out of any political relationship, i.e. to fall out of the human condition. Before the age of nation states, this condition was considered to be undetachable; it was a common conviction that "no tyrant could take [it] away."[23] The experience of modernity is that the opposite of this conviction is true. It is the experience of a fundamental deprivation

---

19 Arendt, *Origins*, p. 293.
20 Arendt, *Elemente und Ursprünge*, p. 607. The situation of absolute rightlessness is not the same as the loss of the "so-called" human rights, i.e. the rights of the citizens. Absolute rightlessness does not just mean to lose all these rights since—on the one hand—"no loss of particular rights necessarily involves the condition of absolute rightlessness which only can be meaningfully called a loss of human rights" and—on the other hand—the "so-called" human rights can often still be enjoyed "under the conditions of absolute rightlessness" (ibid., p. 611). The particular rights of non-members do not change anything in the fundamental situation of absolute rightlessness, which consists of being a non-member (compare ibid., pp. 612–613).
21 Arendt, "Es gibt nur ein einziges Menschenrecht," p. 759, my translation.
22 Ibid.
23 Arendt, *Origins*, p. 297.

of the human condition, i.e. of an absolute exclusion from human communities. The reason for this modern experience was not "any lack of civilization, backwardness, or mere tyranny"; rather, it became possible only "because there was no longer any 'uncivilized' spot on earth."[24] Civilization is not characterized here by technical, scientific or cultural achievements, but by the fact that the nation state has become the decisive juridical-political form in which human communities are organized; "civilization" is the name of the condition in which being part of a community is identical with being a citizen, i.e. a member of a nation state. When the global system of modern nation states had closed the last gaps, the entire globe became "civilized": we have "really started to live in One World."[25] The consequence of this unification of the world is the fact that the exclusion from one part of the system—from one nation state—is equivalent to the exclusion "from the entire family of nations,"[26] that is from any politically relevant community. In an entirely civilized world, "the loss of home and political status [could] become identical with the expulsion from humanity altogether."[27] Paradoxically, this situation of absolute rightlessness is based on an order of states, which entail human rights as their foundation.

24 Ibid.
25 Ibid.
26 Arendt, *Elemente und Ursprünge*, p. 608, my translation.
27 Arendt, *Origins*, p. 297. The legal situation has improved in the meantime. Due to the national and supranational implementation of human rights, stateless people are now also considered as juridical persons and (should) get legal protection. For this comparison, with regard to Arendt, see Hauke Brunkhorst, "Menschenrechte und Souveränität – ein Dilemma?," in Hauke Brunkhorst, Wolfgang R. Köhler and Matthias Lutz-Bachmann, eds., *Recht auf Menschenrechte. Menschenrechte, Demokratie und internationale Politik* (Frankfurt am Main: Suhrkamp, 1999), pp. 157–175, here p. 174. However, it has become evident again in the current situation of refugees that enforceable rights, including the right to live, are not independent of citizenship. The continuing actuality of Arendt is emphasized by Giorgio Agamben, for instance in *Mittel ohne Zweck. Noten zur Politik* (Zurich and Berlin: diaphanes, 2006), p. 25.

A major situation of absolute rightlessness occurred, according to Arendt, in the moment when a vast number of refugees were in search of a new home after World War I. It occurred again during and after World War II, when the "survivors of the extermination camps, the inmates of concentration and internment camps, and even the comparatively happy stateless people" experienced that, after having lost protection as citizens, "the abstract nakedness of being nothing but human was their greatest danger."[28] The experience of this loss procured a twofold insight. Firstly, it suddenly became clear that the human condition—the condition of being part of a community—is nothing merely given, nothing human beings can simply rely on. Rather, it became apparent that this human condition can be lost. Secondly, it became clear that the human condition is something completely different from the "natural" condition, i.e. the condition of "human nature": a human being in its naked natural form is exactly the opposite of a human being in the human condition. The "abstract nakedness" does not involve any protection, but absolute abandonment: a condition in which one is isolated from all relationships (therefore *abstract*) and deprived of the relevance of one's speech.

This twofold insight—that membership in a community is not unlosable and that its loss does not lead to protection, but brings abandonment—includes a third insight. The deprivation of rights shows that what is lost at the same time, namely being part of humanity, has to be secured by being *posited* as a right, precisely because it is nothing that simply *exists*. If the content of "having rights" is to belong to a community, then the form of this content is not natural, but *only* a right, i.e. something we can lose. "Having rights" must have the form of a right essentially different from all citizen

---

28 Arendt, *Origins*, p. 300.

rights.[29] This third insight is the discovery of the "right to have rights." It is an insight regarding the *form* that the content of "having rights"—namely membership—must have. I will come back to the right to have rights and its specific form later. At this point, something else is important to note: the experience that the loss of citizen rights involves an additional loss, and the insight that what is additionally lost does not have the form of nature, but the form of a right. This experience and this insight do *not* mean that human rights as such (as opposed to citizen rights) are a delusion insofar they have failed to protect. Rather, the experience of the loss of citizen rights coincides with the *realization* of human rights as such.

4. The realization of human rights as such

The loss of citizen rights makes clear that human nature itself provides no right. For, in this situation, the claims connected to human rights as such prove to be of no use. When citizen rights are lost, human rights as such are thus not realized *as rights*. What becomes apparent is, in contrast, that their character as rights is a mere fiction. But as explicated before, it is not this lack in effect of human rights as such that makes the loss of citizen rights a situation of absolute rightlessness. Rightlessness does not evolve because human rights as such have no impact and remain a mere idea, but rather because a part of this idea is realized; what becomes real is not the idea of *right*, but the idea of *human*.

The idea of human rights as such is based upon the idea of an essential and stable human nature, which is shared by all individuals independent of any relationship in which they are included. The idea of human rights as such entails the idea of a human being as

---

29 Compare Arendt, *Elemente und Ursprünge*, p. 607.

such. It is the idea that a human individual "belongs to the human race in the same manner as an animal to a particular animal species."[30] In this case, belonging is reduced to a form of biological nature. Arendt's objection is that "something like a human species" doesn't exist, but can only be fabricated.[31] The exemplary place of such a fabrication of a human nature is, according to Arendt, the concentration camp: "Actually the experience of the concentration camps does show that human beings can be transformed into specimens of the human animal, and that man's 'nature' is only 'human' insofar as it opens up to man the possibility of becoming something highly unnatural, that is, a man."[32] This man, a product of a fabrication, has a paradoxical structure. On the one hand, it is a *universal* existence: in its abstract nakedness beyond any human relationship, it is like any other human being in this position. On the other hand, it is an absolute individualized and thus *particular* being: isolated from any common life and not involved in any communication between equals, it has nothing else than its own uniqueness.[33] This two-sided structure of "man" is not only characteristic of the inmates of the concentration camps, but also of those who lost their membership in a community. And what Arendt emphasizes about the camps is not the violation of specific fundamental rights, but the absolute loss of membership in a political community—that is, the experience of absolute exclusion. The "image of man"[34] is, according to the idea of human rights as such, an existence excluded from communal life. The idea of this existence becomes real in the moment when citizen rights are lost. This is the systematic nexus of Arendt's critique of rights: she

---

30 Arendt, "Es gibt nur ein einziges Menschenrecht," p. 764, my translation.
31 Arendt, *Elemente und Ursprünge*, p. 907, my translation.
32 Arendt, *Origins*, p. 455.
33 Compare Arendt, "Es gibt nur ein einziges Menschenrecht," p. 764.
34 Arendt, *Origins*, p. 291.

criticizes citizen rights for being so easily losable and she criticizes human rights as such for fatally coming true when citizen rights are lost.

5. The killing of the juridical person

According to Arendt, there is a relevant common feature in the situation of the inmates of concentration camps on the one hand, and of refugees and stateless people on the other. In both cases, the exclusion from membership in a community is induced by the extinction of "the juridical person in man."[35] In the case of the latter groups, this extinction occurs automatically because they are placed "outside of all prevailing law."[36] In the case of the concentration camp, which is at the heart of total domination, the extinction of the juridical person is "a planned murder,"[37] since concentration camps are purposely put beyond the law.

It is significant how this de-legalization of concentration camps works. It is not accomplished by the removal of the camp area from the domain of law, but by the revocation of the legal status of the inmates. Not the place, but the persons are transferred outside the law; the de-legalization of the camps is not carried out in terms of public law, but in terms of criminal law, namely through the isolation of the camp inmates from the normal penal system. In this respect, the most important guideline was that no one could be imprisoned because of indictable acts.[38] The inmates were separated from law by abrogating the principle "*nulla poena sine culpa*," that is, no punishment without guilt. As opposed to this principle, according to the logic of

---

35 Ibid., p. 447.
36 Arendt, *Elemente und Ursprünge*, p. 922, my translation.
37 Ibid., my translation.
38 Compare ibid.

the concentration camp, it does not matter at all what its inmates have done.

The same holds true for the situation of refugees: "The modern refugees are not persecuted because they did or thought this or that, but because of what they are immutably by birth—born into the wrong race or the wrong class or called up for military service by the wrong government."[39] Precisely their undeniable innocence was their "greatest calamity."[40] That they are *undeniably* innocent means that they are not held responsible for whatever they do. It means that their actions do not count: "Innocence, in the sense of complete lack of responsibility, was the mark of their rightlessness as it was the seal of their loss of political status."[41] "Innocence" here is to be understood in a strict juridical sense; to be indisputably innocent due to a complete lack of responsibility means to have no legal capacity and thus no position in the sphere of law whatsoever.[42] In other words, undeniable innocence results from the denial of the status as a juridical person.

The denial of this status is something else than losing all particular rights; it is the loss of being obligated. Being obligated necessarily involves an intact connection between what someone has done and how she is treated. The killing of the juridical person entails the fundamental and permanent disruption of this connection: what is done to someone by the authorities is then in no relation to her actions any more. That actions don't count, that is, that someone is not at all obligated in her doing, means that this doing is separated from all responsibility; the person in question is penally irrelevant and loses as such her position within the law.

39 Ibid., pp. 609–610, my translation.
40 Ibid., p. 610.
41 Arendt, *Origins*, p. 295.
42 I will point to the problematic consequences of this link between responsibility and juridical status in step 7. For a critique of the category of responsibility, see also Frieder Vogelmann, *Im Bann der Verantwortung* (Frankfurt am Main and New York: Campus, 2013).

Only a person within the law—that is, a juridical person, a person having legal capacity—can have rights. Having rights depends on being held responsible, and to be absolutely rightless means to be released from any responsibility.

The experience of inmates of concentration camps, of stateless people and of refugees made clear that being held responsible is not an inalienable human condition, but rather a capability, which can be lost. As such, it can only be actualized when "secured by a right whose existence was apparently not yet anticipated by those proclaiming the rights of man."[43] Arendt calls this unknown right—a right to a condition of responsibility—the "right to have rights."[44] In the following step, I will outline why it is important to recognize that this right, which is in the center of Arendt's argument, is not a right *to rights*, but a right *to have*—to a position of having. Since this position of having rights is characterized by being obligated, it involves being judged in accordance with this obligation: the right to have rights is the right to be judged in a specific way.

6. The capability of being judged

Arendt identifies the right to have rights with the right "to live in a framework [in the German version: *Beziehungssystem*[45]] where one is judged by one's actions and opinions."[46] This formulation makes unambiguously clear that the object of this right does not entail specific *(legal) claims*, but a specific *(political) having*. The content of this political having is, as mentioned, a political *capability*: not the capability to judge, but the more fundamental capability of being judged.

---

43 Arendt, *Elemente und Ursprünge*, p. 614, my translation.
44 Ibid.
45 Ibid.
46 Arendt, *Origins*, pp. 296–297.

Before elaborating on this, it has to be said that this does not mean that juridical rights in the narrower sense do not play a role in Arendt's considerations. The right to have rights also serves the function of making juridical rights enforceable. In her famous 1949 article "Es gibt nur ein einziges Menschenrecht," Arendt writes that "none of the other rights are realizable" without this one right.[47] However, the right to have rights is not primarily directed towards juridical rights. Juridical rights are rights to do something at will (for example to express one's opinion, cast one's vote, execute an office) or to receive something (for example welfare support if unemployed). The right to have rights is not a right to such activities or benefits. It does not enable one to act without the need for justification. Instead of being a right to an activity, it is the right to a passivity: a right to be treated in accordance with what one has done or said. This passive position has to be understood as a capability: not as the capability of doing something, that is, of being the subject of actions, but as the capability of being the object of the action of others, namely an object of their judgement on what one did or said.[48]

It follows that the right to have rights cannot be a "subjective right." There are two reasons for this. The first reason refers to the enabling function, which this right fulfils, regarding the juridically-installed subjective rights: insofar as it secures the position of having these rights, it cannot belong to them. The position of having rights—also called legal capacity—is logically

47 Arendt, "Es gibt nur ein einziges Menschenrecht," p. 770, my translation.
48 Werner Hamacher suggests another correlation between rights and passivity by emphasizing the "unexpressed implication of all rights," namely the "right not to use rights." However, and in contrast to Arendt, this right does not lead to a transformation of subjective rights, insofar as it still operates in their framework of a freedom of choice. Compare Werner Hamacher, "Vom Recht, Rechte nicht zu gebrauchen. Menschenrechte und Urteilsstruktur," in Werner Hamacher, *Sprachgerechtigkeit* (Frankfurt am Main: Fischer, 2018), pp. 93–126, here p. 117, my translation.

prior. This argument is formulated, for instance, in the *Berner Kommentar zum schweizerischen Privatrecht*: "In any case, it is incorrect to conceive of legal capacity as a *subjective right*, as is sometimes done. It is the presupposition of having rights, but not a right itself."[49] As the enabling condition of having subjective rights, the right to have rights cannot be a subjective right itself. The second reason is not about logical priority, but about logical difference. The logic of subjective rights is that they put subjects in a position which obligates others. They provide the legal power to place others under an obligation of refraining, doing or tolerating.[50] As opposed to this, the right to have rights does not obligate others to acquiesce in the subject's doing; it rather exposes this doing to judgement. It does not open up a space for the arbitrariness of acting (freedom of choice), but obligates its subjects to take responsibility for their doing (to choose judiciously). It is, unlike subjective rights, not a dispensing right—dispensing from justification—but a constraining right: it puts actions under the constraint of judgement.

Arendt illustrates the importance of such a constraining right by pointing to those who are "released" from it. Exemplary of this release are the captives of concentration camps, for under the conditions of totalitarian terror, the concentration camps were often the only place where "a free exchange of views and free discussion" was possible. However, "this did not make them 'islands of freedom,' but of a fool's freedom, which stateless people also enjoyed."[51] This fool's freedom, the freedom that it does not matter at all what one says or does,

---

49 Arthur Meier-Hayoz, "Das Personenrecht. Die natürlichen Personen," in *Berner Kommentar zum schweizerischen Privatrecht*, vol. 1, section 2 (Bern: Stämpfli & Cie., 1976), p. 46, emphasis in the original, my translation.

50 Compare Bodo Pieroth, Bernhard Schlink, Thorsten Kingreen and Ralf Poscher, *Grundrechte. Staatsrecht II* (Heidelberg and Munich: C.F. Müller, 2013), p. 33.

51 Arendt, *Elemente und Ursprünge*, p. 613, my translation.

has the downside that one can be persecuted and chased without any relation to one's actions. Not being judged regarding what one does and says is not the guarantee of freedom, but the sign of rightlessness. The right to have rights does not belong to the category of subjective rights because it is their presupposition and because it is not a dispensing, but a constraining right. Then, however, there is still the question if and in what sense the right to have rights is the opposite of a subjective right, namely an objective right.

The objective character is related to its constraining function: it is not a right which sets the subjects free, but which binds them.[52] The capability it protects is *being bound*. This is, in contrast to a fool's freedom, the capability of the political, the "Fähigkeit zum Politischen,"[53] as Arendt writes. It is obvious that this capability cannot be realized from inside of the subject, but is only enabled and established by the outside: by the attribution of relevance. This implies objectivity in a twofold sense. Firstly, the subject becomes, as I have mentioned, the object of judgement; its actions and opinions *materialize* in a shared world, appear as contributions within and to the community. By this, secondly, these actions and opinions are not just regarded as products of subjective caprice. That they are treated as relevant not only means that they are noticed, but that they are submitted to *objective* standards, namely to the norms of the community. Thus, they are not reduced to mere opinions, but considered as reasoned convictions and have to live

---

52 In his reading of Arendt, Christoph Menke considers the right to have rights to be "objective" in another, although related sense: instead of defining a claim of human beings, this right "defines what is right *for* them," namely "that *it is right* for human beings to be members of a political community." See Christoph Menke, "Dignity as the right to have rights: human dignity in Hannah Arendt," in Marcus Düwell, Jens Braarvig, Roger Brownsword and Dietmar Mieth, eds., *The Cambridge Handbook of Human Dignity: Interdisciplinary Perspectives* (Cambridge: Cambridge University Press, 2014), pp. 332–342, here p. 340, emphasis in the original.
53 Arendt, *Elemente und Ursprünge*, p. 615.

up to this requirement. The capability of the political allows for leaving the space of what is just "personal opinion." Conversely, the loss of a standpoint in the political world—the exclusion from the human condition—means falling back onto what is absolutely *subjective* in the sense of restricted to the individual person. It is in this sense that Arendt makes clear that refugees are "politically (*but of course not personally*) deprived of the capability of having convictions [Überzeugungen] and to act."[54] To have this capability *politically* implicates that the opinions and acts are considered as having a relation to the life in the community.

The capability of being "judged by one's actions and opinions"[55] is not only the capability of the political, but also a political capability: since it is realized as a passivity involving the judgement of others as members of the community, it is not only the presupposition of a political life, but it also presupposes the political sphere. Therefore, this capability is not an aspect of human "nature" and, accordingly, it is impossible to derive the *right* to this capability —the right to have rights—from such a nature. This is the reason why the right to have rights "cannot be grasped in the categories of the eighteenth century," i.e. the categories of natural law which suppose that rights "immediately evolve from the 'nature' of man."[56] The right Arendt aims at requires new categories. It can neither be thought of in the categories of natural rights nor in the categories of juridical rights. Consequently, the conception of what a

---

54 Ibid., p. 614, my translation and emphasis.
55 Arendt, *Origins*, pp. 296–297.
56 Arendt, *Elemente und Ursprünge*, p. 616, my translation. Thomas Khurana makes clear that the right to have rights does not refer to a given human nature, but rather makes it possible to politically determine, i.e. to posit, this nature. See Thomas Khurana, "'Recht auf Rechte.' Zur Naturalisierung und Politisierung subjektiver Rechte nach Arendt," *Rechtsphilosophie. Zeitschrift für Grundlagen des Rechts* 1 (2017): pp. 15–30, here pp. 24–26.

right can be needs to be transformed. I will discuss this question of transformation in the following step.

7. The transformation of rights

The question of transformation is at the core of Arendt's critique of rights, since her critique is directed against a past legal transformation and aims at a future legal transformation. I will now outline these two transformations. The transformation she criticizes is the fact that the question of belonging to a community has turned into a question of rights. This became clear when the loss of (citizen) rights proved to be equivalent to the expulsion from any community. There are two aspects of this transformation. The first aspect is that under the conditions of modernity the only (politically) relevant community is the nation state: only the nation state guarantees an existence in which individuals are recognized in their political form of life, hence the human condition has transformed into a national condition, that is, a condition of nation state citizens. The second aspect is that nation states are based upon human rights: they entail them in the form of citizen rights as the foundation of their national constitutions. These two aspects coincide insofar as belonging to a political community is defined by being a subject of citizen rights. It is this conjunction of the two aspects which makes the loss of citizen rights an unprecedented catastrophe. In this catastrophe, according to Arendt, human rights are not just a victim, but also a cause: their installation in the center of nation states transforms the question of belonging into a question of rights—and the loss of rights into a loss of belonging. This loss involves at the same time, as I have indicated, the realization of human rights "as such": the exclusion of those having lost their rights individualizes them into a mere representative of the human species. As such, they correspond to the idea of a "natural" human individual upon which the idea of human rights is built.

Arendt's critique of rights is a critique of both human rights as citizen rights and human rights as such. The problem of *citizen rights* is their decisive role in reducing political membership to citizenship and thereby limiting the realization of the human condition (i.e. of political qualities) to nationality. And the problem of *human rights as such* is not just their lack in force, but the fact that they identify human life with an existence beyond the political sphere.

Arendt's suggestion regarding these problems is another transformation of rights. As a first and obvious part of this transformation, the fact of membership itself, since it has proved to be losable, has to be brought into the form of a right. Since this right, as I have outlined, requires the judgement of the community, it is not a right that one can naturally *have* as a subject, but a right that can only be politically *given*. To acknowledge such a right to have rights hence means to acknowledge the limits of rights, namely the precedence of the political inclusion over *any* legal inclusion. The transformation that Arendt calls for by proclaiming a right to have rights stresses that only an inclusive organization of the political sphere can constitute rights for all—and that, conversely, no subjective right can guarantee such a political inclusion.

The transformation of rights at which Arendt aims is the overcoming of the alternative of a right either being a positive right or a natural right, that is, either juridical or moral. It is this alternative which leads to the aporia of rights, the separation between two kinds of rights. Arendt's right to have rights belongs neither to the former nor to the latter kind. It is not a juridical right, since it is the right to a position in which one can have such rights. And it is not a moral right, since it does not timelessly exist (but became necessary in history) and since it is not oriented towards others as individuals (but only as members). What distinguishes this right from all rights we know is the fact that it cannot be claimed, because it is not a right one already has, be it juridical or moral. Since it is a politically given right to political membership, one only *has* this right when its content is fulfilled. However, not only does the existence of this right depend on its political provision; the political sphere is also only established by the fact of providing this right, that is, by considering individuals as relevant in regard to what they do and say. Because the provision of this right is the *sine qua non* of the political sphere, it is not a fundamental right of the subject, but the fundamental right of the community: the right upon which a community is based. As the right of the community—not a right which it has, but one which it must give—it is not a subjective, but an objective right. As becomes apparent now, the *objectivity* of this right has a threefold meaning (the first two meanings have already been mentioned): 1) the right to have rights turns subjects into the object of judgement; 2) it gathers actions and opinions under a shared standard, that is, a norm; 3) it is not the right of the individual subjects (since, *if* they have it, they have it (its content) always as a fact, not as a right), but rather the right of the political community.

What I have outlined so far about the transformation suggested by Arendt concerns the *right* to have rights. There is, however, also a transformation concerning the latter part of this formulation, concerning the *rights*. As I pointed out, the right to have rights does not aim at securing rights, but at securing a position in which one is able to have them. It is the position of legal capacity, that is, the position of being regarded as an equal member of the legally organized community, which, in modernity, has the form of the nation state. This position is defined by two aspects or, more precisely, two abilities: the ability to have rights and the responsibility for one's own actions. Arendt changes the hierarchy of these two abilities. Whereas the ability to have rights has been traditionally given priority because it is derived directly from the freedom of the individual human being,[57] Arendt considers the aspect of responsibility to be more fundamental. The reason for this can be found in the fact that, according to Arendt, freedom cannot lie in the individual, but rather is a public affair requiring a community. Since there is no freedom residing in human nature, no ability can be derived from it. This does not mean that freedom is not important at this point; however, the decisive relation is not to be found between (individual) freedom and the ability to have rights, but between (public) freedom and responsibility. In order to understand this relation, it is helpful to consider Arendt's *Lectures on Kant's Political Philosophy*.

Here, Arendt deals with what she calls "political freedom"[58] in Kant, namely the freedom enabling enlightenment, that is, the freedom "to make public use of one's reason at every point" [*die Freiheit, "von seiner Vernunft in allen Stücken öffentlichen Gebrauch zu machen"*].[59] This freedom is not the "freedom of opinion and expression" as guaranteed, for instance, in Article 19 of the *Universal Declaration of Human Rights*: such a freedom to formulate "without interference" (ibid.) what is my personal opinion would presuppose, as Arendt

---

57 However, it has to be noted that, since the eighteenth century, when the idea of human rights gained political influence, this freedom of the individual is not just the freedom of choice, but freedom in the sense of autonomy. As such, it is connected with the requirement of responsibility: whereas human rights enable the freedom of choice, they are based on autonomy. Regarding the relation between these two forms of freedom within the idea of human rights, compare Jonas Heller, *Mensch und Maßnahme* (Weilerswist: Velbrück Wissenschaft, 2018), pp. 294–301.

58 Hannah Arendt, *Lectures on Kant's Political Philosophy*, ed. and with an interpretive essay by Ronald Beiner (Chicago: University of Chicago Press, 1992), p. 39.

59 Immanuel Kant, "Beantwortung der Frage: Was ist Aufklärung?," in *Kant's gesammelte Schriften*, ed. Königlich Preußische Akademie der Wissenschaften (Akademie-Ausgabe), vol. 8 (Berlin: de Gruyter, 1923), p. 36.

writes, "that I am capable of making up my mind all by myself."[60] With reference to Kant, Arendt holds a different view: "Reason is not made to isolate itself but to get into community with others." [*"Die Vernunft ist nicht dazu gemacht, dass sie sich isoliere, sondern in Gemeinschaft setze."*][61] Against this background, the public use of freedom appears as its *only* use: freedom is used publicly or not used at all. Accordingly, political freedom and the freedom to make use of reason are the same.

Arendt explains this at a later point in her *Lectures* in regard to Kant's *Critique of Judgement*.[62] Here, in paragraph 40, Kant distinguishes between *sensus privatus* and *sensus communis* and identifies the latter with a "faculty for judging"[63] [*Beurteilungsvermögen*] which, "in its reflection,"[64] incorporates a priori the considerations of others: "Now this happens by one holding his judgment up not so much to the actual as to the merely possible judgments of others, and putting himself into the position of everyone else, merely by abstracting from the limitations that contingently attach to our own judging."[65] Controlling our own thinking by the possible judgements of others does not restrict our freedom, but, on the contrary, liberates us from our own limitations. This is the decisive point that Arendt takes from Kant. The use of reason—which is always its public use, namely the examination of this use in the light of

---

60 Arendt, *Lectures*, p. 39.

61 Immanuel Kant, *Reflexionen zur Anthropologie*, in *Kant's gesammelte Schriften*, ed. Königlich Preußische Akademie der Wissenschaften (Akademie-Ausgabe), vol. 15 (Berlin: de Gruyter, 1923), no. 897, p. 392.

62 Compare Arendt, *Lectures*, pp. 70–71; see also Hannah Arendt, "Some Questions of Moral Philosophy," in Hannah Arendt, *Responsibility and Judgment*, ed. and with an introduction by Jerome Kohn (New York: Schocken Books, 2003), pp. 49–146, here pp. 139–141.

63 Immanuel Kant, *Critique of the Power of Judgment*, ed. Paul Guyer, transl. Paul Guyer and Eric Matthews (Cambridge: Cambridge University Press, 2007), § 40, p. 173.

64 Ibid.

65 Ibid., p. 174.

the judgements of others—is, as such, the actualization of (political) freedom.[66]

However, according to Arendt, this examination cannot remain a hypothetical one. The faculty of judgement can only be actualized if it is really submitted to the judgement of others, that is, if one's own reasoning is disclosed: "[U]nless you can somehow communicate and expose to the test of others, either orally or in writing, whatever you may have found out when you were alone, this faculty exerted in solitude will disappear."[67] The faculty of judgement, in which our political freedom is comprised, is only maintained by being judged; the faculty to judge, and thus our political freedom, presupposes the faculty of being judged. We have this faculty of being judged if we are considered responsible for what we say and do. In this way, responsibility and (public) freedom are connected in Arendt: the realization of freedom rests upon the attribution of responsibility. This is the reason why, in Arendt's conception of legal capacity, responsibility is prior to freedom. A freedom enabled by the attribution of responsibility is different from a freedom residing in a postulated nature of human individuals. The transformation concerning the concept of rights, as indicated by Arendt, is based on a revision of the concept of freedom. The rights which are intended by Arendt's right to have rights, are rights to freedom in a fundamentally different sense than the established citizen rights. I will conclude by exposing this difference.

---

66 The loss of this public use, that is, the loss of the *sensus communis* and the absolutization of the *"logische Eigensinn (sensus privatus)"* is, according to Kant, the only general feature of insaneness. See Immanuel Kant, *Anthropologie in pragmatischer Hinsicht*, in *Kant's gesammelte Schriften*, ed. Königlich Preußische Akademie der Wissenschaften (Akademie-Ausgabe), vol. 7 (Berlin: de Gruyter, 1923), p. 219; quoted as well by Arendt in *Lectures*, pp. 70–71. In an Arendtian reading of Kant, the deprivation of political freedom thus involves the loss of reason.

67 Arendt, *Lectures*, p. 40.

Since they are grounded in the idea of an essential freedom of human subjects as such, subjective rights (to which all kinds of human and citizen rights belong) necessarily go along with a separation of "the notion of freedom from politics": freedom is private freedom, namely the power over oneself "shielded from outside interference."[68] It is true that Arendt attributes a subjective aspect to the act of liberation; in order to be free, a subject must have liberated itself "from the necessities of life."[69] However, liberation and freedom are not the same.[70] Arendt goes on as follows: "But the status of freedom did not follow automatically upon the act of liberation. Freedom needed, in addition to mere liberation, the company of other men who were in the same state, and it needed a common public space to meet them—a politically organized world, in other words, into which each of the free men could insert himself by word and deed."[71] Arendt's objection against the idea of subjective rights is that freedom is not an individual affair because it does not exist, as the philosophical tradition claims, in the will, but only in the act.[72] And acting is not just what an individual does, but is realized "only with the help of others."[73] For acting is defined, according to Arendt, by interrupting "the process in whose frame-

---

68 Hannah Arendt, "What is Freedom?," in Hannah Arendt, *Between Past and Future: Eight Exercises in Political Thought* (New York: Penguin Group, 2006), pp. 142–169, here p. 146. Similarly, Axel Honneth uses the term "protective wall" [*Schutzwall*] regarding this notion of freedom. See Axel Honneth, *Das Recht der Freiheit. Grundriß einer demokratischen Sittlichkeit* (Berlin: Suhrkamp, 2011), pp. 143, 145 and 152.
69 Arendt, "What is Freedom?," p. 147.
70 A liberation from merely material (socio-economic) necessities has, according to Arendt, no political character and therefore cannot by itself establish freedom. For a critique of this position, see Jürgen Habermas, "Die Geschichte von den zwei Revolutionen (1966)," in Jürgen Habermas, *Philosophisch-politische Profile* (Frankfurt am Main: Suhrkamp, 1981), pp. 223–228.
71 Arendt, "What is Freedom?," p. 147
72 Compare ibid., p. 151.
73 Ibid., p. 164.

work it occurs."[74] An individual as such has only the power to proceed in this process, but not the power to break through it.[75] Arendt's notion of freedom as *strictly* political does not allow for subjective rights, which are based on the concept of a "nonpolitical freedom"[76] within individuals as such.

Therefore, the rights for which the right to have rights strives are not claims that subjects individually have and enjoy. They are not establishing and protecting a private sphere of actions that is not regulated by laws. Rather, rights are the name for a relation. It is not a personal relation to other subjects, but a political one to what is common, shared by the community: to have rights is to participate in the world of norms, that is, to fall under the validity of laws. The ability to be judged is not about being judged personally, but according to the legal standards of a community. And the rights that a subject has are not primarily subjective; they rather grant access to the objective law ("objektives Recht"): to legality. Only by being a member of legality (and not by nature) can one actually have, as a second step, subjective claims. Only as an *object of laws* can one be a *subject of rights*. Arendt's right to have rights is not oriented towards this subjective, but towards the objective side: the side of law. The *right* to have rights is objective because it is the right that the community has to give to its members in order to make them members and, by doing so, to constitute itself as a political sphere.[77] And the *rights* one

---

74 Ibid., p. 168.
75 This brings up the question, however, in what way the liberation from the necessities—as "natural processes which are interrupted" (ibid.)—can have a strong individual aspect.
76 Ibid., p. 147.
77 The constitution of this political community can, in line with Arendt's argument, no longer have the form of the nation state (since the order of nation states is part of the "aporia of human rights"). Regarding the question of how membership beyond the nation state could be thought of following Arendt, see Daniel Loick, "Wir Flüchtlinge. Überlegungen zu einer Bürgerschaft jenseits des Nationalstaates," *Leviathan* 45:4 (2017): pp. 1–18.

has are objective because they constitute the subject as an object of laws; they guarantee that laws are equally applied to the subjects. Rights, at the same time, authorize the subjects to form and enact these laws: participating in the world of legal norms involves contributing to the political process in which these norms, *including* the rights of the subjects, are made. Therefore, the right to have rights is not simply the right to have subjective rights, but the right to participate in determining them.

However, it is important to note that Arendt does not develop a theory of subjective rights at all. What she suggests is to transform rights from a sphere not regulated by judgements towards a sphere in which one is judged. Since this changes the very idea of subjective rights, Arendt's transformation of rights deforms them: it suggests a shift from the subjective to the objective aspect of legality, since Arendt recognizes—against the background of the experience of modernity (the loss of having rights)—that political equality before the law is required for any rights of the subject.

This suggestion for a transformation of rights provokes at least two objections. Firstly, how can it take into account a nonpolitical freedom of the subjects enjoyed beyond their active participation in a community? And secondly, doesn't it lead to excluding consequences if individuals are only guaranteed a life as free and equal members insofar as they possess at least the *faculty* to live up to the norms of the community, that is, insofar as they have the capability of being responsible? Regarding the first objection, it is helpful to pursue a modest reading of Arendt. According to such a reading, Arendt doesn't claim that there should be no right to individual freedom, but that freedom itself is, firstly, not a natural right[78] and that there is, secondly,

---

[78] In this aspect Arendt contradicts Kant, who considers freedom to be an innate right. Compare Immanuel Kant, *Die Metaphysik der Sitten*, in *Kant's gesammelte Schriften*, ed. Königlich Preußische Akademie

no natural freedom from which rights could directly be derived. Rather, a political freedom—which consists of being regarded as relevant—is the enabling condition of any individual freedom (of any subjective rights) and not the other way round. This leaves open the second objection. Admittedly, it is true that Arendt's position allows for individuals to be provided with rights protecting them, including irresponsible members who do not live up to the standards of the community, but prefer to behave like fools.[79] However, according to Arendt, the provision with such rights—with *any* rights—presupposes that the subjects of rights are considered as relevant in the specific sense that they are capable of being judged equally in accordance with their actions: in the sense that they can be held responsible. This is where the question arises if, in Arendt's account, there is room for protection of those who do not have this capability. At the basis of freedom, Arendt places a concept of legal capacity, which links political relevance to the capacity of responsibility. In this aspect, her account of political membership (and hence of freedom) remains juridical in a problematic sense: it does not take into account the situation and thus the limited possibilities of concrete individuals. The kind of judgement upon which her theory of political inclusion rests, must, however, incorporate these limitations in order to overcome the exclusion that is the starting point of her critique.

---

der Wissenschaften (Akademie-Ausgabe), vol. 6 (Berlin: Reimer, 1907), pp. 237–238.

79 Such a protection of a "fool's freedom" (Arendt, *Elemente und Ursprünge*, p. 613, my translation) must, in the framework of Arendt's account, take the form of being judged equally in accordance with the legal norms.

Authors

Fares Chalabi was born in Beirut in 1977. He obtained his BA in philosophy in 2002 from the Lebanese University, and a diploma in architecture at Université De Balamand-Académie Libanaise Des Beaux-Arts (ALBA) in 2004. He continued his studies in philosophy at Paris 8 where he obtained a Master 2 in 2008, and his PhD in 2016. Today Chalabi teaches philosophy at American University of Beirut (AUB), and art theory at ALBA and Université Saint-Joseph (USJ). His main fields of interest are the study of ontological argumentation, ethics and aesthetics—in line with the Deleuzian approach.

Franziska Dübgen is Professor of Political and Legal Philosophy at the University of Münster. Her current research interests include twentieth century political philosophy, transcultural philosophy (in particular African philosophy), critical theory, gender and epistemic justice. She published a monograph on punishment entitled *Theorien der Strafe* (Hamburg: Junius, 2016) and edited an anthology on African political philosophy with Stefan Skupien for Suhrkamp (2015).

Peter Goodrich is epistemically and ontographically transitional, his habitus an eerie space between Cardozo Law, New York; Birkbeck College, London; and New York University, Abu Dhabi. Recent exothermic productions include *Schreber's Law: Jurisprudence and Judgment in Transition* (Edinburgh: Edinburgh University Press, 2019).

Jonas Heller is "wissenschaftlicher Mitarbeiter" at the Philosophy Department of Goethe University, Frankfurt am Main. Within the research association *The Formation of Normative Orders* he is co-leader of the Deutsche Forschungsgemeinschaft (DFG) research project "The Political Difference of Life: For a Reconceptualization of the Crisis of State and Society." His main research interests are in political, legal and social philosophy and in the theory of history. He received his PhD in 2017 with a thesis about the relation between state of exception and human rights. In 2018 his first book, *Mensch und Maßnahme. Zur Dialektik von Ausnahmezustand und Menschenrechten* was published with Velbrük.

Manuela Klaut studied business administration in Halberstadt and media culture at the Bauhaus University in Weimar. In 2012, she organized the first festival for legal cases, *Just in Case*, together with Fabian Steinhauer. After completing her PhD on theories of the legal case as a medium of knowledge transfer in 2019, she is a postdoctoral fellow at the Institute for Theater, Film and Media Studies at Goethe University, Frankfurt am Main and at Leuphana University, Lüneburg.

Susanne Krasmann is Professor of Sociology at the Institute for Criminological Research, University of Hamburg. Her main research areas are: law and its knowledge; dispositifs of security; the future of algorithms; power and truth; vulnerability and political theory. She is co-editor of *Governmentality: Current Issues and Future Challenges* (New York and London: Routledge, 2010) and has published in international journals like *Cultural Studies, Foucault Studies, Leiden Journal of International Law, Policing & Society, Punishment & Society, Security Dialogue, Surveillance & Society, Theoretical Criminology*.

Daniel Loick is affiliated with Goethe University, Frankfurt am Main (as "Privatdozent") and with the Frankfurt University Institute for Social Research. After receiving his PhD in 2010, he held positions at multiple institutes in Germany, Switzerland, and the US. His main research interests are in political, cultural, legal and social philosophy, social theory, and political theory. Among his publications are four books, *Kritik der Souveränität* (Frankfurt: Campus, 2012; English translation as *A Critique of Sovereignty* (London: Rowman & Littlefield International, 2018)), *Der Missbrauch des Eigentums* (Berlin: August Verlag, 2016), *Anarchismus zur Einführung* (Hamburg:

Junius, 2017), and most recently *Juridismus. Konturen einer kritischen Theorie des Rechts* (Berlin: Suhrkamp, 2017).

Liza Mattutat studied literature and philosophy at the Technische Universität (TU) Darmstadt. From 2015 to 2016 she was part of the research group *Beyond a Politics of Punishment*, based at Kassel University. From 2016 to 2019 she worked as a PhD student within the DFG Research Training Group *Cultures of Critique* at Leuphana University, Lüneburg. Her interests lie in philosophy of law, political philosophy, critical theory and French philosophy. She is currently writing her PhD thesis, which relates philosophical critiques of law to current legal politics from a feminist perspective.

Christoph Menke is Professor of Practical Philosophy at Goethe University, Frankfurt am Main. He obtained his PhD in philosophy from the University of Konstanz in 1987; his "Habilitation" in philosophy from the Free University, Berlin, in 1995. From 1997–1999 he was Associate Professor at the New School for Social Research, New York, and from 1999–2008 Professor at the University of Potsdam. His book publications in English are: *The Sovereignty of Art: Aesthetic Negativity after Adorno and Derrida* (Boston MA: The MIT Press, 1998), *Reflections of Equality* (Stanford CA: Stanford University Press, 2006), *Tragic Play: Tragedy, Irony and Theater from Sophocles to Beckett* (New York: Columbia University Press, 2009), *Force: A Fundamental Concept of Aesthetic Anthropology* (New York: Fordham University Press, 2012), *Law and Violence: Christoph Menke in Dialogue* (Manchester: Manchester University Press, 2018), *Critique of Rights* (Cambridge: Polity Press, forthcoming 2020).

Paolo Napoli teaches Histoire des catégories et des pratiques normatives at the École des Hautes Études en Sciences Sociales in Paris. After working on the legal-political thought of Michel Foucault and the concept of "police" between the eighteenth and nineteenth centuries in France and Germany, his interests turned to a genealogy of administrative rational-ity based on theological and canonical sources.

Roberto Nigro is Professor of Philosophy, in particular con-tinental philosophy, at the Leuphana University, Lüneburg. He also is a former head of program at the Collège Inter-national de Philosophie in Paris. His research and teaching interests include aesthetics, political philosophy, and cul-tural theory, with a special focus on French and Italian con-temporary philosophy and the legacy of German philosophy (in particular Marx, Nietzsche, and Heidegger) in contempo-rary thought.

Alisa Del Re taught political science at the Faculty of Politi-cal Science of the University of Padua, where she founded and until 2013 directed the CIRSG (Interdepartmental Research Center for Gender Studies). Her research focuses on issues of social citizenship, socio-economic and demographic transformations, gender issues in political citizenship, and the quality of city governance from a gender perspective.

Nadine Schiel is part of the DFG Research Training Group *Cultures of Critique* and Research Assistant at Leuphana Uni-versity, Lüneburg. After her studies in art, philosophy, sociol-ogy and educational sciences in Wuppertal, Toulouse, Vienna and the Kunstakademie in Düsseldorf, she received her MA in "Theory of *Bildung* and Analysis of Society" in Wuppertal. In her PhD thesis she examines the current potential of *Bildung* in the aesthetics of Christoph Menke and Juliane Rebentisch.

Heiko Stubenrauch is Research Assistant at the Institute of Philosophy and Science of Art at Leuphana University, Lüne-burg. He studied philosophy, sociology, economics, cultural studies and art history in Frankfurt, Lüneburg and Hamburg. From 2016 to 2019 he worked as a PhD student within the DFG Research Training Group *Cultures of Critique*. His main research interests are critical theory, poststructuralism, Ger-man idealism and Marxism. In his PhD thesis, he examines the relationship between critique and affect, especially in the works of Kant, Adorno and Deleuze.

Laurent de Sutter is Professor of Legal Theory at Vrije University, Brussels. He has been visiting researcher at Waseda University, Tokyo, Bonn University and Yeshiva University, New York, as well as invited professor at New York University, Université Catholique de Louvain and Facultés universitaires, Saint-Louis. A member of the scientific committee of the Collège International de Philosophie, he also is associate researcher at École des Hautes Études en Sciences Sociales, Université Paris-X Nanterre and Ponta Grossa University, Brazil. He is editor of the "Theory Redux" series at Polity Press and the "Perspectives Critiques" series at Presses Universitaires de France, and serves as a member of the editorial board of *Law & Literature*; *Décalages: An Althusser Studies Journal* and *Iconocrazia*.

Benno Zabel is Professor of Criminal Law and Philosophy at the University of Bonn, following studies in law, philosophy and comparative literature. He has published on legal criticism, legal and political philosophy, and the cultures of punishment. His most recent publications are *Die Ordnung des Strafrechts* (Tübingen: Verfahren, 2017), *Philosophie der Republik*, co-edited with Pirmin Stekeler-Weithofer (Tübingen: Mohr Siebeck, 2018), and *Sittlichkeit. Eine Kategorie moderner Staatlichkeit*, co-edited with Michael Spieker and Sebastian Schwenzfeuer (Baden-Baden: Nomos Verlagsgesellschaft 2019).